THE CHURCH IN ITALY
IN THE FIFTEENTH CENTURY

THE CHURCH IN ITALY
IN THE FIFTEENTH CENTURY

The Birkbeck Lectures, 1971

DENYS HAY

PROFESSOR OF MEDIEVAL HISTORY
UNIVERSITY OF EDINBURGH

CAMBRIDGE UNIVERSITY PRESS
CAMBRIDGE
LONDON · NEW YORK · MELBOURNE

Published by the Syndics of the Cambridge University Press
The Pitt Building, Trumpington Street, Cambridge CB2 IRP
Bentley House, 200 Euston Road, London NWI 2DB
32 East 57th Street, New York, NY 10022, USA
296 Beaconsfield Parade, Middle Park, Melbourne 3206, Australia

© Cambridge University Press 1977

First published 1977

Printed in Great Britain by
Western Printing Services Ltd
Bristol

Library of Congress Cataloguing in Publication Data
Hay, Denys.
The church in Italy in the fifteenth century.
(The Birkbeck lectures; 1971)
Bibliography: p.
Includes index.
1. Italy – Church history – 15th century. 2. Catholic
Church in Italy – History. I. Title. II. Series.
BX1544.H39   282'.45   76–50652
ISBN 0 521 21532 3

CONTENTS

PREFACE   *page* vii

1   The problems of Italian church history   1
2   Diocesan and parochial organisation   9
3   The Schism in Italy: the emergence of an
    Italian papacy   26
4   The state of the clergy and laity in fifteenth-
    century Italy   49
5   The quality of Italian religious life. Reform   72
6   The Italian Renaissance and the clergy of
    Italy in the fifteenth century   91

APPENDIX

I   Italian sees 1400–1500   110
II   Popes 1378–1534   123
III Promotions of cardinals 1417–1549   124
IV   Italian church archives   125

NOTES   127

REFERENCES   159

INDEX (NOT INCLUDING APPENDICES)   177

PREFACE

These lectures were delivered in Cambridge in November 1971. I must express my thanks to the Master and Fellows of Trinity College, first for honouring me with the invitation, and second for accepting postponement when illness prevented me from coming at the appointed time. I received much kindness from many people during my stay in Cambridge. I cannot thank them all individually, but I should like to mention the names of two fellows of Trinity, the late Dr Kitson Clark and Professor Walter Ullmann.

That I have been able to turn the lectures into a book is due to my University allowing me several months of study leave, and to the British Academy granting me generous aid for work in Italian libraries. I must also express my gratitude to the Rockefeller Foundation's Research Centre at the Villa Serbelloni, Bellagio.

Slight though this book is, it has taken a long time to write. My original intention was to survey the reactions of the Italian clergy (assuming that they must have been a large literate group) to the new ideas and disturbing challenge of the Renaissance in Italy. I did, I confess, at first assume that among recent Italian scholarship I should find surveys of the clergy comparable to those available for England (for instance) in the works of Hamilton Thompson and Dom David Knowles. Such was not the case and I found I was obliged to attempt some sort of picture myself. I should, I suppose, have heeded the warning in the volumes of Professors Delaruelle, Labande and Ourliac, *L'église au temps du Grand Schisme* (in Fliche and Martin, *Histoire de l'église*) where it was stated (1, p. xviii) 'Il n'éxiste pas d'histoire de l'Eglise italienne, celle-ci étant toujours confondue dans l'histoire de la papauté'.

In the event, therefore, I found myself concerned more with men and women than with ideas. I dare say this is no bad discipline for anyone who writes about the Renaissance. At any rate that is what happened and if the result resembles a short manual at times I hope it may stimulate better scholars to more exciting analyses. Two 'ideological' problems did indeed impose themselves at once: why should Italians, whose intellectuals from the author of the *Divine Comedy* to the author of *Christ stopped at Eboli* have been moulded by their love–hate relationship with the church and clergy of their country, have neglected serious study of church history? A brief discussion of this occurs in chapter 1. And how could it come about that the papacy was so identified with the clergy of Italy as to justify the quotation from Delaruelle above? A preliminary word on this now.

Some partial explanations suggest themselves, if no real excuses. The most obvious point to be stressed is the peculiar public rôle of the papacy in Italy, with its persistent and on the whole successful policy of either preventing any rival authority from emerging or, when it has emerged, trying to keep such authority as weak as possible. As far as the fifteenth century is concerned profound changes were occurring in the situation in which the policy operated. The popes were becoming Italian, the curia, even including its non-Italian members, was italianised and the papacy was obliged to haggle not only with the larger European powers, but (and often with more positive results) with the small but aggressive states of the peninsula. Meanwhile the leadership of Christendom as a spiritual aim of the papacy was quietly abandoned; the pope was an Italian prince who happened to have spiritual powers with which to coerce – not France, England or the Spanish kingdoms – but occasionally the Italian governments. Thus the equation 'history of the church in Italy = history of the Italian papacy' has some sense, even before the Council of Trent. But we must not imagine that the popes of the period and their officials were solely absorbed by Italian business. The massive collections prepared by foreign scholarship in Rome are all on a national basis (e.g. the English series *Calendars of Papal Petitions*, *Calendars of Papal Letters*) and would almost suggest the papal machinery operated mainly for non-Italians. Alas, as chapter 1 explains, there are no 'Calendars of Italian Petitions and Letters', nor ever will be.

The undoubted activity at the curia of many non-Italians in soliciting help from the machinery of central church government, which must strike anyone looking through the main administrative series in the Vatican Archives, should however not rule out the likelihood that as the fifteenth century drew to a close, and long before the Protestant reformation cut off chunks of northern Europe, the majority of persons approaching Rome was Italian. I can think of no simple way of positively establishing this and so only advance it as a hypothesis.

In another way the clergy in Italy differed from their fifteenth-century contemporaries in northern Europe: the relative absence of popular heresy. Despite the fascination exercised in recent years by the Waldensians (the first reformed church in Europe), the Fraticelli (wiped out by the end of the fifteenth century), the Brethren of the Free Spirit, these were tiny minority groups. The vast majority of Italian clergy in general regarded the pope as undisputed head of the church after 1417 and to clever clerics he was there to be used and abused through his ability to upset earlier decisions by himself or his predecessors. There can be little doubt that in this last respect the Italians were more alert to their opportunities than Christians elsewhere.

I am so much better informed about English ecclesiastical history in the Middle Ages that I inevitably tend to make conscious (and doubtless unconscious) comparisons between Italy and England. I have, however, emphatically not aimed at a comparison of the 'Church of England', to give that bit of Christendom its medieval title, with the 'Church of Italy', along the lines of Professor Robert Brentano's *Two Churches*, the stimulating comparison of thirteenth-century attitudes, which came out in 1968.

The structure of the book closely follows the structure of the lectures as given and I have deliberately allowed a few turns of phrase to survive to remind the reader that what he reads was originally partly spoken. But the lecture, thank goodness, cannot carry footnotes, although I have heard lectures where the attempt was tried with gruesome consequences. The annotations may appear elaborate for so slender an essay; this is because there is no other manual to which the reader may be referred, as I have indicated. (References are normally quoted in full on the first occasion, thereafter usually by a short title to be consulted in the List at the end of the book.) The only place in which I have extended my Cambridge remarks so much as to constitute an additional section is in the final chapter. Here I have used, by the kind permission of the Society for Renaissance Studies, a few pages from a lecture I gave in 1972 (*Italian Clergy and Italian Culture in the Fifteenth Century*, London: the Society, 1973). A preview of my Birkbeck Lectures as a whole was given as a lecture in May 1971 to the Irish Historical Conference and published by them in *Irish Historical Studies*, ix (Belfast 1974).

The period covered in my title refers more accurately to the years between 1417 (election of Martin V) and 1527 (Sack of Rome). A more tricky problem is constituted by what one means by 'Italy' in this period. What I have done is to follow fifteenth-century practice in completely neglecting the islands of Sicily, Sardinia and Corsica, but in other respects accepting the boundaries of Italy in our own day. This is mainly reflected in the bishoprics I have admitted to appendix 1: Aosta is included (although in the province of Tarentaise) but Laibach (Lubliana) is not, although in the period a suffragan of Aquileia. I am inconsistent in this since I have retained the Istrian dioceses, although as I was revising this book (winter of 1975–6) Italy and Jugoslavia signed an agreement making 'Zone B' Jugoslav territory. For some further notes on 'Italy' see below pp. 26–7. It seemed worth while attempting an accurate list of bishoprics in appendix 1 since the Italian sections of the *Provinciale* concluding each of Eubel's first three volumes are manifestly unreliable.

I owe thanks to Dr J. A. F. Thomson for reading the lectures in their original form and making some useful comments, including the point that medians were more reliable indicators than averages when comparing episcopal assessments for common services; and to Miss Fenny Rankin both for trying to explain to me the different uses of averages, medians and modes, and then working out the medians quoted below p. 11. Dr John O'Malley, S.J. kindly commented on the first three chapters.

My chief thanks go to my wife who has counted bishops, typed chapters, corrected my English, listened to endless diatribes and encomia, and sometimes lived in the cold discomfort of Roman winters. I cannot dedicate another book to her, even if this one would hardly have been written without her assistance. There are many others who have been enormously helpful. I will not name the Librarians in my own University or the National Library of Scotland or other British, European and American centres, but I should like to name Mgr Charles Burns of the Vatican Archives and Mgr José Ruyshaert of the Vatican Library. As a compromise and a much overdue tribute, which covers everything I have ever written, I would like to dedicate this book, without their permission, TO LIBRARIANS EVERYWHERE.

University of Edinburgh   D.H.
July 1976

I

THE PROBLEMS OF ITALIAN CHURCH HISTORY

The difficulties facing the historian of the church in Italy are very considerable and deserve preliminary consideration. This must begin by emphasising a paradox. In recent times church history in Italy has often been written at a very low level indeed. Yet Italy had centuries before been a pioneer in such studies.

There is no need to go behind Bartolomeo Sacchi, called from his birth-place Platina, whose *History of the Popes* is a somewhat neglected work.[1] For the early period of papal history he preserved the legends which were often abstracted in the form he had given them by other writers at the time and for centuries to come. In common with his fellow curialist and contemporary Biondo in the *Decades*,[2] as Platina drew nearer to his own day (he died in 1481) so his work became increasingly a history not, it is true, of the Italian church as such, but of papal policy in Italy. In many ways Platina resembled the many historians working in the princely courts of *quattrocento* Italy. He was indeed to commemorate his patrons the Gonzaga with a history of Mantua.[3] But he had an inestimable advantage, to be shared by later historians of the papacy. In his *Lives of the Popes* he was not writing the history of a dynasty. He was writing the history of an institution of which he was a rather quarrelsome member.[4] This, together with his sharp criticism of some popes and the high level of his accuracy, ensured respect for him among other writers, including Protestants in the post-Reformation period. In the mid-sixteenth century he was edited and continued by Panvinio.[5] In 1601 appeared the first edition of the *Lives of the Popes and Cardinals* by the Spaniard Ciacconius (Chacon).[6] From Platina to Ciacconius papal historiography had progressed solidly, surviving the acerbities of the Reformation, and becoming more scientific and less polemical. As already mentioned, it was Platina's criticism of 'bad' popes which enabled him in some sense to be regarded as a 'reformer' of sorts in the eyes of the sixteenth-century

Protestant reader, so that his influence was exerted in both religious camps.

In the 1620s a number of Italian scholars began to collect material for the revision of Ciacconius. This was officially sponsored, the new edition appearing from the Vatican press in 1630. Some of the papers of this enterprise have fortunately survived and from these we can infer the large part played by the Irish Observant Franciscan, Luke Wadding, and a young Cistercian born in Florence in 1595, Ferdinando Ughelli. Ughelli rose in his order and became abbot of the Tre Fontane, south of Rome, which is now a Trappist house. Ughelli belongs to that group of prodigious scholars who illuminated the seventeenth century with their erudition and their application. He in fact did more than any other scholar to found a truly based church history of Italy by compiling a work which is still indispensable. The *Italia sacra* appeared in nine volumes at Rome between 1643 and 1662, and these folios are the foundation stone on which all subsequent histories of the Italian church are based. It is ironical that they were produced at a time when there was as yet no Italy. How much did they contribute to the emergence of that concept? There was a *natione italica* in only the most limited or geographical sense.[7] Ughelli's *Italia sacra* helped to give life to the idea.[8]

And how much did his work contribute to the practice of sophisticated church history in other parts of what used to be Christendom? The publication of *Italia sacra* began in 1643 and so was coeval with the Saint-Marthes' *Gallia christiana* (Paris 1656), and Henry Wharton's somewhat differently conceived *Anglia sacra* (1691) although it is later than Padilla's ecclesiastical history of Spain (1605) and may have owed a good deal to early seventeenth-century French antiquarians; it is at any rate interesting to note that Ughelli intended originally to publish his work at Lyon.[9] The connection between Ughelli and his Italian and French predecessors deserves investigation. What is not in doubt is the influence exerted by Ughelli on later church historians in his own country.

He was edited again in ten volumes at Venice by a priest called Niccolò Coleti, 1717–22. It is sometimes said that this edition is less reliable than the original, but it is usually in this edition that the work is consulted.[10] Ughelli lies behind most subsequent histories of Italian dioceses.[11] His work is arranged under provinces (where they exist) and in the case of each bishopric it begins with a description of the diocese as it was in Ughelli's day and then deals with the *series episcoporum*; Coleti brings the information down to his own day. Ughelli carefully inserted all early documents he could find and a few later ones and a fair amount of this early material now only survives in his pages. The immediate effects of his work can be seen in his correspondence, much of which can be read in the Barberini manuscripts in the Vatican Library. All over the peninsula he had correspondents, men of antiquarian tastes whose imagination he fired – not least by appealing to the sentiment of local loyalty: if a neighbouring bishopric was well covered by Ughelli it was important to secure a fair share for one's own. Later on, it may be added, when he lacked Italian source material, Gams in the *Series episcoporum ecclesiae catholicae* (1873–86) often took his names from Ughelli, and Eubel, when he failed to find an entry in Vatican records, took his from Gams. So Ughelli laid a heavy hand on the *Hierarchia catholica*.[12]

At the end of the seventeenth century, therefore, Italy had in Ughelli, in his predecessors and in his disciples and immediate sucessors, a wealth of technical scholarship bearing on the history of the Italian church well in advance of similar developments in other parts of Europe. Yet this start was to be lost and, two hundred years after his death, Italian church history had generally fallen on bad days. Perhaps a sign of this is that, despite the Italian mania for centenaries, the three hundredth anniversary of Ughelli's death in 1970 passed without any celebration. It is only lately that a few Italians are taking seriously the remarkable author of *Italia sacra*.[13]

And it is only lately – in effect since the Second World War – that a deliberate attempt has been made to raise the standards of church history in Italy. What are the faults that must be eradicated? Professor Eric Cochrane, in his recent survey of counter-Reformation scholarship in the *Catholic Historical Review* is one of the first historians to speak plainly.[14] He is scathing about the continuing use of history by Italians to point morals, 'philosophy teaching by example', as he says; he stigmatises much of the end-product as chronicle not history; he identifies the absurdities of petty local loyalties, *campanilismo*; he concludes his tale of amateurishness and special pleading with severe reference to the influence of apologetics and homiletics. Cochrane's partial explanation for the neglect, or rather for the pious frivolity, with which Italians have treated their church history is the exclusion of theology and related subjects from the state universities after 1873. This secular and constitutional influence, which a recent monograph has discussed,[15] is undoubtedly important, for it reflected the impressive anti-clericalism of good scholarship in all fields in Italy after unification.

Everything that Cochrane says seems only too true. And one

might argue that he does not go far enough. One aspect of the parochialism which he rightly deplores is the dispersion of source material in episcopal and capitular archives in three hundred cities or more. These are often ill-kept, difficult of access and inadequately catalogued; they were in a bad state often in Ughelli's day[16] and they have not all improved since then. This strikes one as very odd considering the continuity of ecclesiastical institutions in Italy and repeated attempts, ever since the opening of the Secret Archives of the Vatican by Leo XIII in 1883, by the highest authorities to ensure proper care and reasonable access to documents in the charge of the diocesan authorities.[17] This pressure, including recent papal action[18] seems to have mostly been ineffective. Criticism has been both scholarly[19] and hysterical,[20] but all too often a serious scholar has been obliged to abandon an interesting line of enquiry by 'l'ermetismo dell'archivio vescovile'.[21] The matter is further complicated by the absence of 'registers' and the reliance on notarial acts, copies of which may survive in notarial archives even if not in episcopal or repositories. Of course it would be absurd to suggest that all ecclesiastical archives are equally disorganised or inaccessible. It was the existence of the opposite state of affairs in a number of places which enabled Professor Robert Brentano to write his comparison of religious activity in thirteenth-century England and Italy in *Two Churches*.[22] And of course the scholar in the Vatican Archives and Library is superbly treated. But interest locally seems often to be small and in a situation where recruitment of priests is dropping sharply it may well be that bishops are disinclined to take clergy who are competent in Latin off pastoral work for the sake of helping historical research.

Connected with these difficulties there are two others. The first is the large number of places where there should be records. Some 250 or so bishoprics existed in mainland Italy at the period with which this book is concerned and they mostly survive today.[23] Without prior calendaring or publication a survey of existing records by one man or even a sizeable team of men would take years. Second, even if such a survey were attempted it would reap a poor harvest, it may be suspected, for the period with which this book is concerned. The archives which were most cherished were those making grants of land. Of these there were some massive endowments, especially in early centuries, but only a trickle in the later Middle Ages. Documentation of all kinds was demanded as a result of the decisions of the Council of Trent. But for the fourteenth and fifteenth century church archives outside Rome seem to be sparse, even apart from the havoc wreaked by German and Allied armies in the Second World War. Professor Giuseppe Alberigo has explained how, when he was preparing his work on Italian bishops at the Council of Trent,[24] he wrote to a hundred episcopal archivists and was told by half of them that records had been destroyed or dispersed for his period. Cardinal A. Mercati's estimate in 1942 was that 90 per cent of non-Vatican ecclesiastical records were fairly modern.[25] This is borne out by such indications as I have been able to follow up. One of the best regional surveys covers the archdiocese of Florence and it shows (apart from a few early charters) virtually 20 documents prior to 1500.[26] The capitular archives at Cosenza contain 293 pieces, running from 1195 to 1759; of these 29 are prior to 1500 and 9 only from the fifteenth century.[27] The Cesena study by Pietro Burchi already mentioned shows only a handful of documents prior to the sixteenth century.[28] That there are some very important exceptions will, however, emerge from many documents to be quoted later in this book.

Of course the bulk of archival records, ecclesiastical or secular, which have survived are bound to be overwhelmingly modern; the Italian situation regarding church records is in many ways not much different, it would appear, in France.[29] The richness of English medieval material is perhaps unusual; no other country has a series comparable to the publications of the Canterbury and York Society. But the almost total neglect in Italy of such local records as do survive from the later centuries of the Middle Ages makes it hard to generalise securely. With this one must link the deplorable state of the public libraries of Italy and the consequent dependence of scholars on the older books – like Ughelli but alas not always of his high standing.

To these desperate conditions I believe one must add the limitations on the history written by the regular clergy of Italy and of Orders maintaining historical institutions in Rome. The scholars working in this ambience do not, as far as I can judge, betray any confessional bias. Many of them are very good and methodical researchers. My criticism is that they are too often blinkered by their loyalties and concentrate, not on broader issues, but on the biographical trivia of their predecessors in, for instance, the Franciscan or Dominican families. How far this is due to the direction of superiors I do not know, although sometimes one suspects that only the senior members are encouraged to write wide-ranging studies, some of which will be referred to below. Paper, print, scholarship are all hard to come by nowadays, and I fear a great deal of these rare commodities have been devoted to illustrating men and events of no significance whatever: how many man-hours have been spent in identifying the place and time of Savonarola's ordinations?[30] This one might perhaps accept as a question of some general interest, but many of the periodicals list similar details for thousands of dim and insignificant friars. (I shall have more to say on ordination lists later.)

These several handicaps affect to some extent all historians working on the problems of the church in Italy. There is an additional hazard for medievalists. This might be described as 'getting behind Trent'. For years I have been frustrated by the way reference books emanating from France and Italy have in practice neglected the later Middle Ages. I am thinking of the great French series of 'Dictionnaires', of the *Enciclopedia cattolica*. These works, if consulted on historical problems, discuss in detail the early church; and they discuss the post-Tridentine church. But they do not deal with the fourteenth and fifteenth centuries, and they tend to assume that the reforms enacted at Trent were immediately effective. I have now realised that my feeling of discomfort was shared by others. It was with relief that I discovered the views of Eric Cochrane (to whom I have referred already) and John Bossy, editor of the distinguished Birkbeck lectures given by H. O. Evennett, and of course the views of Evennett himself.[31] They tally with my own and I find it a consolation that 'early modernists' want to determine those elements in their world which were old and those which were new.

Some of the results of the difficulties outlined above are worth stressing. A student interested in Italian church history in the late medieval or early modern ('Renaissance') period has no general work on which he may rely, nothing that is to say later than that remarkably informative *Dizionario di erudizione storico-ecclesiastica*, whose 103 volumes came out (at Venice again!) from 1840 to 1861 as a result of the labours of Gaetano Moroni. There are many interesting monographs, but even they are often flawed by an appalling unwillingness to look further afield; for instance the useful study of ecclesiastical law 'in the state of Milan' by Prosdocimi suggests that the author thought mortmain and clerical taxation were phenomena encountered only in Lombardy – let alone in the rest of Italy, let alone in Christendom at large – in short, as though he had never studied European history at all,[32] and behind and beyond such myopia lies the conviction that, if one is interested in the history of the Italian church as a whole one need only consult the history of the papacy.

It will be noted that the argument has come full circle. This brief survey began with Platina. It has in effect now arrived at Ludwig Pastor. Pastor's history of the popes remains in most ways not only the latest but the best available survey of the Italian church in the fifteenth century. His work began to appear in German in 1886 and in translations into other languages soon after (English from 1891 onwards). Just as scholars in Italy from Muratori onwards felt they needed a new Ughelli, so now it would be wonderful to have a new Pastor. It would, of course, be different in many ways; ultramontane views such as his would look grotesque today and, as far as his Renaissance volumes go, the distinction he made between Christian and Pagan now seems quaint as well as tendentious. But his prejudices are readily seen, his care and accuracy have never been surpassed. How could one contemplate a new Pastor, however, since we have no up-to-date biographies of the popes of the fifteenth and sixteenth centuries, and in as much as he was concerned with Italy much the same is true of the important cardinals and curial officers; there is hardly a diocese with a respectable history. As for lives of popes there is, to be sure, the shining example of Pius II who took care to write his own 'memoirs'[33] and has as a result been rewarded by several modern and fairly reasonable biographies.[34] For the rest, modern revision of papal history has concentrated for our period mainly on political and diplomatic questions on the one hand and on the other on the social history of Rome. The student of (say) English church history in the later Middle Ages has two sure guides in Hamilton Thompson and Dom David Knowles, catering respectively for the secular and the regular clergy. Nothing, absolutely nothing, like this exists for Italy.

Yet this situation looks like changing for there is certainly a new critical awareness among some Italian church historians. Besides earlier attempts at turning attention to archives in Italian churches[35] the Vatican has in recent times repeatedly tried to further archival reform at the diocesan and parochial level. The canonical obligation to maintain archives and make them available was repeated in the *Codex* of 1917-8 (Can. 375-8); when he was Cardinal Montini the present pope commented on the matter authoritatively in 1958.[36] In 1955 a papal commission had been appointed to survey local ecclesiastical archives. If these could be better arranged it would make it easier to abandon the assumption that the Italian church and the papacy are coterminous, an assumption fortified by the magnificent records at the Vatican and the working reference library there, superbly useful for church history.[37]

7

It will take time to assess the effects these innovations will have. More immediately apparent is the activity of a group of scholars who have founded the *Rivista di storia della chiesa in Italia*. Since 1946 the new journal has acted as a focus of sophisticated scholarship of a kind long familiar in trans-Alpine lands. Perhaps the erudition of the contributions is over-displayed, their footnotes sometimes vastly exceed their texts, they are still obsessed with bibliography sometimes to the exclusion of reflection. But they are trying to be both wide-ranging in their coverage of the Italian church, and they are trying to bring to their work something like the professionalism expected in other areas of scholarship. This activity is matched by a number of works of excellent scholarship, to some of which I shall refer in the course of these lectures. It may soon be the case that the church of the Italian 'nation' so feared by other 'nations' at Constance and later can be written about in a manner that will do justice to the importance of the theme, and on the basis of well-founded research.

A concluding complication is the continued political tensions which exist in church–state relations in Italy. The constitutional relationships imposed during the Risorgimento and re-negotiated in the Concordat of 1929[38] are all too obviously falling into fragments, but a whole range of current problems until very lately bedevilled ecclesiastical research, the most conspicuous of them being tithes.[39] Nor can one any longer regard the church at the highest level (pope and Italian cardinals) after the reign of John XXIII (1958–63) as speaking with one voice. Conciliarism, recently regarded as dead as a door-nail, is once more raising its head and some clergy regard this as hopeful and some as ugly. Historians who are Italians and who are to any degree devout are often divided between themselves and this is occasionally evident in their work, perhaps even accounting for the excessive documentation to which allusion has just been made.

The upshot of these complicated and interrelated developments must also be seen within the context of a political Italy committed to substantial political devolution and a 'state' which, at any rate since the Second World War, has lacked the means for effective central government. What the results of all this will be for church historians in the peninsula remains to be seen. Those of us working in most other lands on periods as remote as the Middle Ages and Renaissance must be grateful that we are at present exempt from such confusing uncertainties.

2

DIOCESAN AND PAROCHIAL ORGANISATION

Bishoprics

In the course of the previous discussion it was mentioned that Professor Alberigo had written to 100 diocesan archivists and had replies from half of them. This is noted again here not necessarily to justify his conclusion that, since half of the replies suggested that there were no significant pre-Reformation records, a biographical or any other approach based on the systematic use of local church records would be unfruitful – though this may well be true – but to lead the reader to the heart of the matter. Professor Alberigo might, had he so wished, have written to many more archivists. The vast number of bishoprics in Italy was and is one of the central facts about the Italian church.

How many bishoprics were there in fifteenth-century Italy? It is a much more difficult question to answer than one might suppose, since lists of bishops as printed for instance in Tangl's *Kanzleiordnungen*, let alone contemporary early printed *vade mecums* for the clerical visitor to Rome, contain errors and omissions, sometimes of an inexplicable kind.[1] So – perhaps even more alarming in view of the use regularly made of it – does the *Provinciale* printed as an appendix to each volume of Eubel's *Hierarchia catholica*. Nor did the number remain invariable: a few bishoprics were created or recreated; a rather larger number were suppressed or united with other bishoprics. At present the occasion for such changes need not detain us, save to note that new sees were created not because of the needs of the faithful but as a sign of honour, the best example, though not the only one, being Pienza in 1463; the elevation of Florence (1420) and Siena (1459) to metropolitan status had a similar intention and was devoid of administrative or, of course, of religious significance. The unions of bishoprics were often due to poverty and depopulation.

The resulting picture (if we exclude the island bishoprics)[2] can be set out as in the appendix to this book (below pp. 110–22) and summarised as follows:

	1400	1500
Central Italy	64	61
Southern Italy	137	129
Northern Italy	62	63
TOTAL	263	253

When one recalls that there were only 131 sees in France, only 67 in England, Wales, Scotland and Ireland (34 of them in Ireland) one can see how imposing the numbers of Italian prelates were.[3] If we include sees on the Italian islands and in the Italian controlled parts of the Levant and if, for good measure, we add the Italian bishops *in partibus*, Italian bishops were unquestionably more numerous than all the others put together. This for long haunted the consciences of sensitive Italians. Cardinal de Luca writing in 1675 his *Vescovo pratico* is at pains to point out that this is not the result of a dastardly papal plot but a product of history: 'for the most part they are ancient foundations'.[4] This was of course the case, and there is no need here to rehearse the way in which the bishops of the early church established themselves in the towns of the Roman world, which were especially numerous in the south of Italy. Romans and later Italians (one thinks of Flavio Biondo[5] and succeeding historiographers) reckoned the prosperity of Italy by counting the numbers of her cities and regarded a multiplicity of bishops as a very healthy sign. It did, however, raise problems in church government unlike those encountered in the other provinces obedient to Rome.

One immediate consequence of Italy having so many bishoprics was that most of them were extremely poor. Presumably this was always the case, many of the earliest sees in Italy simply withering away. When some sort of comparative figures become available with the imposition of papal taxation in the late thirteenth and fourteenth centuries (the tax known as common services, originally a third of the original gross annual income of a see) we can measure the situation with a little more confidence. The average assessment of a see in England and Wales was 4,000 florins; of a see in Italy it was not quite 400 florins, and it would not have been as high as that save for a handful of rich sees in the north.[6] The break-up is as follows:

Italian sees

Median Assessments		*Highest*	*Lowest*
North	862 fl.	{ 10,000 (Aquileia) { 4,000 (Ravenna)	33⅓ (two)
Centre	328	2,000 (Lucca)	40 (one)
South	184	2,000 (Capua, Naples)	25 (Rossano)

The overall poverty of Italian bishoprics is crudely reflected in these figures. One can argue that to use the level of common services as an index of relative prosperity is unreal and in exact terms this is certainly the case, for it is hard to know how the original estimates were arrived at in the thirteenth century, and, since the taxes hardly changed in centuries, it is obvious that in some cases they would overvalue a concistorial benefice (i.e. bishops and abbots) and in some cases undervalue it as time went on. So far as the fifteenth century is concerned it was likely to be the case that the taxes in general were burdensome, since the thirteenth century had been a period of economic prosperity and in many places, including many parts of Italy, the fifteenth century was still a period of regression. Since virtually all of the common-service revenue came into the curia direct it was a tax which curial officials were most reluctant to diminish though this was occasionally done, notably of course in the concordats after Constance, but also in respect of individual bishoprics. An Italian example is provided by the wretched diocese of Dragonara, in the province of Benevento, where a plea for help was made on grounds of 'Guerram, turbines, mortalitem, pestes', and the bishop was given the income of Lesina as well, i.e. he held Lesina *in administrationem* (see below p. 19); apparently this did not succeed for Dragonara, like one or two other southern sees, was reduced to an archpresbytery in the next century.[7] Thus there were in Italy many bishops who were often not much better endowed than those with titular sees although, however tiny their diocese, it involved in theory pastoral responsibility. The large number of needy prelates in the south is particularly notable, and partly explains why the popes of the period disposed so readily of promotion in what was often enemy territory: no ambitious Aragonese cleric bothered much about such a shabby reward. Popes were able to fill unimpeded sees 'immediately subject', where the rights of the metropolitan had been suspended. All the sees of central Italy (save two) were in this convenient category. So were a surprisingly large number of sees in the kingdom of Naples. It is only in north Italy that this was as rare as it was in the rest of Christendom. Far the greatest number of sees immediately subject go back beyond our period, although a creation of 1474 may be quoted.[8]

The archbishop, as known in the north, was also a stranger to Italy. Here again this is a phenomenon with an explanation in early centuries. It is sufficient for us to note that the provinces of Italy were of little meaning in normal circumstances. I can find only a single metropolitan synod in this period and this is due to the one man who conducted a metropolitan visitation – S. Antonino, arch-bishop of Florence.[9] On the whole the metropolitan sees were wealthier and so they were coveted by important and ambitious clergy; they were grander (at Benevento, for instance, the archbishop claimed 'papal' privileges such as the right to demand from suffragans and abbots visitations *ad limina* of S. Bartolomeo)[10] and this made them attractive to curialists, anxious for precedence as they moved through the corridors of power; and in a few cases they lay at the centre of territorial lordships of which they were in effect an integral part and could therefore not be treated negligently (Naples, most obviously, Milan and, in the second half of the fifteenth century, Florence and Venice). These considerations apart, the 25 archbishops of Italy can be dealt with along with the bishops.

How were Italian bishops appointed? The process had none of the simplicities of the English or French situation,[11] where the Crown directed the chapter to elect the same person who was to be provided at the same time by the pope. In theory all Italian sees were filled by papal provision, whether they were immediately subject to the pope or not. This did not mean that the pope was always a free agent. He was frequently obliged to provide candidates put to him by persons able to make their views prevail over his, and cases of this will be noted shortly. More rarely he was faced with the action of a chapter going through a genuine, old-fashioned election – though here again one suspects that unless the magistrates or the prince supported such action it would not normally have been tolerated by the pope, at any rate after the Schism and its effects had really ended.[12] An interesting case occurs, in fact, just as the Schism was ending. On 5 January 1417 Niccolò Albergati was elected by the canons of Bologna in chapter. Albergati was prior of the Charter-house in Bologna and the citizens were proud both of it and of him, but they must have known that he could be awkward – and indeed he was difficult immediately, trying to get the commune to pay his common services, insisting on the return to the episcopal *mensa* of certain lands usurped by the city. At any rate six months later, his election having been confirmed by the archbishop of Ravenna, he was installed in his cathedral.[13] Would this have happened so smoothly if there had been a pope? For in January 1417 there was no pope: John XXIII had been deposed and so had Benedict XIII; Gregory XII had resigned. In November of that year Martin V was elected at Constance as a result of proceedings even more unusual than those which had just occurred at Bologna, for he had been elected in a conclave where the 'nations' had representatives sitting alongside the cardinals who were in the council. There are other late medieval capitular elections in Italy, but they are less remarkable than Albergati's.[14] We may take as an example what happened at Verona in 1453. There Dom Gregorio Correr was elected by the canons in chapter and supported by representatives of the commune, as well as by the signoria at Venice. But Nicholas V had already translated Ermolao Barbaro from Treviso and this was reluctantly accepted by Venice; Verona and its chapter had no real choice in the matter.[15] Pius II was no different from other popes in insisting on his right to provide to all Italian sees. He nevertheless insisted on capitular elections in the foundation of his own new bishopric of Pienza.[16] A similar provision is to be found in the bull (1433) uniting the sees of Nepi and Sutri, and in that (1437) uniting Città Castellana with Orte.[17] Detailed studies are needed to penetrate through theory to practice.

In the area dominated by a powerful family or commune provision by the pope was tempered by pressure of a political kind. This was what happened, of course, everywhere in Christendom, but the results in Italy were less predictable and the whole process often became intricate beyond belief. The duke of Milan (who normally sent two names to the pope but instructed his ambassador at the curia which one he was to press for) succeeded in getting his brother Gabriele provided to the archbishopric of Milan in 1454; and three years later he was successful in nominating Carlo da Forlì; but in 1461 he failed and had to accept a curialist – albeit a very distinguished one – Stefano Nardini, provided by Pius II, and the first of a series of non-residents. Nor were the Venetians uniformly victorious in their dealings with the popes, even with the Venetian popes, perhaps especially with the Venetian popes.[18]

The Venetians had felt obliged to devise formal machinery for filling vacant benefices, in the optimistic hope that rules and regulations were all that were needed to produce clear answers and avoid lobbying or chicanery. In the senate candidates for vacant prelacies were voted on and the successful candidate was then supported by the signory in a letter to the pope. It was an offence for a Venetian to approach the curia directly; the result of the ballot was unalterable. In this way the patricians hoped to avoid the operation of pressure groups, for there had been a significant rise in the number of aspirants in the 1360s. The vote or *proba* was frequently effective in producing a candidate for whom the Venetians were prepared to exert maximum pressure – often for political reasons – to secure a bishop who would be loyal to the Serenissima and in particular to keep out foreigners, who would drain away Venetian wealth; this problem obviously loomed larger with Venetian expansion on *terra firma*. For instance, the Republic voted for Maffeo Ghirado as patriarch of Venice in April 1466; Paul II (the Venetian Barbo) refused because he wanted a patriarch who would obey him and not be a creature of the Republic. But two and a half years later the senate got its way. A few years afterwards, and towards the end of his life, Paul II gave three Venetian bishoprics *in commendam* to three Venetian cardinals. Giovanni Michiel was given Verona, Marco Barbo the patriarchal dignity of Aquileia, Battista Zeno the see of Vicenza. The Venetians were furious and refused to allow these men to touch the revenues. After six months, in September 1471, the bulls of provision for Marco Barbo were accepted and he became patriarch. There then ensued over four years of convoluted negotiations and arm-twisting[19] before the others were admitted to their temporalities – which they enjoyed only from April 1476; income from the earlier years had been spent (so the Venetians said) on the war against the Turks. Many other examples could be given of the tug-of-war between pope and senate.[20] In all this it should be remembered that the pope frequently heard of a vacancy and filled it before Venetian views could reach him.[21]

Such negotiations are also found all over the peninsula in cases where territories had changed sides owing to the advance of armies, or political intrigue; they will come before us again when we consider the effects of the Schism. Francesco Maria Visconti went to unscrupulous lengths to rid Cremona of its bishop when he obtained the town in 1420. When Venice occupied Cremona she insisted that the former Visconti nominee should be replaced by a trustworthy Venetian (1405);[22] in the 1430s Venice insisted on men she could trust occupying monasteries in Bergamo and Brescia for similar reasons.[23] In any case states bitterly resented having their revenues depleted for the benefit of strangers and perhaps even having enemies established in their midst. One remembers the anti-French sentiment behind the English Statute of Provisors as one hears Francesco Sforza thundering about the need to have one of his subjects as abbot of the great Milanese convent of Chiaravalle and refusing to allow the Venetian Paul II to add it to the papal patrimony, as another Montecassino. The upshot of this affair was that Sforza's son Ascanio was made a clerk and given the house: it was hard for the pope to refuse to provide the duke's son. (This set Ascanio on a career which nearly gave him the tiara.)[24] Much the fiercest competition between the dukes and the pope came with the first Borgia pope, Calixtus III (1455-8), when lavish grants of expectatives and *commendams* were made to Borgia cardinals in Milanese territory – treating Milanese territory with the voracity displayed in Spain itself and the Regno.[25] In 1454 Alfonso V wanted Cardinal Scarampo (to whom he was in debt) to have Montecassino *in commendam*; when Calixtus at first demurred, Alfonso threatened to send troops in to flatten the monastery, and the pope complied.[26]

Even where a strong tradition of Guelf loyalty to the papacy conditioned public action, the need to control senior church appointments manifested itself. This is clearly evident in the Florentine story, which is odd and interesting. Here it had been decided at the end of the fourteenth century not to have a Florentine as bishop, but rather to treat the office as on a par with those magistrates (such as the *podestà*) which went to strangers. This lofty attitude was maintained well into the fifteenth century. Palladini (1410) came from Teramo, and Zabarella (1410-11) from Padua, Corsini, it is true, was a Florentine (1411-35), but he was followed by Vitelleschi (from Corneto – now called Tarquinia – in the Papal States, 1435-7) and by another dubious climber, Scarampo, who was born in Venice (1437-9). Scarampo was followed by another stranger, Zabarella (Bartolomeo, 1439-45). Nearly all these men were non-resident. At this point there seems to have been a change in the attitude of the government. The signoria nominated to Eugenius IV a short list of five names, all Florentine. These citizens were passed over but Eugenius listened instead (it seems) to Fra Angelico and appointed another Florentine, Antonino Forcilioni, the future saint.[27] On Antonino's death the government again tried to get its way. Pius II was in the town at the time that Antonino lay dying and the petition presented to him by the gonfalonier Bernardo Gherardino asked the pope to provide Gianozzo Pandolfo – or at any rate a Florentine. The pope chose a Florentine curialist called Orlando Borlandi, who was succeeded by the Neroni who had been Florentine favourite in 1455. Neroni died in 1473, expelled from the city for his part in the abortive conspiracy of 1466 against Piero di Cosimo. In the 1470s Sixtus IV's ambitions for his family often outweighed considerations of prudence and when Neroni died the pope's nephew, young Cardinal Pietro Riario, was made archbishop of Florence. However, in January 1474, when Riario died, the next archbishop, though a Roman, was the choice of Lorenzo de' Medici. This was Rinaldo degli Orsini, Lorenzo's brother-in-law. He was followed by Cosimo de' Pazzi, who had been bishop of Arezzo since 1497. Cosimo died in May 1513 and Leo X then made his cousin Giulio de' Medici bishop who was later, as pope, to secure an even more permanent Medici victory in Florence. But it is my impression that both republican and later princely Florence was more anxious to secure obedient bishops in the *dominio* than in the capital itself; hence the fuss when Sixtus IV promoted Francesco Salviati to the archbishopric of Pisa in 1474.[28]

As the fifteenth century progressed there is little doubt that the attitude of Italian governments hardened. The papacy was now a medium-sized Italian government itself and, as we shall see, this had significant consequences for papal policy. It became important to the other powers in the peninsula to have a loud voice in the curia and a vote in the conclave. We are, after all, on the eve of the French invasion when a prince entered Italy who had behind him three centuries of almost total mastery over his prelates; and he was to be chased out by Charles V who, from his Burgundian and Spanish background, was equally determined to get his way in senior church appointments in his territories. Papal liberty of action by the 1530s was effectively limited to the Papal States – and even in those there were sometimes intransigent princelings, whose vassalage to the Holy See was not allowed to conflict with family interests. Indeed it was from hungry members of this group that many senior members of the Roman curia were drawn.[29]

Within the framework described above the Italian episcopate, while in certain fundamental matters similar to the episcopate elsewhere, was subjected to unusual pressures and responded in curious ways. In the south were a multitude of impoverished bishoprics, often held by friars who lived as the vicars in spirituals of their comparatively wealthier brethren in the north; and in the centre and north were sees which habitually went to swell the income of curialists or courtiers. The oddities to be seen in Italy to which some attention should be paid are : the exchange of bishoprics, the treatment of office as a property and (related to this) the dominant role of certain families in some sees for several generations.

Exchanges of benefices were, of course, not a new thing. The 'chop-churches' of late fourteenth-century England attracted the censure of Archbishop Courtenay; Italian priests also followed this practice from time to time.[30] But outside Italy were there many cases of bishops exchanging their dioceses? A careful survey of the personnel of rather more than half the bishoprics of the fifteenth century yields the following examples of such changes:

1400	Termoli – Monte Corvino
1406	Pisa – Taranto
1438	Mondovì – Belley
1443	Gallipoli – Motula
1449	Sarsina – Forlì
1454	Orvieto – Penne and Atri
1463	Parma – Modena
1483	Penne and Atri – Telese
1484	Sutri – Nepi-Bitonto
1487	Telese – Lavello
1489	Teramo – Taranto
1493	Città di Castello – Rossano (see below)
1502	Bologna – Vercelli[31]

'Chop-churches' in England were men who were trading in their revenues: a well-beneficed man who was heavily in debt could raise the wind by selling his lush living for cash to a purchaser who had a poorer living but some ready money. This process, 'resignatio ex causa permutationis', in cases where there was a marked disparity of income, suggested a presumption of fraud, according to the great canonist Felini Sandeo.[32] Some of the above oddities may be explained in this way, but this can scarcely be proved since we have no figures for real income but only the assessments of the camera regarding common services. We can, however, hardly doubt that the brokers who trafficked in the sale of offices at the curia acted as intermediaries in some of the episcopal shifts and changes.[33] Some cases are clearly due to straight political adjustments, negotiated between governments and curia. With this collection of exchanges may be associated the curious career of Niccolò Ippolito, a clerk of the diocese of Ariano who became bishop of the small place in 1480. The next year he was translated to the impecunious archbishopric of Rossano (assessed at 25 florins and with no suffragans in his so-called province). Thence Ippolito moved in 1493 to the better-off see of Città di Castello, being compensated for the loss of his status as archbishop by promotion at the same time to the titular metropolitan dignity of Caesarea. Finally our archbishop *in partibus* returned to Ariano whence he had started, in 1498, holding it until his death in 1511.

Goings-on like this are surely uniquely Italian, and a sad comment on episcopal office in the Italian peninsula.

The turn-over of bishops – one is tempted to say the output – in Italy was much higher than in France or England, partly at any rate because something like a *cursus honorum* obtained in trans-Alpine Europe. There a bishop normally moved from a small bishopric to a bigger one, from an unimportant bishopric to an important one or to a metropolitan see. Of course this happened also in Italy. But so also did the reverse. Nor was exchange of church due solely to financial embarrassment or the greed of prelates. One must also not rule out papal anxiety to raise money from a frequent levying of common services and other benefits of a financial kind.[34] After all translation without the consent of a prelate was legislated against at Constance, and in the fifteenth century it was much more difficult to move an unwilling incumbent. All in all, however, it seems likely that the switching about referred to above was normally at the instance of the clergy concerned, who usually had little interest in their flocks. They had never seen them.

The treatment of office as property is nothing new and is not especially Italian: indeed historiographical tradition would have it that the *Eigenkloster* is mainly a northern or Teutonic phenomenon. In the fourteenth and fifteenth centuries the condemnation of simony was maintained, but in practice it was eroded in several ways. The most obvious was the outright sale of appointments at the curia – admittedly without cure of souls – at first in a very small way at Avignon and then in *quattrocento* Rome on a massive scale, income from this source becoming an essential element in papal finance and, since it led popes to multiply offices, directly affecting the machinery of papal government. But in subtler ways doctrines developed which justified the resignation or renunciation of a benefice while either reserving a pension from it, or the right of regress, or both. *Resignationes in favorem* (i.e. resignation in favour of a specified person) became such a scandal that Julius II and his successors tried to control them by insisting in their being registered in camera and chancery, and then by trying to prevent fraudulent entries in the curial records – with results which may be studied in the Vatican Archives.[35] With *resignationes in favorem* went the right of 'regress'; for example if the bishop who had resigned did not get paid his reserved pension regularly he could resume the benefice he had resigned.[36] With this machinery available the traffic in benefices at all levels, and of monastic offices as well, was intense in the fifteenth century in Italy. It is most noticeable in the case of the bishoprics.

Together with the practice of granting the income of a benefice without residence, termed in the case of a monastery *commendam* (technically in the case of a bishopric the grant was *in administrationem*), the right of 'regress' and the reserving of pensions, the way was open for the creation of what Clergeac described as 'les véritables apanages', what Tacchi-Venturi called 'fiefs'.[37]

These probably became much more prominent in the sixteenth century than in earlier periods, despite the legislation of the Council of Trent and the continued criticism of abuses in the resignation procedure. But one is struck in looking at Ughelli or Eubel at the regularity with which members of the same family follow each other in office even in the fifteenth century in Italy. Self-indulgent popes set an example. Aeneas Sylvius Piccolomini who became bishop of Siena in 1450 retained it when he was promoted cardinal in 1456. When he became pope two years later he was succeeded as bishop (archbishop the next year) by his nephew Antonio; and Antonio was followed by Pius II's sister's child Francesco, whose brief pontificate as Pius III was to come in 1503. Pienza from its foundation in 1462 was a Piccolomini preserve, and from 1467 the same clan collared Sovanua. Of those bishoprics for which detailed notes have been made for this study there is one (Alba) in the hands of the Carretto family for eighty years. Marsi and Trevico (both near Benevento) remained under families that did not change for respectively 70 and nearly 60 years; while the list of sees where one family reigned for 40 or 50 years is too long to rehearse. These 'proprietory' churches existed from time to time all over Italy.[38] Certainly many additional family connections existed which are not self-evident to the researcher who is unfamiliar with the locality and its history, and the varied nomenclature within a given dynasty.

What sort of men were Italian bishops? The prominent ones jump to mind – the ambitious men, the scions of great families, the important pluralist cardinals. But, numerous as such bishops are, they are only a fraction of the total. Below that level a much larger group is formed by the sizeable number of what Ughelli calls 'well-born' or 'of gentle birth' – lesser gentry and nobility from town and country, but mainly of urban origin. Often, of course, such men were also members of the papal curia and their ability to gain promotion was partly due to their being favourably placed. It is sometimes staggering how short an interval elapses between an incumbent resigning and another being provided.[39] There is no doubt that on very many occasions two Italians – even if not habitually resident in Rome – paraded together in the offices of the chancery to get their bulls and in the offices of the camera to pay or pledge their common services; often the same day is given for resignation and new appointment. And below this numerous and avid band lie perhaps an equal number of regular clergy, especially friars and, among friars, especially Dominicans. This impressive number of regulars is, I believe, in marked contrast with the rest of Europe where regular bishops become rarer after the thirteenth century. It represents further evidence of the relative poverty of the majority of Italian sees. The bishop's endowment or *mensa* did not attract men of substance, who might accept provision to a poor see but only for the title and honour it carried in Rome or at some prince's court – and they really wanted the fatter sees anyway. So the mendicants stepped in, and often eked out their meagre stipend by acting as vicars for richer bishops. Mendicants also constitute the overwhelming majority of bishops with sees *in partibus*, and Italian mendicants also filled most of the shadowy Italian-controlled bishoprics in the Levant, to which reference has been made above.

Thus it is, in a way, somewhat irrelevant to ask who the bishops were, since most of them did not reside in their bishoprics. In the bigger centres they usually took possession by proctor fairly rapidly, at any rate within six months of the provision. Then at some time in the next six months or so the new bishop might make a ceremonial entry, which was an occasion for much ritualistic pomp, civic processions and bad temper.[40] After that the bishop often withdrew permanently to his normal area of operations – Milan, Naples, Rome – drawing his stipend and hiring deputies as necessary.[41] Frequently the poorer cities never set eyes at all on their shepherds, only on their proctors.

If one had endless space one could illustrate the bishops of Italy in considerable detail for this period, and catalogue those that were bad and – for there were some, as we shall see later on – those that were good. In fact, even in Italy the bishops remain a significant cog in the machine of church government and they will crop up in subsequent chapters. A very good survey of the quality of the Italian episcopate at a slightly later date (the early sessions of the council of Trent) is provided in Professor Giuseppe Alberigo's book.[42]

Parishes

This chapter will conclude with some remarks on the secular diocesan clergy. If this were to be done thoroughly it would require some elaborate analysis of the cathedrals and their chapters. These contained, in Italy as elsewhere, large numbers of often rather litigious clerics, whose quarrels occupied much of the time of bishops and their officials; one or two wretched bishops were especially unfortunate, like the bishop of Bergamo who suffered from two warring co-cathedrals each with its own chapter.[43]

Capitular organisation was in many cases very different from what one is familiar with in England and other parts of northern Europe. This partly reflected the smaller size of most dioceses (markedly tiny in the south of the peninsula), and the dominant position in public life of the baptistery and the cathedral. But two important differences seem independent of this: the rarity – in effect the non-existence – of the monastic cathedral in Italy; and the relationship of archdeacon, dean and provost in capitular importance. Monastic cathedrals were, it may be supposed, commoner in areas of more recent conversion and the vicissitudes of Montecassino, a bishopric for a short time in the fourteenth century, reminds us that arrangements, if temporary, such as are found at Canterbury or Durham, were not entirely unknown in Italy.[44] But Montecassino did not survive long as a bishopric, and only one Benedictine house in our period remained a see – Nardò (near Lecce), permanently from 1413; Cava, near Montecassino, reverted to monastic status in 1471.

As for the chapter in Italy the archdeacon tended to have the most seniority, whereas in the north of Europe this dignity went to the dean. The dean in many Italian churches was even less grand than the provost, somtimes even lower than the cantor (or precentor). On the other hand, since the diocese was small the archdeacon never acquired territorial responsibility, whereas parochial duties had to be attributed to a chapter member, usually the archpriest.[45] Here are a few not untypical chapters, one big, one small (both being old) and one small but recent.

Ferrara[46]	*Brescia*[47]	*Montefiascone*[48]
Archpriest	Archdeacon	Dean
Provost	Archpriest	Sacristan
Archdeacon	Provost	6 canons
'Primicerius'	'Vice-dominus'	
Custos	Precentor	
Treasurer	Dean	
Dean	17 canons	
14 canons	Penitentiary	
2 prebendaries	Theologian	
(one the penitentiary, one the theologian)		

This, in fact, is far from giving a true picture. Every big cathedral had a large number of other clergy. For example at Ferrara there were 8 *mansionarii* (resident canons) and 50 beneficed chaplains in a college separate from the rest. The chapter at Milan was as aristocratic as any German body, after Archbishop Ottone Visconti so ordained in 1277 (later they were drawn from a book called the *Catalogus centum familiarum*, though there were often more than a hundred). The chapter in the fifteenth and sixteenth centuries consisted of five 'dignities' – archpriest, archdeacon, 'primicerius', provost, dean;[49] three *personatus* – theologian, major penitentiary, *doctor prebendatus* (presumably the 'scholasticus'); and three further groups – 15 priests, including the archpriest (all called locally 'cardinals' – not unusual in large cathedrals), 10 deacons including the archdeacon, 5 subdeacons. These were collectively the canons, termed *ordinari*. In the fifteenth century there was added a small section of *ordinarioli*, who had the insignia of canons and had the right to be nominated as canons when vacancies arose in the *ordinari*, but who meantime drew no income.[50] The Brescian clergy, besides 6 *mansionarii*, or residents, included 11 chaplains and 150 other clerks.

It will be evident from the previous remarks that the bigger (and probably the smaller) cathedrals had difficulty over non-residence, pluralism[51] and a combination of both; and that, despite the number of men technically qualified as clergy, it was difficult to have adequate choir service as required by law. Various remedies were attempted. The 'canon in residence' and the vicar-choral (to use English terminology) make their appearance.[52] What is quite overwhelming is the number of *chiericati*, 'priestlings', found in some northern dioceses, clustered in vaguely collegiate fashion around, drawing tiny stipends from, some ancient foundation. This invoked the wrath of Eugenius IV in 1440 when he found '769 ecclesiastical benefices called *chiericati*' in the diocese of Verona, held by separate individuals who took their small stipends but performed no services, however small. Eugenius took sharp action. The 'benefices' were reduced to 190, and the saving thus attained was to be devoted to providing a teacher of grammar and music in Verona cathedral. This was bitterly resented by the Veronese. The council sent a deputation to explain that the *chiericati* were poor clerks, who had drawn small sums from parochial revenue from time immemorial; and in fact Eugenius climbed a long way down, allowing the bulk of the *chiericati* to fade out.[53]

Chiericati (indeed those at Verona) were not solely the product of city churches but are found also in rural communities. The rural

'Italy'. When two Italian cameral clerks struggle over a living at Chambéry is this an episode in Italian church history or French?[1] Is Chambéry at this stage French? In dealing with the diocese I have explained that Aosta has been treated as an Italian see, but its bishop was suffragan to the archbishop of Tarentaise.

Anyway it is evident that the popes were Italian (except for Calixtus)[2] and so were most of their curial administrators, as well as the bulk of their revenues, on which more later. It seems likely that a careful study of the clerical background of each pope would do much to illuminate the assumptions he took for granted as a result of his earlier experience. Pastor gives thumb-nail sketches of each pontiff as he became a cardinal. More is needed. The attitudes (for example) of Gregory XII, Eugenius IV, Paul II cannot be understood unless one examines the position in the Venetian scene of the devout patrician, and unless one explores in the case of each man the tensions between a republican political tradition and the autocratic papacy.[3]

The effects of the Schism

The most important influences on the popes of the fifteenth century derived from events that had little directly to do with the Italian church. The Schism of 1378 was produced by long-standing tendencies in the curia (at that time overwhelmingly French) and notably by the resentment of the cardinals, all-powerful in conclave but helpless in concistory. But once the dust had settled the division threatened Italy with direr consequences than other parts of Latin Christendom. The effects of the Schism were directly proportional to the structure of government and in Italy government in many areas was exceedingly divided, thus encouraging the popes to try to exercise their jurisdiction in ways that would be an embarrassment to their rivals. In the initial stages of the Schism the effects were not so severe as they became later.

The Neapolitan who took the title of Urban VI at his election in April 1378 was soon (September 1378) faced with a rival 'French' pope, Robert of Geneva, who took the title of Clement VII. Failing in a military effort to rout Urban, Clement took himself off to Avignon and the clergy of France had their own pontiff – a privilege they came later to regard as dearly bought. Europe divided round these 'obediences' on purely political grounds and European rulers took advantage of the opportunities offered for hard bargaining. But it is my impression that under the first two rival popes (Urban VI died in 1389 and Clement VII in 1394) the game of beggar-myneighbour was not undertaken seriously at the expense of the church in Italy. With the election of a Catalan Pedro de Luna to succeed Clement (with the title of Benedict XIII) and the election of another 'Roman' pope, Boniface IX (Tomacelli) the situation gradually changed. Under Clement VII the position of the French pope was not seriously queried in France and he made few if any provisions to Italian bishoprics; Urban VI and Boniface IX likewise seem in the main to have kept to their own obediences and not deliberately sought to inflame passions by provisions which could not be literally effective.

With the 'Roman' Innocent VII (Migliorati), who reigned from 1404 and with the French attempts to put pressure on Benedict XIII to end the Schism (siege at Avignon 1398–1403, final withdrawal of obedience 1406), and the departure of Benedict to Valencia in 1408, one begins to find evidence of awkward rivalries. Curiously enough these do not affect very much the college of cardinals. There were, it is true, occasionally two cardinal bishops with the same title, but few cardinal priests or deacons. This relative absence of competition was chiefly due to two factors. During the Schism popes created relatively few cardinals, since the election capitulations during the period signed by the elect pledged him not to prolong the Schism and large colleges would obviously have done that. Apart from Urban VI, who created 43 (many of whom deserted him or were disposed of by him) and whose election, after all, had started the whole business, the others, three Roman, two so-called 'Avignonese' and two 'Pisan', over a period of 40 years accumulated only 97 – an average of just over two a year (kept as high as this by the 49 of the two Avignon popes),[4] as we shall see the popes of the later fifteenth century were to do better than that.[5] More important, what mattered to a cardinal financially was the right to share the main source of papal income and the ability to accumulate benefices despite the normal prohibition of pluralism. This, of course, had also led to capitulation undertakings not to increase the numbers sharing in the income.

There are some, but not nearly enough, studies of the effects of the Schism in Italy. The muddle it created not unnaturally provoked Eubel to some thoughtful reflections as he tried to list the bishops for his *Hierarchia catholica*; no one could have given a better overall picture, but this unfortunately he did not provide.[6] One generalisation he did venture to make: there are far more cases of competitive appointments, i.e. bishops provided at about the same time by different popes to the same see, in border areas, areas touching on rival obediences; and he implied, which was certainly the case, that this was particularly so when there was political rivalry between authorities anxious to extend or retain power in territories where it was challenged. There are several signal examples of this. One is Venetian–Austrian ambitions in Friuli, which turned on the person of the patriarch of Aquileia.[7] This was (at the critical moment) Antonio Panciera, promoted to the patriarchate by Boniface IX in February 1402, who had lands in Friuli and was regarded by the Venetians as essential to their interests in the region. Hence the Republic exerted enormous diplomatic pressure to prevent the summoning of the Council of Pisa lest it should lead to the patriarch being replaced by someone else. When Gregory XII at the end of 1408 was reduced to being taken care of by the Malatesta the Venetian viewpoint changed and, having failed to get Gregory to come to Venice, they withdrew their obedience from him and instructed all clergy in the *dominio* that they must follow suit.[8] The Venetians, like Italy and most of Europe, recognised the popes of Pisa, Alexander V and John XXIII. The struggle went on to control Friuli, and grew more intense after Panciera was induced to renounce the patriarchate (against compensation).[9] The contenders were Jacopo da Ponte provided by Gregory XII in 1409, and Ludwig duke of Tek, favoured by Sigismund who became emperor in 1410–11. Tek finally had his title approved in 1418, as part of the settlement after the Council of Constance. Meanwhile the inhabitants of Udine vainly protested, soldiers marched over the land, and no one could pretend that any pastoral functions of the patriarchate were being considered for some 20 years.

So much (and more could be adduced) of the tensions on the Italian–German front. In the north-west Ligurian and Piedomontese bishoprics faced France and were much at risk. Vercelli, for example, was regarded almost as a Savoyard parish. Innocent VII provided Matteo de' Giselberti in 1406, having in the process deprived of the see one of Urban VI's surviving cardinals, Lodovico Fieschi. Meantime actual possession of the see lay with Jacopo de' Cavalli, whom Clement VII had provided in 1379. Subsequently John XXIII deprived Giselberti and provided Ibleto Fieschi (26 August 1412) while translating Jacopo de' Cavalli to what was, in effect, a titular see in Wallachia.[10] Ventimiglia is another example, which has been investigated already.[11] Here there are a dazzling series of bishops, *catolici* and *scismatici*; the former were sometimes in Ventimiglia, the latter in Sospello, now a small place inside France. Here they are:

Ventimiglia	*Ventimiglia (Sospello)*
Jacopo Fieschi, provided by Urban VI, 1380, translated to archbishopric of Genoa 1382	Bertrando Impati, O.F.M., provided by Clement VII, 1380, d. 1386
Benedetto Boccanegra, provided by Urban VI, 1382; d. 1418	Pietro Marinacco, provided by Clement VII, 1386; translated to archbishopric of Famagusta by Benedict XIII, 1409
Tommaso Rivato, provided by Martin V in 1419; d. 1422	Bartolomeo de' Giudici, provided by Benedict XIII, 1409, d. about 1420
	Zaccaria Degna, provided by Benedict XIII, 1421

What happened in the end to the shadowy Degna is not clear. De' Giudici was confirmed in the see by the Pisan pope Alexander V. The series then becomes more or less rational again. Benedict XIII had then been deposed (1417). Genoa itself had a tough time and so did Naples.[12]

Another, if rather different, border area lay to the east and south of the Papal States, in the kingdom of Naples. Here again the 'Avignon' popes could and sometimes did find local support. For an early example we may turn to L'Aquila. Here Giacomo Donadei had been provided by Clement VII in 1391, but he prudently turned in 1405 to the obedience of Boniface IX; Benedict XIII then gave the see to the bishop of Lucera if he could evict Giacomo, but this he failed to do.[13] Much the same fate befell the bishop of Teramo in 1412.[14]. Fortunately by the time the Aragonese had conquered the kingdom in the early 1440s they had long since deserted their Catalan compatriot Benedict XIII, who in any case died in 1423.

One could go on with many more examples. I have counted some twenty sees where there was confusion in the period of the Great Schism, and no doubt there are a good many more. The later and smaller upset over the Council of Basle and the election of the Antipope Felix V seems to have produced, as one would expect, far less trouble. At Cortona Eugenius IV deprived Matteo Ughi or Ghinotti because he adhered to the Council and provided someone else, but this seems to have been quite ineffective and Ghinotti held the see until he renounced it about 1454, reserving a pension.[15] At Chiusi (where earlier in 1410 Alexander V had deprived the bishop as an adherent of Gregory XII), Alessio Cesari, provided in 1438, was challenged in 1443 by a bishop appointed by the Council of Basle.[16] The troubles of Domenico Capranica, appointed cardinal by Martin V in 1426, but not recognised by Eugenius IV, and who betook himself to the Council, belong to a different set of pressures.[17]

An aggravation of these troubles, and an aspect of the situation which prolonged the consequences of a double appointment was that once a man had been consecrated as a bishop (which is not technically a matter of ordination) he was and remained a bishop. This was explicitly recognised by the Council of Pisa as it grappled with the problem of bishops (most numerous in Italy) each with an entitlement, so to speak, to the same see. At the 22nd session on 27 July 1409, just after Alexander V's election, the Council decreed that 'all elections, postulations, promotions ... provisions regarding prelacies . . . all consecrations of bishops made by the two pretenders and their predecessors in favour of persons who now recognise the Council are valid if they took place before the sentence of deposition and in canonical form. If for any reason in particular cases this would damage any individual's interest, being a supporter of the Council, the pope will seek an equitable solution'. And the Council stated further 'that all who possess benefices should continue to possess them in all security provided they were legitimately acquired and will not cause to suffer any supporter of the Council'.[18]

This doubtless covered most of the cases it was designed to cope with. But it emphatically did not deal adequately or at all with the problem of two bishops each claiming the same see, each with a valid claim. Eubel printed the bull of Boniface IX validating Giacomo Donadei to the see of L'Aquila in 1401 when he switched his allegiance; in this Boniface formally absolved Giacomo from censures levelled against him as a schismatic and confirmed him as holding office as a properly consecrated bishop.[19] Such action, which resulted in a plurality of claimants, was often healed by translating one of them to another see, sometimes *in partibus*, with a pension drawn on the contested bishopric. As an immediate measure a pope could order what amounted to an *ad hoc* division of the revenues. John XXIII did this in the disputed see of Ventimiglia, where in 1412 he directed that De' Giudici should remain in possession of part of the see until his rival died, in terms of the Pisan decree.[20] In this document the other legitimate bishop, Benedetto Boccanegra was referred to as *episcopus in universali ecclesia*.[21]

The consequences of these divisions were thus long in being solved and in part account for the ease with which secular rulers often stimulated changes in the episcopal succession in their territories. Gregory XII's subservient grants to the Malatesta when he was a client of the court at Rimini, notably of papal vicariates, were not to be reversed (if that is the right word) until Pius II's violent confrontation with Sigismondo Malatesta. But other lords, big and small, and republics like Venice, took advantage of conflicts between popes and the muddle that survived when the Schism technically ended in 1417, to further their interests through the clergy in their domains. That sometimes it paid them to do a deal with the pope we have already seen.[22] Broadly speaking, however, the evidence for princely and municipal interference in episcopal elections, in capitular nominations and in securing abbots of their own choice is overwhelming and would take far too long to rehearse.[23] Obviously divided allegiance among the clergy during the Schism and its aftermath facilitated this process of lay erosion of clerical immunities.

The effects of the Schism also affected papal policy in other ways. By encouraging and then stabilising the divisions in religious orders – especially the Franciscans, but to some degree other friars and even orders of monks – the Schism and the Council of Constance which ended it greatly complicated the Italian branches of the rival families. By making heavy demands for papal intervention they were to further discredit the efficacy of central direction, and this will be discussed later.[24]

At Constance the doctrine had been accepted by the Fathers that in the last resort popes were subject to properly convoked general councils, and arrangements were made for regular meetings of general councils in the future. The doctrine of conciliar supremacy (to reduce the complex programme of Constance and Basel to a convenient formula) had long been of concern to a few canonists, aware of the dangers that might lurk in the untrammelled sovereignty of thirteenth- and fourteenth-century popes.[25] The crisis of 1378 was a striking instance of the condition for which conciliarism (another familiar piece of shorthand) was a drastic remedy. The senior clergy who in 1414 faced the scandal of three popes accepted the notion that Christ's purposes were reflected in the whole church as represented in a council. In the winter of 1417–18, after Martin V's election (in effect by the whole council, since delegates of the five 'nations' joined the cardinals in the conclave) it seemed that the pope had also assented to the ultimate superiority of a general council. In fact this was far from being the case. Although Martin and subsequent popes did not dare to reject the terms of the decree *Frequens* (a council to be held five years after Constance, another seven years after that, and then every ten years) they could and did do their best to avoid summoning them. And they entirely repudiated the concept of papal responsibility to a council, however summoned, however ecumenical. In this their instinct was sure so far as their temporal power was concerned. Of course every prince in Christendom invoked the Constance decrees *Sacrosancta* and *Frequens* when he wanted to influence the pope. But in practice kings allowed the prelates whom they continued to nominate to pay common services to the papal camera and this, it must be admitted, was the pope's main interest in the Christian world outside Italy. Charles VII or Louis XI of France might huff and puff, but French bishops and abbots paid their dues, however belatedly, and so did English prelates until the break with Rome, and this despite the Statute of Provisors.[26] Where conciliar doctrine was a more immediate threat to the popes was Italy. There any lordling could defy the pope on grounds that righteousness would prevail at the ensuing general council.[27] Everyone could play this game, from disgruntled cardinals down to unfrocked priests: the Council of Basel had its share of both and a few cardinals two generations later staged their own *conciliabulum* at Pisa in 1511, at the instigation of the French government. None of this happened, of course, in well-regulated monarchies where baronial reliance on ancient liberties was by now a thing of the past, and where lords were becoming courtiers. But the popes for four hundred years had made it their policy to prevent the emergence of any strong government in Italy and they were now to pay the price, first by promoting endemic disorder, ultimately in their own political insignificance.

The election of a Roman noble, Oddo Colonna, in 1417 inaugurated a practically unbroken series of Italian pontiffs. In the circumstances after Constance this had far-reaching consequences. Those circumstances were: a depleted papal treasury and a reduced regular income for the popes as a result of the concordats which halved papal taxation in France and Germany: a need to establish political control over the Papal States, both for fiscal reasons and for considerations of security – lest another Ladislas of Naples, or another Giangaleazzo Visconti, should have Italian ambitions; and gradual acceptance that papal action was now necessarily to be undertaken with due respect to the interest of the pope's family, just like the public programme of any other Italian prince.

Belief in the propriety of helping friends and relations was deeply engrained in medieval man – even, perhaps, more deeply engrained

than it is in modern man. Popes were not exempt from this sentiment. They also knew how divided had been the conclave which
had elected them, how desirable it was to have dependable members
in the college. At Avignon all this had been reflected in a large
number of cardinals drawn from the province of the reigning pontiff
(a predominant number of Limousin cardinals had been, after all,
one factor in the unsatisfactory conclave which elected Urban VI
and precipitated the Schism) and in a very large number of papal
relations attaining the purple. Professor Guillemain reckons that 27
papal relatives became cardinals between 1307 and 1376: that is a
fifth of the total.[28] His laborious work, which has yet to be repeated
for the fifteenth century, shows a similar disposition of the administrative and other offices of the papal curia.

For a time after Constance these practices seemed to have been
abandoned. Martin V inherited the remnants of three colleges. In
addition he inherited a conciliar decree limiting the college to a
maximum of 24, as well as a memory of earlier election capitulations
which had also tried to limit the creation of cardinals. All of this
doubtless accounts for Martin's caution so far as cardinals were concerned; at his death the number had dwindled to 19. It may be
noted also that he took seriously another Constance injunction – to
appoint cardinals from all over Christendom. He created three
cardinals from France, two Spaniards, an Englishman, and a
Greek.[29] His successor Eugenius IV behaved in a similar way. For
somewhat different reasons he had also to elevate a number of
foreigners; the total college rose by 1447 to 24.[30] In the short
pontificate which followed, Nicholas likewise had to accom-
modate within the college some of the former rebels of the Council
of Basel, but the total had dropped to 20 when the pope died in
1455.[31]

The three pontificates which run from 1417 to 1455 were thus in
marked contrast with the pre-Schismatic papacy in regard to the
promotion of relatives and friends: the decree *Frequens*, one might
guess, if not the outright doctrine of conciliar supremacy, was partly
responsible. Nevertheless one should not exaggerate the purity in
this respect of Martin V and Eugenius IV. Martin promoted his
nephew Prospero Colonna and thus encouraged Colonna interests
in Rome so as to arouse the suspicions of Eugenius at his accession
that a plot was afoot against him. As for Eugenius, he promoted
his nephew Francesco Condulmer in 1431 and another nephew
Pietro Barbo (the future Paul II) in 1440, when Lodovico Scarampo,
another Venetian, also got the cardinal's hat.[32] There were thus

three Venetians in the college in the second half of Eugenius's reign, a bigger representation than that of any other region of Italy. Finally, while applauding Nicholas V's 'perfect freedom from nepotism'[33] we should note that he made his half-brother Filippo Calandrini a cardinal. It is also perhaps worth noting that at the conclaves of both 1447 and 1455 the issue seemed to observers to be a straight fight between the two Roman families of Colonna and Orsini.

The pontificate of the elderly Catalan Alonso Borja (20 April 1455 to 6 August 1458) was short but critical in establishing a new trend. Of the three cardinals of the promotion of 1455 two were nephews of the pope, one of them, Rodrigo, destined to be a mighty nepotist in his turn. All the pope's military and civil power soon came into the hands of a third nephew, Pedro Luis. Not only was the personal household of the pope staffed with Catalans, which was reasonable, but they became sufficiently numerous in the administrative offices of the curia to make for bad feeling.[34] Do what one will to justify Calixtus by stressing his merit in fighting the Turk and in resisting the outrageous demands of Alfonso V of Naples, there can be no doubt that the pope did his best to endow his family as rapidly as possible.[35] He doubtless did need friends in Rome; he would have needed fewer if he had not behaved with such ruthlessness. His support for Pedro Luis anticipates Alexander VI's support for Cesare Borgia.

Pius II promoted as cardinals two relatives and an adopted member of his family (Ammanati) and he secured a lustrous future for two lay nephews.[36] Paul II raised three nephews – Marco Barbo, Giovanni-Battista Zeno and Giovanni Michiel – to the purple, but restrained himself from further patronage of relatives, perhaps because of his alleged 'austerity', perhaps because the Republic of S. Marco was jealous of the success of Venetians.[37] Paul had also promoted Francesco della Rovere, Franciscan general and theologian, of a poor but honest family from the east end of the Riviera di Ponente, who succeeded as Sixtus IV. Sixtus's brother and sisters had a good many children and papal bounty was generously bestowed on papal relatives. In 1471 two nephews were promoted cardinal, Pietro Riario and Giuliano della Rovere. Pietro died early in 1474. Three years later three more nephews became cardinals, Cristoforo, Girolamo Basso and Raffaelo Sansoni; after a few months Cristoforo della Rovere died and the old pope at once promoted Cristoforo's brother Domenico. This proliferation of red hats was, of course, only part of the story, as was the formidable accumulation of prelacies by each of these princes of the church. Other children were given secular promotion (notably Girolamo Riario) and married with the best dynasties – Naples, Milan, Urbino. It would be tedious to catalogue the duchies provided for his kinsfolk in the end of the day by this Franciscan pope, so innocent of money matters and hence so careless of *meum* and *tuum* (this is the traditional defence).[38] From completely obscure beginnings the della Rovere in a generation had become one of the great families of Italy. Cardinal Giuliano della Rovere failed to get himself elected pope but he got the tiara for a pliable Ligurian, Giovanni Battista Cibò. The latter, who styled himself Innocent VIII, was the father of two illegitimate children born before he had been ordained a priest, and he had for them and their children a cosy family feeling: marriage into the Medici family and the Aragonese of Naples were the immediate fruit of his policies. Other pickings went to his brother Maurizio, and Maurizio's son Lorenzo was made a cardinal in the one promotion of this short pontificate. And so finally to Alexander VI, dealt with here as an Italian and not as a Catalan. Though Alexander at different times made cardinals of his son Cesare, a nephew, two great-nephews and a cousin, he was not supported in concistory at any one time by more than three of them since Cesare was permitted to resign his cardinalate on 17 August 1498 and the pope's great-nephew died in 1500. As with the two predecessors, however, the success of the Borgia family was secular rather than ecclesiastical. Their origins, though reputable, would never otherwise have led to their becoming one of Italy's leading noble dynasties, related to everyone who mattered, rewarded with countries, duchies, principates in Italy and Spain.[39]

There is little need to insist on the way family ambitions circumscribed the Italian policies of Calixtus III and succeeding popes. The way in which Italian politics were disturbed by this was due to the haste with which the popes, already elderly at their election, had to act if they were to succeed in establishing their relatives in strong positions in secular society. The Pazzi conspiracy was a good example of this; so was the career of Cesare Borgia. By promoting relatives to the college of cardinals a pope not only gave himself immediate allies in the curia but provided a modicum of protection for his relatives exposed to jealous rivalry when he died. He might even hope that one of his kinsmen might become pope and – who knows – turn the extraordinary elective absolutism of the papacy into a hereditary monarchy of traditional shape. We have encountered two Borgia popes and two Piccolomini. With Julius II we will meet another della Rovere and very soon after that there were two Medici. I do not suggest for a moment that Eugenius IV calculated the result but the fact remains that Paul II was his sister's son. Thus in the century after Martin V there were thirteen popes, but they were drawn from only nine families.

The rôle of the college as a source of popes became intensely important to Italian princes as soon as popes began to play Italian politics at the dynastic level and on this scale. And so we find popes under pressure to nominate cardinals from the dynasties of the peninsula. There had indeed been a secular tradition for old Roman families to be represented. But Orsinis and Colonnas were small beer in the Italian power game. It is arguable that Amadeo, ex-duke of Savoy, soon to be ex-pope Felix V, was in a way the first cardinal of the new kind when Nicholas V promoted him in April 1449 after the Council of Basel was dead and buried; it is not as absurd a point as it sounds – the family provided bishops of Geneva from 1444 to 1482, thus removing a tiresome pocket in the ducal domains. At any rate there is no doubt about what was happening when we find Pius II promoting the first Gonzaga cardinal, Sixtus IV promoting Giovanni, son of Ferrante of Naples, in 1477 and Ascanio Sforza in 1484. The first Medici cardinal was promoted by Innocent VIII and he was in due time to become Leo X;[40] the first Este and the second Aragonese by Alexander VI.[41] It is true that by the end of the fifteenth century princes all over Europe were anxious to have their own cardinals, though not necessarily princely ones. But such non-Italian cardinals did not normally reside in the curia[42] and concistorial business, as of old, was usually in the hands of a retained curial cardinal. The Italian cardinals were frequently high officials of the papal administration, held important legations in papal territory, and above all were able both to influence the recruitment to their own college and to elect a future pope in conclave.

The college as a whole became a little larger: (and this trend was to continue until the maximum was – notionally – fixed at 70 by Sixtus V in 1586).[43] On New Year's Day 1500 there were 35 cardinals alive compared with 21 in 1450. Mainly as a result of Alexander VI's lavish creations several old titles, not used since the thirteenth or early fourteenth centuries, had to be revived and one new title invented. More significant are the numbers in conclaves: when a cardinal in a hurry averaged only 10 or 15 miles a day it will be clear that only those already resident in Italy had much chance of being present.[44] This information is best shown in the form of a table:

Date of Conclave	Number of Italian cardinals present	Other cardinals present	Election of:
1431	6	6	Eugenius IV
1447	11	7	Nicholas V
1455	8	7	Calixtus III
1458	9	9	Pius II
1464	11	8	Paul II
1471	6	2	Sixtus IV
1484	21	4	Innocent VIII
1492	22	1	Alexander VI
1503	27	11	Julius II
1513	18	7	Leo X
1522	36	3	Adrian VI
1523	34	5	Clement VII[45]

The figures tell their own story – of dwindling non-Italian influence at papal elections, with the exception of the two conclaves of 1503 (Pius III and Julius II) which display the large number of Spaniards promoted by Alexander VI. The election of Adrian of Utrecht in 1522 was a freakish result; the papacy had in fact become Italian. It might still interest Charles V to secure his nominee, or tempt Henry VIII and Cardinal Wolsey. But such pressure had to be mainly exercised through the Italian members of the college, and only had international significance because of the wars in Italy between the emperor and the king of France.

Another way in which the fifteenth-century popes confined themselves, or were confined by circumstances, to the peninsula lay in their finances. A good many of the older papal revenues from Christendom had been reduced by concordats and conciliar legislation. A contemporary estimate of 1429 said that papal revenue was a third only of what it had been before 1378.[46] This is, it seems, an exaggeration, but income had certainly halved. Although common services continued to be paid by all prelates, other papal taxes were in effect only collected in Italy, and in most of the country only with the consent of the local ruler, prince or commune. Even in the Papal States the older 'spiritual' revenue (*decimae* and so on) shrank. In the place of these sources of income the popes had perforce to raise money in other ways. The direct and indirect taxation of Rome and other papal territory was stiffly increased.[47] In the latter part of the *quattrocento* the sale of offices in the curia was systematically pursued and extended to attract substantial and regular sums; other high offices (cardinalate, masterships of military orders) were sometimes sold.[48] There was also, of course, the Tolfa alum which popes tried to enforce with spiritual (but not economic) sanctions on the cloth manufacturers of Europe at the high price commanded by the Levantine product. We must not forget the way in which the papal plenitude was boosted by more frequent jubilees, by an active exercise of the dispensing power and by multiplying indulgences. But the picture that emerges shows the heavy dependence of the popes after the Schism on their Italian revenues. 'Reform', as will appear, usually meant tightening up the rules for collecting money.

Various soundings have been made for Martin V's pontificate (1426–7), Eugenius IV's (1436) and Pius II's (1461–2).[49] These are based on the real revenue of the papacy, on the books of the Introitus and Exitus, though substantial sums were routed into the papal privy purse. On the earliest date the accounts show revenue totalling just over 100,000 florins, though Dr Partner reckons the real total to be 170,000. In 1436 the accounts show revenue of 60,000, a measure of the effects on taxation of the pope's troubles in Italy and with the Council of Basel. The efforts of Pius II to pacify the Papal State and raise funds for the Crusade are reflected in an income shown in the Introitus of 470,000 florins. This sum should be compared with those 'budgets' prepared in Sixtus IV's pontificate, which are based on what should have come in, not necessarily on what did come in. They do, however, enable an assessment of the character of the revenues: 'We may perhaps take 170,000 ducats as a conservative figure of the net profit made on the Papal States by the Apostolic Chamber, and 120,000 ducats as an average figure for the product of the "spiritual" taxes and the venal offices, giving a total income for Sixtus IV of about 290,000 ducats.'[50] These proportions are, roughly speaking, the reverse of what they had been in the fourteenth century. Finally a similar sort of estimate of papal dues is available for 1525.[51] Here the total 'appears to have been in the neighbourhood of 432,000 ducats, made up of 220,000 ducats from the temporal power and 212,000 ducats from the spiritual power'. By the early sixteenth century papal revenues thus appear to have recovered, as a result of a careful exploitation of the papal state, and an increased 'spiritual' revenue from the sale of graces of various kinds as well as of venal offices. These last were a very ingenious device for a time. In effect they were for the office holders an investment and for the camera a way of borrowing. In order to guarantee an interest of 11 per cent the camera had indeed to allocate some funds itself – but half the interest was in effect paid by the persons who were doing business with the curia and who had to pay taxes to officials on scales laid down in advance.[52]

These developments, it will be evident, had a clear message for the popes – to maintain and extend their Italian resources, in Rome and the Papal States. The prolonged campaigns of Martin V, Eugenius IV, Pius II, the prominent position of unsavoury cardinals like Viteleschi and Scarampo, these can be justified since the late fifteenth-century popes were placed more securely in control of their lands than they had been for centuries and – it seemed until 1527 – especially firmly entrenched in Rome. It is fashionable nowadays to justify the exploits of Cesare Borgia in these terms. If he and his father the pope had not been struck down in 1503 by the fever which killed Alexander it is perhaps not certain that the papacy would have continued to get much revenue from the Papal States, unless the popes had all been Borgias. But that Julius II's bellicosity was in the proper tradition we may not doubt.

The figures quoted show of course that the papacy did not count and had never counted as a European power, comparable to France, England or Aragon, so far as physical resources were concerned.[53] Even in Italian terms the popes from Pius II onwards were not in the front rank; in financial terms a contemporary reckoned the papacy as a medium-sized Italian power towards the end of the fifteenth century.[54] This admittedly ignores those spiritual powers which the popes disposed of so influentially. They could not only oblige with a divorce; they could (as Henry VIII discovered) refuse to oblige. The pope, that is to say, could win friends and influence people in ways that are not always available to a modern autocrat.

Nevertheless the relative insignificance of the pope as prince may go some way to explaining the policies which were to turn Rome into the leading Renaissance city by the end of the fifteenth century. This will be discussed later and at this juncture I shall merely indicate one feature which does not directly derive from Renaissance motives although it is expressed frequently in the Renaissance manner. I refer to papal self-advertisement. As one walks up from the Porta Sant' Anna to the Cortile del Belvedere, where one goes into the Library and the Archives, one goes under an arch of the corridor built across the gardens from the old palace to Innocent VIII's *villetta*. This corridor was constructed by Julius II and over one's head as one goes in the fact is proclaimed in 'handsome and large capital letters in white marble which stand out against the dark brick': JULIUS II PONT. MAX. LIGURUM VI PATRIA SAONENSIS SIXTI IIII NEPOS VIAM HANC STRUXIT PONT. COMMODITATI.[55] When does this massive manifestation of papal possessiveness begin? The display of papal coats of arms is nothing new, as any visitor to Viterbo will recall. It is in the thirteenth century that popes begin to distinguish themselves with personal arms; it is not surprising that Boniface VIII was a pioneer – perhaps because his wretched predecessor Celestine V had no coat of arms at all. The fifteenth-century popes still sometimes used papal insignia alone, perhaps when, like Nicholas V, they were not proud of their lineage. Nevertheless Nicholas began the process of putting his name with his insignia (on the city wall, near the Porta Ardeatina) and, when rebuilding the Ponte Milvio, Calixtus also put his name besides the Borgia shield. From then onwards the popes commonly spell out their connection with buildings, as well as indicating it symbolically. Julius II is, it seems, the first pope to spell it out without the shield. This practice was to culminate in the preposterous frieze which runs across the façade of St Peter's, commemorating Paul V and subordinating the Prince of the Apostles, one might say, to a place in the wings, almost off-stage.[56]

The Roman curia

One immediate effect of an Italian papacy was the 'Italianisation' of the papal curia, the collective name given to the offices of papal government and the men who ran them. These ranged from the cardinals at the top down to ushers, messengers and other menial servants at the bottom. The curia was remarkable for its sense of solidarity. This was marked by two features: the groups within the curia acted *collegialiter* and they all helped each other – at the expense of their clients, the public lay and clerical which sought their services and paid for them. The habit of acting in a corporate or collegiate manner had been established first by the cardinals themselves, who shared some papal revenue and had their own chamberlain and accounts.[57] The habit of standing by one's colleagues against the outside world is shown by the frequent abatement or cancellation of customary fees when the individual was a member of the curia: phrases like 'gratis pro cardinale', 'gratis pro socio' are frequently found in the marginalia of all records where payment was involved; and so with cardinals' familiars and the colleagues' servants.[58] In these ways the whole curia was a team, with strong allegiance to the machinery they operated and from which they benefited.

The officials of the central administration of the church were already numerous when the papacy gradually established itself again after Constance. One of Martin V's first actions after his election was to re-enact the rules of papal administration which had technically lapsed between the deposition of John XXIII (29 May 1415) and the resignation of Gregory XII (4 July 1415), and the election of Martin V (11 November 1417) over two years later.[59] The curias of Gregory and of John were redeployed at Constance and this side of the council – the council as head of the church and employer of the apparatus of central government – still awaits its historian, so far as I am aware. Some of the abler men (one thinks of Poggio Bracciolini) kept out of mischief by pursuing literary interests; one, Leonardo Bruni, resumed a career as Florentine chancellor; others became secretaries to important prelates; and some were employed by the council – which had its rota, its penitentiary, its camera and its chancery.

If we are ignorant of the administrative personnel at Constance, it cannot be said that we are well informed regarding the papal administration after 1417. The substantial volumes of von Hofmann on 'the offices of the curia from Schism to Reformation' are extremely helpful, and (like everyone else) I have relied on them very heavily;[60] but the material in them is less ample and much less satisfactorily presented than the equivalent information about Avignon in the masterly book by Bernard Guillemain.[61] It is certain that Italians were in a large majority in all departments, even during the pontificate of Calixtus III when the immediate servants of the pope, his *familia*, in the sense of his personal household, were overwhelmingly Catalan. The predominance of Italians should not be taken to mean that other nations were not represented, sometimes at the very highest levels.[62] Martin V inherited a French vice-chancellor, Jean de Brogny (1409–26) and appointed as his successor Jean de la Rochtailée (1436–7), and Sixtus IV made another Frenchman, Guillaume d'Estouteville, his *camerarius* (1477–83). The Strasbourgeois Johann Burckard, whose *Liber notarum* furnishes so many details for the pontificates of Alexander and Julius, was master of ceremonies. And so one could go on. Yet such strangers were becoming less common and were reaching less exalted positions. The current language of inter-departmental business in the offices of the curia was Italian by the end of the fifteenth century – doubtless a relief for the northerners who had learned a Latin regarded as barbarous at Rome.[63]

For Italian clergy the most remarkable development was the growth in the size of the curia, and this despite the undoubted contraction of business as time went on. In the Avignon period the size of the administrative units varied a good deal from pope to pope within each pontificate. It was, however, roughly between 450 and 500 persons, of which two-thirds were in the main departments of the camera, the chancery and the penitentiary and the rota, the rest being in the *familia* (household) and the bodyguard, police and so forth.[64] By the early sixteenth century (1514) numbers had risen to something over 2,000. This staggering rise was part of a deliberate policy, which created offices in order to sell them.[65] The history of this development is hard to trace with precision since the prohibition of simony remained a prominent plank in all programmes of so-called 'reform', conciliar and papal. There can be no doubt that offices were sold from time to time at Avignon and during the Schism (John XXIII seems to have been active).[66] Martin V seems to have encouraged the process and despite his high moral qualities Eugenius IV was evidently aware of the traffic in the papal guard, for it was then laid down that no sergeant could sell his office before he had served in the curia for at least four months.[67]

The pressure for regularising the situation arose probably as much from the administration itself as from an ever poverty-stricken pope. Office was to a great extent rewarded by fees from the clients of the curia, as was of course the case in all administrative machines at this time. Now if one depended for one's living in large measure on fees it was necessary to ensure fair shares. Hence the pressure for collegiate organisation – a pressure first exerted long ago by the cardinals themselves, who carefully divided their joint revenue under their own *camerarius*, and who were insistent in trying to restrict their number to a decent and profitable minimum – both points to which reference has already been made.[68] Cardinals' hats were never regularly sold by popes; only from time to time. The collegiate system of sharing income did lead, however, to the regular sale of offices. The abbreviators, secretaries, protonotaries and all the other corporations of officials held appointments which came to be venal. By abolishing the abbreviators Paul II earned the dislike of humanists who had found employment there; Sixtus IV earned their praises by re-establishing their college. And it was Sixtus IV who of all fifteenth-century popes did most to extend the multiplication of saleable offices. This policy, albeit at a slower pace, was followed by Innocent VIII and Alexander VI. With Julius and Leo there was another leap forward. By this time the sale was, in many cases, of posts which had no function, that is, no rôle in involving fees from the public. It was therefore necessary for the *camerarius* to pay an annual interest on the purchase price. In effect the system was in large measure a not unreasonable if usurious way (11 per cent) of anticipating revenue.[69]

The technical term for these venal offices was *vacabilia*, since they were vacated and available for resale at the term of the holder's life or if he obtained promotion.[70] It was reckoned that there was a complete turnover of all *vacabilia* every 15 years. Here was a further reason for the award of prelacies to curialists and for the rapid rotation of Italian bishoprics. Thus the curia became more and more Italian and more at any rate of the senior curialists found promotion in the church of Italy – at every level. One should perhaps add that the 'expectative' (the entitlement, other things being equal, to a future vacancy), long established for papal provisions to benefices, was now applied to *vacabilia*. Promotion to a benefice seldom meant that individuals went from Rome to an archdeaconary or a bishopric in the provincial church to which they had been provided. They stayed in the curia, or if they left it they went as papal officials to the cities of the Papal States. Put in another way, many members of chancery, camera, penitentiary, datary and so forth who had purchased their posts in the curia (and others who had not) later got stipends from Italian benefices. Only exhaustive study would establish how far this process had gone, but everything suggests that it had gone a long way by the end of the fifteenth century. I have analysed the fifteenth-century bishops of 30 Italian sees (18 in the south, 6 in the centre and 6 in the north) and for what it is worth the figures are as follows: of the total of 223 appointments there are insufficient clues readily available to make a guess in 22 per cent of the cases: about 18 per cent look as though candidates had been promoted as a result of local pressures of some kind: princely protection probably accounts for about 27 per cent. Of the balance, some 32 per cent were promotions of men who had been or still were members of the papal curia. We may note in passing that senior curialists and the clergy protected by princes were mainly interested in the richer sees – not that many of these would have been regarded as such outside Italy, where of course similar use of rich benefices was common enough. All over Christendom canonries, archdeaconries and bishoprics went to civil servants whose stipends as public officials were usually inadequate and in any case were hardly ever paid with regularity. Now two developments in fourteenth-century administration deserve to be carefully noted. Outside the papacy and the Papal States there is a distinct trend towards the employment of laymen and away from the employment of clerks: the English Signet Office is a case in point.[71] By all accounts the *reverse* was happening in the curia and in the provincial administration of the popes. Whereas laymen were not uncommon in the early fifteenth-century papal service, they became rarer in the later fifteenth century where we encounter fewer figures like Poggio Bracciolini or Flavio Biondo. The system of *vacabilia* clearly encouraged this trend since it was more profitable to sell as many posts as possible to clergy who could then be promoted out of them.[72]

Within the curia precedence was of prime importance and we may recall in this connection the upheaval over the papal pronotaries. Martin V had allowed them precedence over bishops and at the appeal of Domenico de' Domenichi, who wrote a book *De dignitati episcopali* on the subject, Pius II deprived them of this privilege.[73] How important was precedence may be guessed at when one examines, for instance, the procession which took Innocent VIII to the Lateran after his coronation, the celebrated *possesso*. After the pope's barber and tailor (very necessary on such a long and exhausting day) came the household servants and courtiers, the nephews and kinsmen of cardinals, papal and civic heralds, flagbearers (note that the papal arms were carried separately from the arms of the church) chamberlains and ambassadors who were not prelates, various clerical officials, then the secretaries and advocates (*mixtim* by papal order since they had just had a row over precedence). Then went the acolytes, cameral clerks, auditors of the rota, papal subdeacons, the Greek deacon and subdeacon, and the *abbates forenses*. Finally in degrees of growing proximity to the pope, the bishops, the archbishops, the bishops and archbishops in attendance on the pope, the abbots of Roman convents, the patriarchs and then the cardinals (deacons, priests and bishops). This was the supreme stage in the procession. Behind the pope under his baldachino came his marshal and soldan, throwing coins to the crowds, and the procession wound up in a group of officials – the dean of the rota down to the *corrector literarum apostolicarum*.[74] A beautiful miniature picture of Martin V's *possesso* procession survives which gives one some idea of the panoply.[75] One can, incidentally, see how princes and kings, Italians being no exception, found it desirable, if only for questions of prestige, to have a prelate as envoy to the Holy See, and preferably a cardinal.

Such were the great public displays in which curial officials and especially curial prelates were given a special pre-eminence. There was a similar importance attaching to the attendance at a secret concistory. Here the pope sat facing the centre of a semi-circle of cardinals, ranged around him according to seniority and custom, then rows of archbishops and bishops in order of seniority. At the concistory of 20 December 1484 there were 19 cardinals present, 4 archbishops and 55 bishops. Further there were 2 protonotaries, 2 subdeacons, an auditor of the rota, the *magister palatii*, a cameral clerk, a concistorial advocate, the procurator fiscal, 2 chamberlains and the master of ceremonies to whom we owe the list. Of the 59 archbishops and bishops at least 37 were Italian.[76]

I have referred repeatedly above to the bishops who owed their rank, and perhaps some of their whirligig translations, demotions, exaltations, to their membership of the curia. This, however, is merely because with Eubel and Ughelli reference works are to hand which make it relatively simple to identify many men of episcopal rank. (Relatively simple: as already noted, there are astonishing gaps and uncertainties in both works.) But there is no account available of cathedral dignitaries, no Le Neve, let alone a new series of Le Neves, such as historians of the church of England are blessed with. Some churches have publications which are helpful in this regard: the cathedral of Milan is a good example.[77] But for most great Italian churches the work of compiling *Fasti* remains to be done and I very much doubt if it can be done for many cathedrals prior to the seventeenth century. The churches of Rome were also often generous to curialists – the Lateran, Sa Maria Maggiore and, of course, St Peter's are found associated with curial officials, especially with officials on the way up to a bishopric or a cardinal's hat.

On the Italianisation of the curia and the effect this had on the *ecclesia italica* much therefore remains to be discovered. A rather better known story – though with serious gaps in it – is the Romanisation of the church in Italy. Prior to the Avignonese period the popes had not spent much time in the city from which they derived their title. As Mgr Mollat has insisted,[78] for the two hundred years prior to 1304 the popes were more frequently not in Rome than in it. Viterbo and Orvieto, Naples and Perugia, even for long periods France, these were the places where the pontiffs were more likely to be found by weary supplicants and ambassadors than in the City itself. For so prolonged an absence as was afforded by the Avignon period there was, however, no real precedent and the election of 1378, when the mob howled at the conclave to elect a Roman or at least an Italian, reflected the frustrations of a large if decrepit non-commercial town which had very much less significance and so a very much less comfortable time when the pope was absent. Yet not all of Rome's magic departed with the pope. The thresholds of the apostles did not leave at the same time as St Peter's successor and *visitationes ad limina* had at any rate to be paid for whether the pope was in Rome or not. The Jubilee was proclaimed by Clement VI at Avignon in 1350, attracting large numbers of pilgrims to Rome.

But Rome as a fountain of grace, as the Capital of Prayer,[79] flourished much better when the pope was there to keep a degree of order not only in the turbulent city but in the approaches through the Papal States. The election of a Roman at Constance was in many ways a turning point in this. Martin V steadily and securely obtained a fair measure of authority in Romagna, the Marches and the Patrimony. When he entered Rome in 1420 it was to stay there, not to treat the place as a temporary refuge. His successor, it must be admitted, had to make a hurried exit in 1432; Eugenius's ten years in Florence have always been recognised as contributing much to humanising – literally converting to the humanities – many members of the curia. After his return in 1443 no pope left Rome involuntarily until the Napoleonic conquest, though Clement VII must have wished to get away in 1527. And very few of them left the city even voluntarily until our own day. Two of the popes who did so, Pius II and Julius II, travelled, so to say, on business. Pius went to promote the interests of the papacy and of his own family in Tuscany (a trip where business was combined with pleasure) and again left Rome for the abortive crusade and his death at Ancona.[80] Julius's expeditions were more evidently related to mastering and protecting papal territory, if not to driving barbarians out of Italy.

From 1443 onwards with only the briefest of intervals Rome thus became permanent headquarters of the curia. No one seems to have asked or answered the question, when did the administrative departments stay in Rome even when the pope moved, when did they 'go out of Court'? I suspect that the process began with Pius II, who on one occasion reassured a nervous ambassador that, though he was leaving for Siena, his servants were to stay near Rome at Viterbo.[81] (Pius, on the other hand, stressed how advantageous it was financially for other towns to harbour the curia from time to time.) It was not merely that Italians and especially Romans feared another Avignon, though they did as late as Julius II's departure for Perugia and Bologna in 1506. Predictably, it seems to have been a law court that went out out of court first: the rota seems to have become a fixture sooner than the other department.[82]

This permanence in Rome led popes to those striking developments in the Borgo and in the Vatican palaces which have been chronicled respectively by Magnuson and Redig de Campos. The culmination of these programmes was the new St Peter's. This project had been conceived by Nicholas V. It was Julius II who really got the new building started, encouraging Bramante on that career of destruction which earned him the soubriquet 'il Maestro Ruinante'. Perhaps the old basilica was really unsafe, as Nicholas said and

Julius repeated, even on the foundation stone which, needless to say, carried Julius's name on it. He laid the stone on 18 April 1506, just before his expedition to Romagna.[83] There was soon to be a new church in more ways than just a fresh St Peter's.

The background to the Reformation in Italy ('reform before the Reformation') and the connection between clergy and Renaissance will be discussed later and it will bring us back to the Vatican and St Peter's. In the next chapter an attempt will be made to analyse the state of the clergy in fifteenth-century Italy, seculars and regulars, and the machinery of synod and visitation which in theory should have provided inspiration and prevented abuse.

4

THE STATE OF THE CLERGY AND LAITY IN FIFTEENTH-CENTURY ITALY

Secular clergy

In this chapter some impressions will be given of the clergy of Italy, seculars and regulars, and of the laity to whom many of them ministered. In approaching in this way somewhat nearer to the actual religious life of the period it is important not to forget how varied were the organisations in which Christians found themselves, even in the one obedience, even in one country or region, before the sixteenth century. I remarked before how difficult a problem it was to get behind Trent, when a mask of uniformity was laid on Roman Catholic Europe. We must constantly remind ourselves that the concepts of the parish, of the bishop and perhaps even of the cloister, were much more fluid in the Middle Ages, at any rate after the twelfth century, than in the epoch of the Counter-Reformation, or the Catholic Reformation as one is nowadays encouraged to call it. Despite papal leadership, despite canon law, a thousand years of Latin Christendom had left many oddities and variations; it is far from being the case that the services of the church were the same all over the Latin west; and the organisations that supported these services varied to an even greater degree. The discussion of the diocese and the parish in chapter 2 will have made this pretty evident to anyone at all familiar with the medieval churches of England or France.

This deserves to be stressed at the outset, since in England and in other northern European countries we are accustomed to find out about the pre-Reformation situations – both of laity and clergy – through the records maintained by bishops and their chanceries. The form this normally took was the copying of all the episcopal *acta* in large volumes called registers. England's series of bishops' registers is one of the most remarkable sources available for medieval history. By the end of the thirteenth century keeping records was increasingly regarded as an obligation by all bishops,[1] but it could be accomplished in various ways, or not at all. In Italy, as elsewhere in southern Europe, certification of records was the province of the notary whose books constituted an authoritative, legally valid, account of a formal act. It is mainly in the form of notarial instruments that we find the surviving evidence of the activities of Italian bishops and their officials – records of conveyancing of land and rights of all kinds, records of visitations, records of ordinations. Now all of this must be set against the relatively poor state of the episcopal and capitular archives which has already been mentioned; some do contain copies of the notarial instruments, but these are just as likely to be found in the notarial archives of the town, where such survive, though to find the material there often involves a very laborious search. It is one's impression that archives for the later medieval period kept in Italian churches big and small for the most part consist of titles to property of all kinds. If this is so, it is hardly surprising, since from property came the bread and butter which the clergy depended on. Without doubt more and more documents bearing on capitular election, ordination, visitation and synods will be discovered in notarial archives and in some capitular records.

As it is, a surprising amount has already been unearthed, especially for northern and central Italy. A number of ordination lists have been published, some general ones (for Bologna, Florence and Padua for instance)[2] and rather more lists in which the modern scholar – a Dominican or Augustinian friar, let us say – has extracted ordinations of members of his own order.[3] Besides this we have the series of more or less unpublished ordinations *apud sedem apostolicam*, in the Vatican Archives.[4] As for visitations and synods we have records of a fair number. Visitations, partial or complete, for one or more years, are available in print of some sort for the fifteenth century at Bologna, Brescia, Cortona, Milan, Padua, Piacenza, Pisa, Siena; and S. Antonino carried out metropolitan visitations of Fiesole and Pistoia in 1451.[5] For the regular clergy we have a good many records of general chapters and some visitation material, of which the most famous, but not the only, example is the *Hodoeporicon* of Ambrogio Traversari.[6] Canons promulgated by episcopal synods are not lacking: in the fifteenth century those for Bologna, Brescia, Florence, Padua, Piacenza and Sabina have been published.[7] There is a distinct correspondence of synods with the sees for which surviving visitation material exists; this is as one would expect. A half dozen towns with visitations in a hundred years and two hundred and sixty bishoprics is not a great deal, perhaps, and does not indicate a very active supervision of the clergy in Italy by their pastors. Much more such material doubtless exists, as observed already, and there is surely a good deal in print which I have failed to note. But it is pretty clear that visitations were rare. When those mentioned are examined it will appear evident that they do not indicate a high level of spirituality in either visitors or visited.

First, however, it is proper to discuss ordinations. Canonically these involved certain external and certain internal requirements, though we must remember that regulations on these matters were far from systematic and are found scattered in various parts of that systematic jungle, the *corpus juris canonici*.[8] The external requirements which had to be met were:

1. Ordination had to be by the ordinary of the clerk involved, or with his permission (through the issue of letters dimissory). The point of this was that the candidate's bishop might be expected to know the propriety of his entering the ranks of the clergy.
2. Ordination had to occur at the appointed times. First tonsure could take place on any day, but minor orders could only be conferred on holy days and major orders only on the Saturdays of the Four Seasons (*Quattro tempori*, or Ember days) and on the Saturdays preceding Easter and the fifth Monday of Lent (Sitientes).
3. The recipient of orders had to have a 'title', i.e. a means of support: a benefice, an office (for instance at the curia) or private income; membership of a religious order constituted a title, since all orders were in theory vowed to individual poverty and the friars also to corporate poverty.
4. Finally, a due interval had to occur between the conferment of one order and the next.
5. No money was to be charged for any ordination.

As for the internal or personal requirements these may be listed thus:

1. A candidate must be of decent appearance, and there must be no scandal, no repellent disease or deformity.
2. He must have attained the appropriate age: about 7 for first tonsure and minor orders; 18 for the sub-diaconate; 20 for diaconate, 25 for priesthood, 30 for bishops. (Friars were privileged and might be ordained priest at the age of 22.)
3. He must be of good conduct and virtuous background; in

particular illegitimacy was a bar unless a dispensation had been obtained.

4. For major orders (sub-diaconate and higher) chastity was essential.
5. For all orders a proper intention.
6. A level of education appropriate to the order involved; for a priest this was interpreted as the possession and understanding of books needed for the Mass, the Office, sacraments, penitential canons, and homilies, from which he could preach on Sundays and holy days. A bishop should have a higher level of instruction so that he could instruct the priests in his diocese.

All these requirements were to be enforced by the candidate's bishop, who was charged with his examination in order either to ordain him or issue him with letters dimissory which he could then take to some other bishop.

This prosaic information is set out above, in a cold and systematic fashion, partly because, oddly enough, it is not always easy to find these details in the works which historians usually consult[9] and partly because without some clear picture of what ought to be done it is impossible to measure the propriety of what in fact happened. And what in fact happened fell very short of what was laid down. It is difficult to know how to tackle the question of the level of education of parish priests. Visitation records make it clear that at the parochial level this was often poor or almost non-existent and the reason is not far to seek: the majority of priests were taught by a system of apprenticeship, in Italy as in every part of Christendom. A boy acted as server, was taught a modicum of letters and, thus prepared, was ordained. Virtually no simple curates resident in parishes had university degrees at any point or any place in the later Middle Ages. The Third Lateran Council in 1179 had laid down that every cathedral should endow a master 'to teach the clergy of the church and, without payment, poor scholars as well'. And the Fourth Lateran repeated the injunction in 1215, adding to it the direction that every metropolitan see should also have a teaching theologian.[10] These provisions did something to encourage the development of cathedral schools in France and England, and elsewhere in trans-Alpine Europe, but they had little effect in Italy where the universities, though numerous (there were 19 by the time Martin V was elected) were not in any meaningful way a source of priests. A good many doctors of civil law or canon law (or of both) became priests and reached high promotion in Italy; a few Italians continued well into the sixteenth century to frequent the celebrated theology schools at Paris and Cologne. The history of the Sapienza,[11] the Roman university, in the fifteenth century is a sad one, while the so-called Palatine university, the school presided over by the theologian in the papal curia who was entitled *magister palatii*, is obscure indeed at this time. The Italian universities were slow to acquire faculties of theology, or to incorporate within themselves the teaching sometimes available in an adjacent Dominican convent.[12] Nor was formal teaching in the arts (the *trivium* without which reading and writing Latin was hard to perfect) always available. Some cathedral churches did have a *scholasticus*: there was one at Pisa, but he taught (it seems) only the cathedral clergy, not the candidates for ordinations of the diocese as a whole.[13] We know there was one at Verona before 1440 when Eugenius IV took drastic steps to endow the office.[14] In the noble chapter of Milan the archbishop had dutifully provided a *theologus*, but his influence on education seems to have been minimal.[15] Several attempts were made to found seminaries in the fifteenth century: at Pavia, Bologna, Rome – but none were effective save those in Rome, about which more will be said later in connection with reform.[16] In any case the effective influence of the colleges established by Capranica and Nardini at Rome came at the very end of the fifteenth century.

The examination of ordinands by the bishop or his deputy was perfunctory in even well regulated dioceses in north Europe.[17] In Italy, as elsewhere, it seems often to have been avoided, if not entirely at ordination at any rate before collation to a living, so that the topsy-turvy situation arose of a beneficed clerk later seeking the appropriate orders with a title but sometimes without any other of the required qualifications. When Nardini was archbishop of Milan he legislated on this question in 1468.[18] But in Italy, as throughout Europe, there was an easygoing acceptance of the rightness of property and where a family held the advowson even a saintly bishop like Antonino of Florence, who took examinations of ordinands seriously, seems to have seen nothing improper in the granting of minor orders to sprigs of patrician stock merely to enable them to enjoy the income from a family church; in 1459 Antonino conferred minor orders on Filippo de' Canigiani who a fortnight later was inducted into the family living of S. Severo in Valla Marina.[19] A further factor contributing to slackness was the absence of a bishop, the regular way in which a vicar in spirituals performed those actions for which a bishop was required. In the 343 ordinations of which details survive in Bologna between 1341 and 1508, the bishop himself was present on only 18 occasions – and Bologna, let it be remembered, was a great see and had one or two devout bishops, including Niccolò Albergati.[20] In 16 ordinations at Pavia between 1464 and 1498 of which we have details the bishop was never present, only a suffragan.[21] The letters dimissory and the title were also productive of inadequate supervision. As has been pointed out, the whole intention of episcopal responsibility lay in the assumption that the bishop knew the youths he was ordaining as members of his flock; most Italian dioceses were indeed small enough to make this reasonable – which is one reason why we find no territorial archdeacons on the northern model in the peninsula. But this intimacy was frustrated not only by employing a deputy, some bishop *in partibus* or a hungry prelate from Calabria or the Abruzzi, but also by the extravagant and uncritical use of letters dimissory. Sometimes this can be partly explained by a see being celebrated, so that ordination there had added lustre, or perhaps might help a candidate to win important friends. Avignon, for instance, was magnetic in this way in France and adjacent countries. Long after the popes had left it the presence of a legate and the connection with Rome caused a high proportion of ordinands there to come from far afield.[22] Other places which attracted ordinands were seats of great universities. At Padua, of the 677 clergy ordained between 1396 and 1419, nearly a third came from outside the diocese, including a fair number of *stranieri*, especially Germans.[23] But we may suspect that candidates often went to a distant diocese in order to avoid too close a scrutiny. When Savonarola was ordained deacon at Bologna in 1477, of the 21 seculars ordained 6 had letters dimissory, 3 subdeacons, 2 deacons and 1 priest. As for titles we may note in this same ordination that nearly half the seculars were received *ad titulum patrimonii*, that is, the family guaranteed the cash; 6 were beneficed; 2 apparently had no title, which is the sinister aspect of the affair.[24]

All the problems touched on in the last few pages are found, in an aggravated form, in the practice of creating clergy in the curia itself. There are 14 volumes in the Vatican Archives called Formatori or Libri formatorum, from the name given to some of the documents (mostly letters testimonial) therein registered. The letters testimonial, together with a few letters dimissory, refer to the general ordinations which are also listed by the cameral notaries. A few consecrations of bishops and abbots (the episcopal dignity was not an *ordo* as such) are also recorded. The volumes cover the period 1426 to 1524, but the last ordination is recorded in 1500.[25] These volumes have been carefully scanned by scholars from Germany, from Poland, from

Ireland and Scotland. But – and it will be recalled that this is not untypical of the Vatican Archives – they have not been looked at by anyone directly interested in the Italian clergy as a whole, though Father Kaeppeli has extracted the Dominican names. They deserve consideration here since, even if every bishop in Italy had been resident and scrupulous in examining ordinands, it would still have been possible for the ambitious and the unscrupulous to obtain orders with a minimum of trouble in the Roman curia which still conveniently moved a good deal in the fifteenth century, as has already been mentioned. With a minimum of trouble, certainly, but, it should be added, with a maximum of expense – prohibited though it was to charge for the conferment of orders as a clear case of simony. And technically, of course, it was the letters and their registration that were taxed, though many candidates must have associated the orders with payment of cash.[26] All the acts registered in the Libri formatorum were undertaken in the name and by the authority of the *camerarius*; ultimately they derived from the powers of the pope as universal ordinary. None of this need necessarily have been corrupting, but contemporaries had no doubt that these ceremonies were a dangerous feature of the contemporary church. Numbers were often large: 58 received first tonsure on 21 December 1471, when there were also 16 minor orders conferred, and 31 holy orders – 105 in all. When General Ordinations occurred in Rome (and they probably did after 1449 – this too had 'gone out of court') notice was posted on the doors of the Castel Sant' Angelo, at the Campo dei Fiori and at San Celso (opposite S. Angelo across the bridge), adjuring those interested to present themselves during office hours on the Wednesday, Thursday and Friday preceding the Saturday of the ceremony.[27] Often these proceedings must have lacked dignity, and usually they must have involved only the most superficial verification of qualification and title. The ill-arranged, not to say slatternly, organisation of the registers themselves confirms that a certain degree of disorderliness pervaded the whole process. Naturally many foreigners are found – Germans, French, Spaniards, and a few natives of the British Isles. But there are also a very large number of Italians, more especially on the occasion when the curia found itself in Florence, for instance, under Eugenius IV when Tuscans often formed the largest group.[28] One would like to know what happened during Pius II's migrations but the registers covering his episcopate are missing. Is this a sign of commotion? True, general ordinations were by then available regularly, but would presumably have been arranged also in the part of the curia which was still itinerant.

The reason for recalling how easy it was to obtain ordination is that it goes a long way to explain practically unanimous evidence of the low quality of many Italian clergy. Some of this evidence must now be presented, but it must be recalled that the Italian picture is perhaps only marginally more dismal than that provided by the abbé Toussaert in his book on *Le sentiment religieux en Flandre à la fin du moyen âge*, or by the abbé Paul Adam in his study of the parish life in fourteenth-century France.[29] By comparison studies of the English clergy reveal a pattern both less depressing and with fewer gleams of a higher level of devotion.[30] It will be easiest to proceed in a roughly chronological way.

1. Albergati visiting the diocese of Bologna (1417–25) found not only crumbling buildings and a general neglect of material resources, but also priests unable to identify the seven mortal sins or to read the breviary. He found it necessary to reiterate an injunction of one of his predecessors that no one could celebrate mass who was not ordained as a priest.[31]

2. It seems that the notarial instrument registering Saint Antonino's metropolitical visitation of Fiesole and Pistoia which has never been printed in full (it is at Pisa) cannot be published because it is in such a bad condition. The conditions it describes are also pretty awful: dilapidation, even abandonment of churches; sacristies and service books in a deplorable state; the priest often, perhaps usually in the better livings, absent and a casual curate in his place. In many villages there were no services at all: the young married themselves, the old died and were buried, without benefit of priest. A fair number of parishes were served by irregular regulars – I mean monks or friars, who had no faculties permitting them to break this part of their Rule. Priests with mistresses and children were far from uncommon. One priest could not read at all.[32] Let us remember that we are talking of rich, urbanised Tuscany, home of Dante, Petrarch and Boccaccio.

3. Let us turn to Pisa in the second half of the fifteenth century. Here patriotic Pisans could and did (indeed still do) blame the depressed state of the clergy on the occupation of the city and its *contado* by Florence in 1406 and it seems clear that at that time there was some depopulation not only in rural areas but even in the town itself where one church was a complete ruin.[33] There were not enough priests; often canonical services were not celebrated; a number of priests had not taken proper orders and the economic position of many was precarious – to a surprising degree they relied for subsistence on rents in kind. And there was, of course, absentee-

ism and pluralism – the latter often because of the shortage of priests, which often drove priests to pluralism like the priest Alberto, *pievano* at Torciano S. Martino and rector of seven other churches. Service books were usually, but alas not always, present.[34]

4. Finally, Piacenza, for which a series of visitations between 1476 and 1554 have left surviving injunctions. In this diocese the city churches were visited more thoroughly than the country parishes where – on the rare occasion of visitations – only a few of the *chiese plebane* came under scrutiny, and not the *filiales*, which (as noted earlier) were in many cases rapidly becoming separate from the mother church. The overall picture is of sluttish conformism, a climate (says the author I am quoting) of general depression.[35]

It is obvious that the picture[36] one gets varies in part with the zeal of the visitor. Antonino's searching enquiries and sharp rebukes are far removed from the rather perfunctory surveys conducted elsewhere. At Pisa, for instance, only Bishop Filippo de' Medici personally conducted a visitation; his successors invariably commissioned as vicars eminent but not very inspiring jurists, whose questions have a mechanical ring about them, who were concerned only to detect breaches of the law. It is exactly the same at Piacenza. Now this kind of observation, it must be conceded, comes close to that erroneous attempt to make post-Tridentine norms the real touchstone, and to dismiss as empty all the bishops who do not approach the standard of Carlo Borromeo. This is of course absurd. What one can say is, first, that the impression one has of the secular clergy, the parochial clergy, of Italy is no better, perhaps a little worse, than in other provinces of the church. And that visitations, when they took place, are mechanical and legalistic.[37]

There were other and numerous groups of secular priests who cannot be dealt with here. At one end there were the cathedral clergy, numerous, aristocratic in the richer and bigger sees, often absentees living in the papal curia or employed by a prince, their places supplied by what in English parlance were called vicars-choral. At the other end there were the multitudes of clerks in minor orders, scholars sometimes, children of impoverished but gentle families often, who took some small and ancient revenue and gave nothing in return. There were 769 such *chiericati* in the diocese of Verona in 1440.[38] With such persons we are in effect dealing with a group which in many respects was composed of laity, to whose spiritual condition we must turn after a brief consideration of the regular clergy.

Regular clergy

Our information on this subject is partly derived from the visitation material already discussed, but this can be supplemented by the internal visitations of their houses conducted by some regulars, and by the legislation of the chapters-general of the friars. Normal visitations often passed over the Benedictine houses, many of which were exempt. But in grave cases bishops could and sometimes did obtain a mandate from the pope empowering them to disregard privileges.

The decline in rigour common to most monasteries had already gone far in Italy before the fifteenth century. Claustration was very imperfectly observed. The dormitory was divided up into separate rooms; individual monks sometimes held livings *in commendam*.[39] And the zealous ordinary was confronted with the laws's delays, the reference to ancient rights and present protectors. San Paolo a Ripa d'Arno at Pisa was an exempt house of the Order of Vallombrosa, one of the more austere offshoots of the Benedictine rule. Its visitation by the archbishop of Pisa was quite an event in 1470, for the house was not only exempt, it was held *in commendam* from 1457 to 1483. The archbishop, fortified by a brief of Sixtus IV, arrived flanked by three abbots, but was kept outside in an undignified way waiting in the rain. Finally admitted he questioned the monks, none of whom were professed. The evidence adduced suggests a depressing decline in discipline, a terrifying degree of ignorance, and, among the laity of the neighbourhood, an utter contempt for the abbot, so-called, and the so-called monks.[40]

Of the monastic groups who at the time conducted their own reform programme none is more celebrated than the Italian Order of Camaldoli, visited by one of their own number Ambrogio Traversari, now one of the unofficial *beati* of the *quattrocento* as well as a disciplinarian and lover of classical Latin. His peregrinations are recorded in the *Hodoeporicon* and in his letters.[41] Ambrogio's commission as Visitor derived from his election in 1431 as minister-general of an order which combined awkwardly a hermit wing and a traditional monastic side, the latter being now easily in the ascendant. His travels reveal again an almost uniform tepidity: claustration was not observed; once rich monasteries were ruinous and inhabited by a prior and one or two monks; there was a good deal of incontinence and occasional dishonesty on a large scale as well as violent crime. There is (so Ambrogio said) virtually no difference or distinction between the lives of the religious (he means monks) and the secular clergy. Nearly all religious wear linen underclothes and at night sleep naked under the coverlets. 'Indeed', he adds 'I believe we monks are the winners in the competition with the seculars for wealth and self-indulgence.' Rules of austere eating, of chastity, above all the fundamental law of obedience, these have gone save in a handful of convents. The censorious remarks scattered about Ambrogio's writings are all the more telling since he was in practice extraordinarily gentle and long-suffering, tactful and imaginative, in dealing with the offenders he encountered.

Another group of visitation documents refer to the Greek or Basilian monasteries of southern Italy.[42] The inspiration behind this was Bessarion's. Soon after the latter was made a cardinal, in November 1439, he was made Protector of the Basilian monks. In 1446 a chapter-general of Greek houses in Sicily, Calabria and Apulia was held in Rome and it was the canons of this chapter which were treated as the basic minimum for observance in the visitation ordered by Bessarion ten years later by one of his trusted priests, Athanasius Chalképoulos, who subsequently became a bishop in Calabria – a resident one. Athanasius visited 78 houses; there were still others, but nothing suggests that they were different from those he did see. The monks, with the rarest exceptions, were few, ignorant and in some cases illiterate, at any rate in Greek. Hence the necessity of providing many convents with the extracts from S. Basil of Caesarea, which Bessarion had himself prepared for their spiritual guidance. The visitation revealed sordid dilapidation and sluttishness. Consider, for example, the case of the convent of Santa Maria de Tripizometa, near Reggio. The house had two inhabitants, an abbot and a monk. The abbot had a concubine by whom he had had a child before the chapter at Rome in 1446 and – perhaps more serious – five children after the rehearsal at Rome of the rules regarding chastity. He told Athanasius that 'he could not relinquish the woman because of his affection for the children she had borne him; and further, his doctor advised sex as useful treatment for his complaint, the stone'. And elsewhere Athanasius encountered a fighting abbot, armoured and armed; he reproved him, but one feels no improvement would result, though it is hard to know what the Visitor could do without a troop of soldiers at his back. But the overall picture, the average house, displayed not wickedness on this scale but torpor, tiny numbers, and minor corruption.

The moral state of the friars was, perhaps of more general significance, so largely had they contributed in the past to a general leavening of society. Here it is almost impossible to be so positive, to make brief generalisations of a safe kind, as it was with the monks.

All the orders had experienced an Observant reform of some sort in the last decades of the fourteenth century and the early decades of the fifteenth,[43] and in all – Franciscans, Dominicans, Austin Hermits and Carmelites – the result had tended to create a state of tension, of competition. This was most celebrated and most productive of good and ill in the Order of St Francis, where the Observants in Italy numbered a series of great preachers – Bernardino of Siena being the greatest of them. These inspired men and their evangelism must be set against a century and a half of intense bickering locally and centrally on buildings and control of organisation, not ended till Leo X finally accepted a division on a permanent footing in 1517. Pope after pope tried to bring the two sides together and failed. Pope after pope rescinded, *plenitudine potestatis*, the arrangements made by his predecessors in favour of the Observants or the Conventuals. Some Observants were saints; the Franciscan Order was nearly killed by the movement as a whole. With it should be coupled the new branches – in effect new Orders of the Minims of S. Francesco de Paola (1417–1507)[44] and the Capuchins, hiving off in the 1530s.[45] Altogether a story of bigoted devotion and inspired blindness.

The Dominican troubles were less dramatic, perhaps, but equally persistent. Raymond of Capua had envisaged a reformed house in each province, under the provincial, but existing reformed houses would not relinquish their vicars-general; Boniface IX confirmed this on 9 January 1391, but since vicars-general were not expressly mentioned in the bull it became merely the first of a series of contradictory papal interventions – despite the advocacy of Giovanni Dominici and, later on, Leonardo Dati; despite popes who were sympathetic to reform, and popes who legislated energetically for reform, there were others who listened to a vocal unreformed complaint and put the clock back. The wrangle was still going on in the 1530s.[46] Maybe the Dominicans were more wrapped up in politics than other orders, including the Minors: the tortuous negotiations over creating the reformed Congregation of S. Marco at Florence under Savonarola were involved in high diplomatic issues since the main Observant group, the Lombard Congregation, was, or was regarded as being, under the control of the duke of Milan. Certainly the local prince did in fact treat the friars he favoured as his lackeys and the Medici may have rightly regarded Lombard Observants as dangerous interlopers in Florence. Likewise the Gonzaga rulers ordered about the provincial ministers, chose confidential messengers from friars who were exempt from all normal restrictions and complained if their nominees were troubled by conventual business.[47] We have seen how jealously bishops were removed from newly acquired territory; the same could happen to friars. Yet, as we shall see later, the principal supporter of reform in the Mendicant Orders was the local prince or communal government.[48] In my opinion there is no doubt that political intervention for good and ill was far more prominent in the church life of Italy than elsewhere in Christendom.

When we look at the more humdrum legislation of chapters-general, however, we find, as with the monks, an atmosphere which would have appalled Francis and Dominic. Real mendicancy, it need hardly be said, has gone for good. The Franciscans in early fifteenth century chapters reiterate prohibitions of separate bedrooms (with a fairly lengthy list of exceptions), of extravagant dress, of actual trafficking,[49] the repetition of these laws shows – as does all the other evidence – that they were neglected.[50] In particular many Franciscans took secular benefices, with or without dispensation: without them, as we have seen, the shortage of priests in some areas would have been much worse than it was. Or consider the Dominicans of the Lombard Congregation, that is the Observant group. Their capitular acts have been published by Father A. D'Amato, O.P. for the years 1482–1531.[51] In 1483 the *multiplicationem fratrum inutilium* was to be avoided by insisting that no one should be received *nisi fuerit in grammaticalibus sufficienter instructus*. At Mantua in 1516 severe criticism was levelled at luxurious linen underwear, ostentatious headgear and expensive habits. Meat is not to be eaten – at any rate in the refectory or as often as twice or thrice a week (Bologna 1521). And throughout, with monotonous regularity, legislation is passed dealing with supervision of nunneries. Only elderly friars are to hear confession, and they are to be frequently changed. The number of nuns is excessive and maxima are laid down for each nunnery (Brescia 1486). 'No brother of our congregation shall carry letters, notes, gifts whatsoever for or to the nuns of our order or any other order without authority of his superior; none is to visit a nunnery without permission' (Bologna, 1529).

This brings us to the nuns of Italy and thence to the laity – an all too easy transition.

The nuns were particularly vulnerable because they were often girls given to religion by parents who found the dowry to be paid to a convent less than the dowry to be raised to secure a husband: in Florence the latter was ten times larger.[52] One suspects also that many nunneries were extremely poorly endowed, and suffered sharply in the cold economic climate of the fourteenth and fifteenth centuries. The absence of vocation which one sees among monks and friars is very much more pronounced among nuns of all orders; of that there can be absolutely no doubt. The evidence of corruption, widespread and accepted by all, is overwhelming. One well-known piece of evidence must suffice. It is a summary of two sulphurous pages from the patrician chronicle or 'diary' of G. Priuli, regarding the nuns of the fifteen convents in Venice.[53] These Priuli describes as brothels. The nuns were connected with the best families and this is his explanation for the state of affairs. The girls were luxuriously brought up, well educated and able to sing, embroider, make music. Young foreigners and Venetians frequented the convents (rather than normal houses of prostitution, one gathers), paid big money for the privilege of satisfying the nuns' lust, which, when it was not so satisfied, they appeased by themselves hiring boatmen. There was severe legislation against all this, of course, but it was ineffective because the *monache meretrice* had close relatives among the most important senatorial families; and so did the girls' patrons. Indeed the important nobles, while condemning the immorality of the nuns in public debate were often enjoying their favours themselves. Excommunication was totally ineffective; even children of twelve or thirteen were sometimes sexually assaulted, and in church. And then our diarist says much the same thing about the way in which sodomy was tolerated – and not only by the old and wicked nobles of Venice and their effeminate sons, but by the highest ecclesiastical authorities: *et erant patientes in curia Romana*.[54] Priuli is careful to say that he is not condemning everyone; some good people there are among the city of the lagoon – more than God could find (one feels) among the cities of the plain. But Casanova's Venice was much the same as Priuli's.

As with men regulars, so with the nuns, claustration was neglected, especially in the larger towns and in convents where the ladies came from good families, as they tended to do in all cases since a dowry, even if small, was necessary.

Within a few years in the 1450s Capranica enforced claustration on a convent of nuns at Genoa, and the archbishop of Messina on some nuns in that city.[55] Both attempts were frustrated. Capranica had to accept lengthy postponements as a result of the pressure of relatives, and in Messina the sisters argued, successfully if surprisingly, that claustration was not part of the vow they had taken on making profession. To insist on this pettifogging requirement would therefore involve a kind of breach of contract; besides, they added, it would deprive them of 'many legacies and last gifts which were made on men's death-beds by reason of the visitation of many persons' – i.e. they need social contacts in order to live it up, and doubtless they did.

This is not to say that the absence of claustration necessarily led to the worst excesses. One might, indeed, hazard a guess that the best as well as the more respectable convents were in towns and recruited from well-to-do families – for whom a *noblesse oblige* sentiment imposed a kind of restraint.[56] In any event claustration of itself was no protection, as the many horrific stories of Italian convents in the century before the Reformation bear witness. Here too the problem could be more complicated in the towns where men of position normally married girls ten or even twenty years their junior: that is, they seem to have married relatively late and, among other diversions, found the local convent walls easy to scale, if they could not be penetrated by doors or windows.[57] Florence in 1421 established a civic commission to deal with such offences. In 1436 Eugenius IV ordered its dissolution since in effect it meant that citizens were taking over the disciplinary problems properly belonging to the clergy. But it survived because it was needed, because young men continued to break into nunneries.[58] This was not only an urban problem. Ambrogio Traversari found the convent at Querceto to be inhabited by harlots and not nuns and there as elsewhere the male religious themselves – including the members of his own order – were as culpable as the nuns.[59] The prohibitions of the Dominican chapters confirm that this was the case. We have no reason to suppose that Aretino would have chosen a nunnery as the scene of the first part of his pornographic *Raggionamenti* if this had not seemed entirely plausible to his readers.[60]

We can perhaps turn to two other Camaldolese monks – or rather hermits – to sum up the overall view of the regular clergy at the end of the *quattrocento*: Fathers Giustiniani and Quirini, who presented in 1513 a 'Libellus ad Leonem Decem', to which we must return later, since it is one of the most important plans for a general reformation in Italy. What they chiefly deplored was the ignorance of the regular clergy, insinuating itself day by day into more and more and ever higher places, consuming and corrupting Christian purity. Many thousands of regulars (say these two Venetians) cannot adequately read and write. 'In the whole multitude of religious scarcely two in a hundred or perhaps ten in a thousand can be found who can read the daily services.' And of this few there are still fewer who have mastered grammar and followed a systematic course of instruction. And of this minority of a minority, of this élite of learned monks and friars, the luminaries are those who are obsessed with sterile arguments about scripture rather than with scripture itself – their interest is not with the Gospel but in *quaestiones*. No monk (they conclude) should be given the habit unless he is competent in scripture, sacred history, doctrine. What we need (they say) are not *doctores* but *docti*.[61]

The laity

The bulk of mankind and womankind, even in an Italy where one sometimes feels that every other person was clerical in status, consisted of the laity. Did all these bishops and the lesser clergy to match, the archpriests and canons, the parish priests and their assistants, the monks and the friars and the nuns, the clerks in minor orders – did they have no effect at all on the quality of religious life in pre-Reformation Italy? What, one might ask, was the church aiming at, if not at the instruction or at least the edification of the laity?

The formal evidence is fairly unanimous for this period. S. Antonino's visitation in Tuscany laid bare villages where there was no priest, where many people were married and buried literally without ceremony. The Pisan visitations at the end of the century confirm this. Often there were no services and it seems established that, when services did occur, there was no attempt to explain Christian teaching (nor, incidentally, did the visitors seem to think that there should have been). The priests deposed that the people did not come to church or even confess and take communion once a year, as laid down in the Fourth Lateran Council. The church buildings, neglected by the clergy, were often used as meeting places or barns and here too the sacraments other than mass were sometimes not kept reverently, or even at all. Nowhere is there evidence of confirmation – but then that is true of almost the whole of Christendom and nearly all the later Middle Ages. These remarks, it should be stressed, are based on evidence from Tuscany, one of the most developed parts of Italy.[62] In remoter, less well governed areas the situation was presumably worse as far as church institutions and knowledge of doctrine was concerned. In the sixteenth century in a small place near Fano in the Marches (i.e. in the Papal States) a survey showed that 366 out of 584 members of the community had never communicated in their lives, and few knew how to make the sign of the Cross or to what it referred. Father Tacchi-Venturi, S.J., from whose book this information is derived, also relates how the Jesuits regarded the moral and religious barbarism as worst in the kingdom of Naples, in the Abruzzi, Apulia and Calabria – calling it *India italiana*, the India of Italy, a land, very near Rome, that awaited conversion.[63]

As I have said, one must not automatically assume that matters were worse in Italy than elsewhere. One must also steer carefully between an imaginary world of good Christians after Trent and Reformation had done their work, and the other imaginary world of some earlier more idyllic period – a golden Middle Age. These assumptions are surely equally wrong. Italian ignorance and superstition, if they seem more noticeable than in northern Europe, may be so at any rate in large measure because much of the peninsula is mountainous and difficult of access, and was (still is) politically divided, culminating in terrible wars and the cruel invasion of foreign armies. After Trent nothing changed dramatically: the Reformation (in both Roman Catholic and Protestant areas) was to come in the nineteenth century, apart from dogmatic quarrels and dogmatic definitions. As for the illusion that there had once been a time of maypole innocence, this recedes backwards in time as one tries to grasp it. It is as evanescent as the yeomen of England – and perhaps not entirely unrelated to that bit of fustian idealism.

Nor must we forget that the old tradition of atheism in the Italy of the *quattrocento* does not stand up to scrutiny.[64] There were wicked men, and there were many men who were both evil-livers and blasphemous as well. Their deeds are occasionally chronicled in the novels and in the court proceedings – like that terrible Tuscan who was beheaded in 1413 after a career which twice involved incest and culminated in his slashing a picture of the Virgin.[65] And up and down the peninsula there was rumbling anticlericalism. This was frequently produced by the financial relations of clergy and laity, both in the clergy trying to levy tithe in its various forms, mortuary fees and other church taxes condoned by tradition but usually uncanonical; and it was exacerbated by attempts of the clergy to evade their share of direct taxation in some of the bigger states, as they did all over Europe. It may be added incidentally that Professor Elio Conti has somewhat surprisingly shown that in the Florentine *contado* more land was held by the church at the end than at the beginning of the fifteenth century – and this may have added to public frustration.[66] The *privilegium fori* also roused passions from time to time, as did the activities of the papal Inquisition, an institution from which northern Europe was mercifully almost free. On the other hand (and not, we may presume, as a result of the activity of the Inquisition) there was very little heresy in

Italy. There was no Wycliffe, no Huss. There were a handful of lonely Fraticelli, some of whom became infected with Joachimite views.[67] If in many ways the Italian laity were ignorant of traditional religion, the persecution of the Waldensians went on fitfully.[68] Pico della Mirandola and Savonarola ran into trouble with Pope Alexander VI, but the former made his submission and the latter was regarded at the time by many and by far more people today not as a heretic but as a saint. In another way they displayed remarkably lively religious convictions: the proliferation of lay confraternities. This is a field much cultivated in recent years but there is no adequate and up-to-date survey of the whole question, let alone of the Italian side of it. It appears to be certain that we are faced with a very ancient impulse, festive, penitential, charitable, whose origins will always defeat precise investigation. There is not much doubt that religious sentiment – using the phrase in its largest sense – came before economic aims in the evolution of the craft guilds of Europe and of Italy. It is the clubbable part of man, and the part of him that longs for demonstrations of collective joy and collective devotion, for the outward manifestation of solidarity, neighbourliness, *vicinanza*, in processions and pageants, in the high moments of birth, destitution and death. Therefore it may not be helpful to make the distinctions recently attempted between confraternities of discipline, of charitable works, of liturgical observance, and so on. Most of them shared in some of all these things.[69] Nor is it the case that confraternities were restricted to the towns or to the people of substance in the towns. They are found in villages and in country districts and they sometimes embraced the *minuto popolo*, as Professor Heers reminds us that they did in both Genoa and Pisa. Most commonly, at any rate in the fifteenth century, they embraced men of different social classes – men and women too, for many of these confraternities had women members though never, it is likely, allowing them to hold office.

The confraternities which have attracted most attention have been, perhaps, those devoted to discipline, to flagellation. At the time such groups sprang up with mysterious rapidity – as the famous 'Bianchi', spreading all over north and central Italy about 1400, a product, so it is now said, of disorientation due to the Schism. Not all Bianchi groups were flagellants; all were a worry to public authority and they were forcibly excluded from Venice (despite Giovanni Dominici's leadership) and Florence.[70] What appears to have happened in the fifteenth century is a diminishing of the importance of public discipline; where flagellation survived in confraternities –

and it did so survive until at any rate the late sixteenth century – it was normally practised in private. And in what Professor Alberigo grimly calls the *storiografia flagellentesca* he invites us also to observe that wild, popular and unlicensed activities, with mob inspiration, gave way gradually to episcopal or parochial controls.

Dare one venture one or two other generalisations in this difficult matter? Lay initiative seems at first to have lain behind this form of corporate organisation. There are confraternities of priests, as at Milan, where a *pio consorzio sacerdotale* was formed in 1460 – evidence, perhaps, that the aristocratic chapter was squeezing the clergy of the town out of their cathedral.[71] But normally and at first the lay confraternity employs priests, or enlists priests, for liturgical purposes – for example as chantry priests. Gradually, as noted, this tends to change and as we move on to the sixteenth century the movement becomes often more literate, composed of rather better-off people, more tied to books and so to clerical organisation. Likewise there was an increase, one suspects, in the amount of energy devoted to charitable activity, to providing the funds and the services for hospitals and to relieving poverty, not least that scourge of noble poverty which afflicted a society where distressed gentlefolk were not allowed to work.[72] But charity was by no means confined to the *poveri vergognosi*; it had enormous and beneficial consequences for the lower orders.[73] Eugenius IV in particular gave impetus to charity in a city where the papal absence in the fourteenth century and then the Schism had virtually destroyed, for instance, Innocent III's great institution of Santo Spirito in Sassia. Such works of mercy were, however, also popularly promoted.[74]

And sometimes one detects a moderation, a sense of measure and prudence, which might be supposed to conflict with the ardours of the spiritual life, or even with the bonhomous joys of membership of a living community. Listen to the regulations of the penitential association of S. Domenico at Bologna. They called themselves the flagellants of the saint – *li Batudi di misser Santo Domenico*. But their guild aimed just as much at mutual support in trouble, their ordinances display not so much divine retribution as divine love, and they aimed to hear Mass daily, to confess and communicate four times a year. As for discipline, it is clearly only one form of devotion not the norm. 'We are men of the world', say these canny flagellants, 'and we have responsibility for property and families and so cannot always be occupied in the service of God like men of religion'.[75]

In one field of religious activity there is no doubt that fifteenth-century Italy was pre-eminent: preaching. The competition to get famous preachers occupied governments all over the peninsula, especially for the Lenten sermons. It was in this field that the Dominican Observants were pre-eminent, led by S. Bernardino da Siena, and we are fortunate that a fair amount of sermon literature has survived, some of it in remarkably vivid form.[76] How closely interwoven with public life such preaching could be is illustrated most dramatically perhaps by the dominant rôle played by Savonarola at Florence for a few years after the French invasion of Italy[77] We know independently of this how attentively some Florentine merchants listened to them. There are several private collections of sermons, one of which covers the years 1467–1502 and has in it only one of Savonarola's.[78] A more permanent and widespread byproduct of preaching (especially that of Bernardino da Feltre) was the criticism of Jews and usury, and the establishment in nearly every big Italian town (save Venice), and in many smaller ones, of *monti di pietà*, official pawnshops where interest rates were rigidly controlled and where the poor could raise the wind at moments of financial crisis. By 1515 there were some 88 such places in the peninsula and a very strange list they make – the introduction of official pawnshops depending not only on preaching and the inspiration of Christian charity but on the current availability of local small scale money-lending sources, notably by Jews.[79] These *monti di pietà* were probably the aspect of revivalist religion which most affected humble members of society, together with charities devoted to dowries and hospitals for orphans and unwanted children.

We shall notice below that S. Bernardino da Siena was accused of inventing a new form of idolatry in promoting the cult of the Holy Name. This emblem is still to be seen on the Palazzo Pubblico at Siena, *JHS* surrounded by radiating rays; his critics claimed that the symbol was widely copied in many places and attracted a worthless and unthinking veneration.[80] The border-line between superstition and devotion is a fine one, and it cannot be discussed here. There is, however, plenty of evidence that a desire for a concrete contact with God was prominent in later medieval Europe and perhaps more in Italy than elsewhere.

The saints are one aspect of this[81] and the almost universal conviction that possession of relics or prayer to a protecting saint was efficacious everywhere. Even towards the end of the sixteenth century a Venetian could assert that Venice's true walls of defence were her saints.[82] To give a relic to the Republic was an act regarded with particular favour by the State which went to extraordinary lengths both to take care of relics and acquire more.[83] It is worth stressing how large a part 'religion' played in the life of the cynical and hard-boiled merchant patricians and citizens; the doge had a 'sacral rôle', was *princeps in republica* and *princeps in ecclesia*; foreign observers were surprised that Venice's attitude to the church prior to the sixteenth century was not based solely on *raison d'état.*[84] At the other end of the peninsula the mid-fifteenth century saw the culmination of the cult of S. Gennaro at Naples, with the miracle, frequently repeated, of the liquefying blood.[85] None of these features of popular religion were new. But it is important that we remember there was a persistent need of outlets for emotion of this kind and that – while it was in some sense devotion of a limited sort – the church had to come to terms with it.

Processions and propitiations, for good weather, against the plague, and in time of war are found everywhere, and everywhere with official sanction and organisation – a very good example being the Florentine cult of Sa Maria Impruneta. Impruneta is a small town to the south of the city and at moments of crisis the picture of the Madonna there, regarded as painted by St Luke, was paraded; and the authorities and private benefactors lavished embellishments on the church throughout the *quattrocento.*[86] Similar ceremonies, involving the whole population, took place in every Italian town (and, of course, in many towns all over Christendom).

In popular religion Mary figured with particular prominence. The Ave Maria, formalised in the Rosary (especially associated with the Dominicans) and the Angelus, when the bells remind the faithful of the Virgin at dawn, midday and dusk, reached their full development in the fifteenth century and were especially cultivated in Italy.[87] With this went, of course, the ancient habit of crossing oneself, the kiss of Peace and the Pax – the metal or wooden cross on a handle which was passed among the congregation at high mass (this mainly, under Franciscan inspiration),[88] and the *Agnus Dei*, an impression of the Lamb and Flag (or other representation of the Cross) on wax, and blessed by the pope; Martin V undertook to consecrate the wax tablets every seventh year of his pontificate.[89] Mass itself had acquired this concrete aspect. The elevation of the elements enabled men to see Christ;[90] the pyx or the Tabernacle, with its light, told men and women who entered a church that they were in the house of God.

It is extraordinarily difficult to disentangle devotion from magic in observances of this kind; as noted earlier, the Jesuits in sixteenth-century Italy found 'Christians' crossing themselves but ignorant of what the Cross represented.[91] Nor can we begin to calculate the proportions of vulgar entertainment and biblical instruction in the *Sacre rappresentazione*, as the religious dramas, which developed from the earlier *Laude*, were called in Italy – the mystery or miracle or Passion plays of northern usage.[92] S. Bernardino da Siena argued that it was better (if the choice were open) to go to a sermon than to attend mass and presumably he was an acute observer of a visit to a service as a kind of perfunctory precaution.[93] On the other hand some preachers were alleged to use all the tricks of mountebanks to attract audiences – not only choosing scabrous subjects on which to talk but clowning in the full sense of the term – like the friar supposed to have preached in the nude at Anagni and the Milanese preacher of the Crusade who suddenly revealed armour under his habit: both cases were Franciscans,[94] and it goes without saying that similar gimmicks are noted north of the Alps. A good preacher had to be entertaining and entertainment was all that some of them attained.

That the more exaggerated forms of discipline were regarded with suspicion because they did excite the mob seems certain. Civic authorities were prepared for confraternities, and even (though unwillingly) for the high class group which met secretly at night, and thus offered opportunities for conspiracy of a political kind.[95] But the flagellation of the Bianchi was another matter, and, as we have already observed, both Venice and Florence banned the hysterical mobs which arose so alarmingly and spontaneously at the turn of the fourteenth and fifteenth century.[96]

Popular heresy as found in the north was almost unknown in *quattrocento* Italy, as we have already noted, and the only real problem was posed by the popularity of the *Speculum animarum simplicium*, attributed to Marguerite Porete (*Mirouer des simples âmes*). Marguerite Porete had been condemned and burned as a heretic in 1310, and there is much debate whether the wide diffusion of the doctrine that God = Perfect Freedom was in any sense directly derived from her (given the sound biblical foundations for the belief) and whether, even in the fourteenth century, there was any organisation which could reasonably be described as a sect. What there is no doubt of is that the book itself had become almost bedside reading among Italians (and other) mystics, and in Italy was particularly favoured by the members of the Gesuate Order and associated with Venice. In 1433 the chapter-general of the Benedictine Congregation of Sa Giustina prohibited monks from reading the book and it was condemned by Bernardino, Giovanni Capestrano and Giacomo della Marca; in 1437 Eugenius IV ordered an enquiry into the errors of the book and its influence in Venice, Padua and Ferrara; it had already been condemned by Ludovico Barbo. Paradoxically (or maliciously) an anonymous critic of Eugenius at the Council of Basel accused the pope of propagating the *Speculum* because his emissaries had cleared the Gesuates of heresy.

With this work and its limited influence we return to the literate, and the association of mystical literature with Venice will become of interest when, in the next chapter, we consider some of the impulses and impediments to reform of the Italian church at this time.

5

THE QUALITY OF
ITALIAN RELIGIOUS LIFE. REFORM

Pre-Reformation reform has been much studied in recent years – almost the sole aspect of church life that has been given extensive treatment in later medieval Italy. This is not least, one suspects, because recent changes in the Roman Catholic Church have stressed popular religious movements or the popular element in religious change. Just as conciliarism is now in favour with many highly-placed ecclesiastics (though by no means all), so confraternities of all sorts, charitable activities of all sorts, the church seen as an element in the social situation in which all men were involved, has led to movements being studied which have been somewhat neglected before, and to a new interest in heretics, especially those Italian heretics who survived the shock waves from the north after the 1520s.

With these last this book is not concerned. But I believe it to be helpful to study the question of reform beginning with reform from below because it provides a useful yardstick for comparison with reform from above. By reform from below I mean the efforts of clergy (of all kinds and up to the bishop and even the cardinal) and the laity (again of all kinds from burgess to prince). By reform from above I mean attempts by councils and popes to identify causes of decline and devise means of recovery. Even that sometimes has an inbuilt assumption that things spiritual and ecclesiastical were in a more parlous condition than they had been. Is this true? We know enough of the early centuries of the Christian era to say with conviction that religion down to the eleventh or twelfth century produced more sinners than saints, at any rate in the public record, which is all we have to go on. It would, we may suspect, be erroneous to suppose that, because literacy was rising in the thirteenth century among many clergymen and laymen, because for a moment here and there the magic of the *poverello* of Assisi touched many hearts, that overall the quality of religion was fundamentally affected for long for the vast majority. Ignorant and incontinent priests (and soon even friars) are plentiful, and if universities produced theological giants and lawyers by the score, they also encouraged pluralism since a benefice was the easiest way of supporting a boy at school, his spiritual duties (which in any case he was too young to perform) being undertaken by some underpaid, ill-educated curate. Thus it pays to be cautious in talking about 'reform' prior to the Reformation, Protestant and Catholic, when a brief attempt was made to achieve the purity of the primitive church, or at any rate this was regarded as the aim with the top priority.

With these reservations I turn now to reform 'from below'.

Reform from below

There were certainly plenty of reformers in fifteenth-century Italy and plenty of movements of reform, if by that we mean group organisations trying to make permanent a higher standard of moral and religious behaviour. Such groups display certain common characteristics. They are found among the laity as well as among the clergy.

I have already mentioned[1] that the regulars all developed observant or quasi-observant movements in the fourteenth and fifteenth century, designed 'strictly' to adhere to the rule. That strictness should not be taken to mean the full rigour of – let us say – early Franciscan life; St Francis would, one suspects, have been hard put to it to distinguish between the Conventuals and the Observants of the fifteenth century. The arguments between the two Franciscan wings, exacerbated by the Schism, turned on the relative claims of poverty on the one hand and obedience to the various papally-approved relaxations of the rule on the other. The level of observance aimed at has neatly been expressed by a recent historian of the order as observance of the rule 'as interpreted by each generation'.[2] I mention the Franciscans first because their troubles were so stormy, their divisions so profound that they culminated in Leo X's division of the order into two orders in 1517, primacy going to the Observants; and partly because the tensions were experienced more in Italy than elsewhere, despite the attempts of saints and reformers like Bernardino and Giovanni Capestrano and also of popes to paper over the widening cracks. What made the whole business particularly absurd was the popular respect which the Observants rapidly acquired, which loaded them with buildings and income and all the trappings to which the Conventuals had allegedly succumbed. But this is hindsight. All sides in these disputes, we may note, shared a common loathing of the few surviving Fraticelli, who were more or less obliterated by the late 1460s.[3]

The Franciscan upheavals are well known. Similar problems arose among other orders of friars, and again seem to have been particularly acute in Italy. All of these cannot be described in any detail but we may glance briefly at the other three large orders – Dominicans, Augustinians and Carmelites. The vicissitudes of the Dominicans, already alluded to, have been well outlined in an admirable paper by the Dominican Fathers R. Creytens and A. D'Amato.[4] The story bears striking resemblances to the troubles of the Franciscans and, as with them, papal intervention produced no effective results (on this see below pp. 89–90). We have a succession of ministers-general with different views, vicars-general elected by Observants and one group after another sucessfully upsetting papal and capitular decisions. The main difference in the Dominican division was that, despite the existence of reformed and unreformed houses, in the end the reforming wing, the so-called 'Lombard Congregation'[5] had dominated most of Italy, and in the final upshot the order was not divided – as the Franciscans in effect were by the mid-sixteenth century – into four. There remains one Dominican order, although the storms in it were not over in 1532. The Augustinian Hermits' observance, organised by Congregation, was also a relatively peaceful affair starting in the convent at Lecceto in Tuscany but ending up (in Italy) as five Congregations of reformed houses; the reform does not seem to have been very profound, the impetus dying down by the end of the fifteenth century.[6] The Carmelites also survived on a congregational basis, the first Observant group being approved in 1442.[7].

But monks too attempted reform and so did the regular canons, so noticeable a feature of Italian church life. Among monks and regular canons – there is really little at this late stage to distinguish between them – three particularly noxious corruptions complicated the task of improvement: the *commendam*, the appointment of conventual superiors *ad vitam*, and poverty – not the theory, the reality. To these disabilities should be added exemption from the ordinary and therefore lack of supervision, although really determined bishops had no difficulty in getting letters from the pope suspending exemption and granting plenary powers of reform. Few bishops asked for this but that was the fault of the bishops more than of the peccant monks.

The *commendam* was an old way of transferring income from a convent to someone who had the title of abbot or prior but who did not in effect occupy the office. (The word is used loosely also to apply to bishoprics granted *in administrationem* but I here refer only to the grant of a monastic house).[8] The evil flowing from the *commendam* was due to non-residence and all that that meant in careless administration, creaming off income instead of conserving resources, lack of discipline among monks, the alienation of neighbouring laity and thus added resistance to paying rents, let alone adding fresh endowments: hence further poverty – the downward spiral is self-evident. But it was possible to reverse this process, and there are several cases (one example was the grant *in commendam* to Ludovico Barbo of the derelict house of S. Giorgio in Alga from which was to stem both the Paduan Congregation of Sa Giustina and the Order of Lateran Canons) where a virtuous commendator actually initiated reform. Unhappily such men were rare. The commendator was often highly placed and very unwilling to listen to reformers. He was often a cardinal, for cardinals were not bound by the normal limitations on pluralism. Ambrogio Traversari had a particular loathing for Antonio Correr, the Venetian cardinal of Bologna who would only surrender an abbey against a substantial pension, 'and let him go with it' writes the future *beatus*, 'into hell'.[9] The size of the bite taken by Italian cardinals out of Italian conventual income remains to be investigated but as one turns the pages of the Vatican Archive series Resignationes (which runs from 1458 to 1514), one is struck by the bulk of the Italian material. And as time went on it may be suspected that Italians contrived by various devices to replace their foreign *commendams* (for instance those in Germany) with ones nearer at hand, less likely to go by default. The reformers, like Ambrogio or later on those other Camaldolese hermits Giustiniani and Quirini, attacked the *commendam*, but grants were to flow from a more or less powerless papacy for many years to come.

A more immediate step to improve monastic discipline was felt by some to be the removal of superiors whose appointment, being for life, led them to treat the property and the members of the convent rather like the improvident beneficiaries of an entail – indeed, with regress and *resignatio in favorem* some houses, like some bishoprics, really were entailed among the males of certain families, and not always among the males lawfully begotten, for legitimacy was one of the most commonly granted papal graces. The friars, of course, had in general avoided life appointments by having regular elections at each centre, although it might be an embarrassment with ministers who sometimes clung to their posts; the fifteenth century saw many attempts in other regular orders to have short term, elective abbacies and priorates; so to arrange things that officials moved from one house to another; to make the chapter-general a feature of all regular communities, and not just among the friars and one or two Benedictine-based orders such as the Carthusians, Cistercians and Camaldolesi.

The device by which these changes were affected was the 'Congregation', that is, a group of houses having the same reform programme and permitted to cut themselves off to some degree from any larger association. This arrangement might be fairly easily attained by Benedictines and by the regular canons, which had never (despite some papal prompting) developed a corporate existence comparable to that of the friars, who had remained either under episcopal control or directly under the pope (exempt). Hence we find that the famous house of Santa Giustina at Padua, reformed by the Venetian Ludovico Barbo, was recognised by Martin V in 1419 as the centre of a Congregation of four houses.[10] Barbo's re-establishment of Benedictinism of a purer kind in houses in Genoa, Florence, Venice and Padua was only the first stage in a very complicated development, for often Barbo's zealous monks were invited into decaying but earnestly penitent convents and effected reform without the convent itself joining the Congregation; but by the time Barbo died as bishop of Treviso, in 1443, there were 16 great monasteries formally united, including the great and rejuvenated house of San Paolo Fuori le Mura at Rome. Later stages in this Benedictine revival culminated in the union of a number of convents with Montecassino, which gave its name to a Congregation in the early sixteenth century. We must again remind ourselves that we are not here witnessing a reversion to anything remotely like primitive monachism. Barbo's monks, for example, slept in separate cells and one of his recent biographers, also a Benedictine, regards this as an important step towards spirituality.[11] It probably was, but it was a step away from earlier corporate life and a recognition of what had already happened everywhere else in western Christendom.

If it was relatively simple for zealous monks to organise in Congregations, similar arrangements were often a reflection of unhappy rivalry among the friars. The Franciscan divisions and sub-divisions tell their own story, with no help needed from the Congregational idea.[12] I have already referred to the Lombard Congregation of reformed Dominicans which in effect took form when a few reformed Dominican houses were put under Giovanni Dominici as vicar-general in 1393. The whole of the fifteenth century was not sufficient for the ensuing controversies. I shall refer to the story in a moment. Meanwhile it is fair to summarise it by saying that until the 1530s reformed Italian Dominicans were grouped under a vicar-general and that the Lombard Congregation was something of a misnomer since their houses covered the peninsula; in the 1490s by invitation of the king they introduced reform in the Regno at much the same time that Savonarola and the Florentine signoria were trying to form a separate observant Dominican Congregation for Tuscany, being fearful (as noted above) that 'Lombard' Dominicans would be agents for the Sforza rulers of Milan.[13]

Moreover the flexible structure of the Congregation could shelter a nascent order. This is what happened with the remarkable development of the Lateran Canons.[14] This company began as a curious mixture of Tuscan decay and Venetian enterprise. The regular canons at Sa Maria di Fregionaia (near Lucca) had sunk in 1401 to one professed member; it was to this derelict convent that Leone Gherardini, prior of the canons of Padua, went – knowing its state – in order to lead a life of observance. Gherardini came from the same spiritual background as Ludovico Barbo, who had founded the Benedictine Congregation of Sa Giustina in Padua – a Venetian world of patrician piety. In ten years Sa Maria was flourishing and the main danger to the revived community was that it was constantly depleted by sending its canons to undertake reform elsewhere. In 1421 there were eleven houses in what was recognised by Martin V as a Congregation. The constitutions then established remained basic thereafter. They are worth rehearsing since they clearly reflect attempts to solve contemporary difficulties:

1. An annual chapter-general (or if necessary at an interval of not more than 3 years); this was the sovereign body.
2. The rector-general and other officials were to be elected annually but could not hold office for more than 3 years at a time.
3. Any canon transferred from one house to another belonged to the second as though he had made profession in it.
4. The chapter-general might receive other houses into the congregation or construct new houses.
   Subsequently (1453) it was established that
5. There should be complete individual poverty.
6. The chapter should consist of rector, *socii* and priors (the *socii*, who were not to be priors, were to assist the rector).
7. There should be annual visitations.
8. The rector's office was to last only for a year; he was then ineligible for 2 years. In certain houses the superior might be called an abbot, but he was still limited in tenure of office.

These members of the Congregation at first called of Sa Maria di Fregionaia got their name of Lateran Canons when Eugenius IV (before he was driven from Rome) and again in 1439 (when he had returned to Rome) handed over to the Congregation the basilica of St John Lateran in Rome. It is hard to know whether this move was disliked more by the existing secular canons of the Lateran or by the northerners to whom the pope was handing over the basilica; the latter disliked Rome, its immorality, its unhealthy climate, its business; the sitting tenants, so to speak, regarded the incomers as foreign (i.e. non-Roman) intruders. It will be necessary to return later to this curious story. At the moment it is enough to note that, although they failed in the end to establish themselves in the Lateran they were in the end to be known as Lateran Canons. This new corporation had some 39 houses by 1485 and was to play an important part in the dissemination of Lutheran ideas in Italy.[15] Once again let us remember that its strictness was not that observed by groups of canons in the twelfth century. All sorts of differences can be observed: while the dietary regimen was at first austere and there was corporate flagellation, we again meet with private bedrooms and there was a firm distinction between the canons and the lay brethren, between the *domini* and the *fratelli*.

The so-called Lateran Canons were an Italian order and conformed in this national limitation to normal trends in late medieval religious activity, whether heretical or orthodox. But the other novel orders of Italy, the Minims founded in the south by S. Francesco da Paola in 1435 and confirmed by Alexander VI at the end of the century, had a more rapid expansion, to some extent transcending national frontiers as the friars had done in the thirteenth century, as the Capuchins were to do in the sixteenth. In the Minims we see some of the old austerities and the old exaltations of St Francis and his first companions.[16]

The characteristic mark of the Catholic Reformation religious order – the regular priesthood – is absent from these manifestations, although the Lateran Canons have some of its features. But the new orders I have mentioned, as well as some among the old (to which we should add the fourteenth-century Order of Gesuates, also confined to Italy)[17] did stress works of charity and concern themselves not only with preaching but with the sick, the plague ridden – including those suffering from that new plague, syphilis. Here we have a strong link between not merely the fifteenth and sixteenth centuries but also between laity and clergy.

The development of confraternities in the fourteenth and fifteenth centuries has attracted much attention in recent years, as we have already seen, and the number of studies devoted to confraternities in Italy is very large.[18] The aspect of such associations of laymen, especially well-to-do laymen, which must be briefly considered here is the development of confraternities – intially usually of a charitable nature – which were to culminate in the Oratory of Divine Love. It has been argued that the initial pattern should be traced back to Bergamo and the fourteenth century where the bishop took a major part in approval and control.[19] More immediately, we find confraternities in the late fifteenth century with such titles as 'Divine Love', 'Name of Jesus', 'divina Sapienza'. There seems no doubt that the inspiration for these developments – paradoxically, because so often designed to relieve the *poveri vergognosi* – was from Franciscans vowed, at any rate in principle, to poverty themselves. About a dozen have so far been identified as being established between 1494, when Bernardino Tomitano da Feltre, O.F.M. (later beatified) established the Company of S. Girolamo in Vicenza; the first using the name 'divine love' was founded, it seems, in Genoa in 1497.[20] The aims of these associations were all more or less the same: restricted membership (including a priest to minister to members), late and frequent meetings (to avoid notoriety), works of mercy both corporal and spiritual, frequent and fervent prayer, mortification or discipline and more frequent confession and communion – sometimes as often as four times a year.

An area of contact between priest and layman which one would like to be able to explore lies precisely in the emphasis placed on frequent confession. In the Middle Ages confession was normally an annual event preceding Easter Communion, and it seems it usually took the form of the *Confiteor* or general confession, much as in the Anglican service today; only if a man or woman felt particularly guilty of some heinous offence, or if on the point of death, was confession heard more frequently. The encouragement to more frequent communion should probably be connected with the development in the thirteenth and fourteenth centuries of a growing literature for confessors and as the layman took to reading instructions for those confessing. This literature, which may have been growing more rigid, more legalistic in the fifteenth century, is to be associated with the manuals becoming increasingly common on 'holy living and holy dying'. The confessional, as an enclosed and private place, is a post-Tridentine innovation, but confession as systematic soul-searching was beginning to be a more regular feature of religion. In Italy the great name in this field was that of S. Antonino of

Florence who wrote three short works (on cases of conscience and the confessional) which are in a sense preparatory to his great *Summa theologica*; he was also much consulted on doubtful cases.[21]

This mixture of laity and clergy in confraternities, with the laity playing the leading rôle, did undoubtedly do a good deal not only to encourage confession and communion but, in larger ways, to bridge the gap between clergy and laity which had always been immense and perhaps had become even more oppressive as laymen became more aware of their spiritual obligations by reading the Bible,[22] prayer books, devotional manuals of all kinds. Here one is referring, of course, to the more prosperous layman, or those who at any rate came from a prosperous background even if they had become poor. It was from such a background that were to come the original members of the Theatines, the new order formed in 1524; the four were ecclesiastics[23] who belonged to the Roman Oratory of Divine Love, and the new order of 'priests-regular' was ecclesiastical, leading on to other groups of clergy, also 'regular', i.e. following a rule – the Barnabites, the Jesuits, and the Oratorians established by St Philip Neri. We have thus in the fifteenth century transformation of a certain type of confraternity, the beginning of a trend towards a new type of Roman Catholic order; and a new type of spirituality which, it might be argued, appealed more to the rich than the poor and, like so many other actions both Protestant and Roman Catholic in the sixteenth century, once again raised barriers between the priest and the people.

Behind organisations such as these touched on here lies a generation of charitable activity by the great and – let us stress the word – the good. Caterina Fieschi Adorno (her name is a sonorous evocation of Genoese history) had been directly involved in the great hospital at Genoa since 1478 and became director of it in 1489. This practical element in works of charity and in the confraternities, referred to in the previous chapter, formed a very important constituent in Italian religious sensibility in the century before the Reformation. From it was to stem an interest in the catechism and devotion to the Eucharist.

Caterina Fieschi Adorno was canonised, but not until 1737. A more immediately appealing type of saint in our period was undoubtedly still the great preacher – the great Observant evangelist Bernardino, who died in 1444 and who was canonised five years later. If from Pastor's list of Italian saints between 1400 and 1520 we subtract the layfolk (27) and nuns (10) we are left with 49 who had obtained beatification or canonisation by the time Pastor wrote this volume: of these 17 were Franciscans, 15 were Dominicans, 13 were other regulars, and only 4 were secular clergy – of whom there were two bishops, Niccolò Albergati and Giovanni Ravelli of Ferrara; a third, if we add in Antonino of Florence, was reckoned already as a Dominican. Much I think could be done by examining the lives of the officially-recognised *beati* and of the many more (one thinks of Savonarola) who attracted a local cult. At the moment, however, I propose to turn to bishops. The heroic days of bishop-martyrs were over, indeed, and especially in over-bishoped, absentee-ridden Italy. That 2 per cent of Italian saints in the fifteenth century were bishops suggests that at any rate a fair proportion were men of worth.

Some indeed there were who were admirable pastors and not least Albergati, whose election by the clergy and people of Bologna in 1417 was described before (pp. 12–13). He was a Carthusian, visited his diocese, held synods, besides being a careful manager of the episcopal lands, a supporter of reform (he introduced the Lateran Canons to Bologna, did his best to support the Gesuates and so on). But two activities in particular deserve to be stressed: he founded a confraternity, composed of clergy and 'noble citizens' to teach children a catechism. And he instituted a seminary for priests. Little seems to be known about this seminary: but then (apart from Guarino and Vittorino, the two heroes of teaching) hardly any work has been done on practical educational history at this time in Italy, although plenty has been written on the easier topic of the theorists. We must not therefore suppose that Albergati's seminary was necessarily ineffective. We do know that the seminary for 12 poor clerks founded by the bishop of Tortona in 1435 had folded up by 1450. We hear of seminaries at Perugia in the mid-fourteenth century, founded by Cardinal Niccolò Capocci and termed the 'vecchia sapienza', and another cardinal, Branda Castiglione, is stated to have founded one at Pavia early in the fifteenth century.[24] And we have seen that the odd cathedral had or was compelled to establish one of the canons as *scholasticus*.[25] But the continuous story of this side of reform dates, I believe, from the Roman foundations of Cardinals Capranica and Nardini towards the end of the century.

Capranica's will is dated 1458, the year of his death. The college for 32 poor students destined for the priesthood did not open till 1475. Capranica made very careful and elaborate provisions for the government of his college which was intended to train half the scholars in theology and half in canon law – a neat balance between the contemplative and the active life; the governors were, significantly enough, laymen – the *conservatori* who (under papal management) ran the city of Rome.[26] Nardini's college for 20 poor students opened its doors four years after his death in 1484; this lasted until the eighteenth century and the building stands, adjoining Nardini's Palace which became the Vecchio Governo.[27] Both of these colleges thus significantly antedate the ineffective attempts of Leo X to put some life (and theology) into the decrepit Roman university, the Sapienza, and both were destined for a long and useful life. Indeed the Collegio Capranica is still in operation – next door to the cinema of the same name in the *piazza omonima*, as the guide books say.

The reforms of prelates like these are paralleled, among the laity, by the fitful but powerful operations of princes. It was Coulton's constant refrain that reform could only come when the reformer had the prince behind him, with the coercive force necessary to effect change.[28] And there is much truth in this, although the Italian princes, like their trans-Alpine opposite numbers, were capricious in their choice of men and movements and often possessive towards the objects of their sympathy.[29] It is incontrovertible that laymen still admired austerity among the religious and that powerful laymen protected and endowed convents which they regarded as virtuous – the Lateran Canons, the Franciscan Observants, the Minims. Hardly a princely family in Italy but has its honoured place among favourers of some exponents of religious zeal. They need not be catalogued here. It must, however, not be overlooked that the prince sometimes wanted to be repaid here below as well as in Heaven. For instance the Gonzaga family supported reformed Franciscans at Mantua, but expected instant obedience; they were not used to their Franciscan chaplains being bothered with conventual business.[30] In Milan Visconti and Sforza rulers arbitrated in the affairs of the friars in Lombardy; it was impossible to hold a chapter there without the benevolence of the prince. The Este family were no different in the territories of Ferrara[31] nor the Aragonese in Naples.[32] Though these Italian princes wielded much less power than kings of England or France, they pursued similarly drastic policies. Could one rely on the true reforming instincts of a ruler like Giovanni Maria Visconti who, in 1409, directed that the word *pax* must be dropped from the Mass to be replaced by the less seditious word *tranquillitas*?[33]

Reform from above

In the foregoing we have ascended high, but there is an even higher authority from which reform of the Italian clergy might have flowed

– the papacy, where responsibilities were, it is true, far wider than the mere provinces of Italy, but who were (as I have argued) circumscribed by *italianità* in the fifteenth century.

Perhaps one should in fairness begin not with the pope but with the councils, whose programmes they so successfully frustrated at the time. Professor Alberigo has studied the rôle of Italian bishops at the early sessions of the Council of Trent.[34] There seems to be no comparable work covering the councils of the first half of the fifteenth century. It is one's impression, however, that both at Constance and Basel Italian reformers as such were not of much significance. At Constance the Italians were distracted by the rivalries of the two Italian popes John XXIII and Gregory XII and (unlike the French or the English or the Castilians) had subsequently no one strong prince to protect them from the fiscality of the re-established papacy. At Basel, though Haller has printed some petitions by a reforming Italian Benedictine,[35] politics predominated throughout and the prelates from Italy attended at the will of their rulers, mostly to embarrass Eugenius IV. Duke Filippo Maria Visconti of Milan ordered prelates in his territories to attend Basel, as a lever against the pope, accepting a rôle as 'conciliar vicar for Italy'.[36] The Aragonese had Niccolò de' Tudeschi, Panormitanus, one of the leading canonists of his day, playing for time at the council in order to drive the pope to accept the new régime being established in the Regno.[37] When it came to the election of Felix V in 1439, supreme moment of conciliar crisis, the only 'Italians' to be found to take part (for, as at Constance, so at Basel, the 'nations' participated – indeed only one cardinal was present) came exclusively from Piedmont and Savoy.[38] In the event, as Paolo Sarpi shrewdly observed in his *Trattato delle materie beneficiari*, the conciliar legislation of Basel was not received in Italy as it was in France and Germany.[39] If it was not received in a formal way, Italian powers, like governments elsewhere in Europe, did not forget the decree *Frequens*, and ten year councils. During Calixtus III's stormy dealings with Alfonso V of Aragon the king threatened to depose the pope at the future council,[40] and the Milanese ambassador in 1465 told the pope that if he dared to excommunicate the duke, Italian governments would adopt the terms of the Pragmatic Sanction of Bruges (i.e. the antipapal legislation of Basel).[41] Sforza clearly regarded the behaviour of Eugenius and other popes as the betrayal of an ancient convention. He had no desire to alter the former arrangement:

We will not be deprived of rights, nor damaged, nor be trampled on by these clerical bosses, with their insatiable appetite which is not satisfied with spiritual income only but demands also the temporal. We have never accepted such practices but have continued in the way of the Visconti our predecessors; and so have done and still do many princes big and little everywhere in Italy.[42]

One feels for a moment back in the days of Gregory VII and Henry IV, when the papacy in the eleventh century suddenly tried to change the accepted rules.

It has already been observed, however, that the papal power now depended on control of the Papal States as never before (above p. 38). And popes were also vulnerable to cardinals, not unwilling to remind the pope of Constance and Basel – and indeed the power of cardinals in certain circumstances to call a council had achieved a kind of orthodoxy by the end of the seventeenth century, when it was no longer needed.[43] But (especially with the backing of the larger powers), some cardinals could call a council and did in 1511 when the *conciliabulum* met at Pisa. The interest of this episode is not in the political intrigues that lay behind it, but the fact that it prompted the pope to convene a 'true' or ecumenical council, which met at the Lateran from 1512 to 1517. Summoned by Julius II (18 July 1511) it was really Leo X's responsibility and recently considerable work has been done on its activities. Lateran V may not have been as Italian in its composition as used to be thought,[44] but there is no doubt that the reform proposals put before it were mainly by Italians,[45] and notably by the two Camaldolese monks, Paolo Giustiniani and Pietro Quirini.

These Venetian scholar–hermits saw the pope as the sole hope of reform; a quarter of the 'Libellus', violently radical as it is in many other ways, is devoted to an exaltation of the papal office. This extraordinary work of 1511 (to which reference has already been made regarding the literacy of the clergy and the importance of benefices in ordination)[46] extends its aims to the whole world; Jews and idolaters are to be converted, Moslems are to be converted if necessary by force; all Christian princes should be at peace with one another; all Christian communities in 'Africae et Asiae regiones' are to be united to 'omnes Europae Christianos'. But it is Italy that these Venetians knew best and which is in the forefront of their speculations, despite their in-built consciousness of the Greek world and the far east. Peace among Christians (for example) would particularly benefit Italy. They then attack *ignorantia* (as has been observed) and their drastic remedy is the prohibition of the use of modern authors; and such writings should be submitted in advance for papal approval. The Bible should replace the orators and poets of antiquity: priests should be prepared for pastoral duties, the jungle of the Canon Law should be simplified (as it was to be by 1917–18). We want *docti* not *doctores*, they exclaim, in an Erasmian aside: morals are what matter not cleverness. The Bible should be translated in an official version, superstitious practices (e.g. prayers to special saints for relief of special complaints) should be discouraged. Diversity of church services should be replaced by a unified and simple liturgy. There should be only one lot of monks and so with other religious; stupid quarrels on the Conception of the B.V.M. should end. The hierarchy should be pure and active, of good birth and good morals. The pope must be an example to all princes.

A summary, however, does not do justice to this vehement document which ends with a personal appeal to Leo X. It may be added that it was pope and council to whom they appealed and that their 'Libellus' advocated general councils every five years, not the ten of the Constance decree *Frequens* re-enacted at Basel.[47]

This conviction that pope and council were the only instruments of reform is less surprising, perhaps, in Venetians than it might have been among other Italians. I have hinted already more than once at the strong Venetian strain in Italian reform and this applies to reforming popes, if that is not too strong an expression to cover Gregory XII (Correr), Eugenius IV (Condulmer), and Paul II (Barbo), all of whom were cousins or half-cousins. Gregory made cardinal the future Eugenius and Eugenius promoted the future Paul. But their connection with a revived spiritual life in Italy goes far beyond the selection of some good cardinals from their many cousins (they also selected some shockers). It was Gregory XII whose nephews, with his encouragement, began that religious revival at S. Giorgio in Alga which was to lead both to the Lateran Canons and the Benedictine reformed congregation of Sa Giustina at Padua (above p. 76). Eugenius's interventions on the side of reform are far too many to list and his efforts are all the more remarkable if one recalls he was for ten years an exile in Florence and the victim of the criticism of the Fathers at Basel who ultimately tried to depose him. The Lateran Canons, Camaldoli, the reformed Friars, all enlisted Eugenius's help; like others he tried to give Rome a decent university; his mandates of a reforming kind in various dioceses of Italy remain to be collected. As for Paul II his reputation as a zealot used to rest on his dissolution of the College of Abbreviators, a meritorious act which roused the ire of Platina, whom the pope also had tortured as a suspected revolutionary. Platina undoubtedly exaggerated the hatred of Paul for the new learning and the humanists.[48] But he too was active in furthering the interests of, for instance, both the Lateran Canons and the Dominicans. I do not mean that other popes of the period were uninterested in reform; only that there is a connection worth investigating between reforming currents and the patricians of Venice, which in fact persists well into the sixteenth century.[49]

In fact the popes I have just mentioned did not address themselves expressly to the problem of reform as much as did Pius II, Sixtus IV and – in a brief moment of repentance – Alexander VI.[50]

Pius II's reform commission, appointed as soon as he became pope, was directed partly at securing an aggressive policy for Christendom against the Turk, and partly the reform of the Roman court. Of the memorials left from this episode (the details of it still seem somewhat obscure) there are memoranda by Nicolas of Cusa and Domenico de' Domenichi; and a draft bull by the pope himself.[51] Cusa's proposals are extremely interesting but they are addressed, as was proper in a non-Italian, to a general reformation of the whole church and I will not discuss them. Domenichi was a Venetian, let us note in passing, and had for years taught philosophy at Padua. He was very hostile to the pomp surrounding the papal protonotaries and in his book *De dignitate episcopali* produced 34 reasons why they should not be accorded precedence over bishops. He was, in short, a conservative, in the good old Venetian way.[52] His suggestions for reform of the curia are therefore all the more telling. They are pretty sweeping; luxury and nepotism are condemned among popes; cardinals should lead simple lives and have no jewels and gold plate; bishops should be compelled to reside; papal offices, especially members of the rota, should have salaries paid regularly and not live on perquisites;[53] simony should be rooted out of the papal chancery. Some small reforms were actually enacted by Pius but the great bull of reform *Pastor aeternus*, drafted in the summer of 1464, was never promulgated. Pastor prints a summary and paraphrase in an appendix to his account of Pius II[54] and, apart from the Pope's assertion of good intentions in regard to his own life and in the selection and wealth of cardinals (Pius's promotions were not to have more than 20 servants, older cardinals not more than 60), the bull is almost entirely restricted to tightening up and slightly rearranging the details – especially those affecting finance – in the traditional administration of the curia; it is a reform mainly of executive procedures. Much the same might be said of Sixtus IV's *Quoniam regnantium cura* which also made grand denunciations of abuses and then pro-

ceeded to proposals for minor alterations in the work of referend-
aries, secretaries and so forth. This bull in any case also remained
unpublished. Tangl prints portions of these documents among the
'Reformationes' in his collection of *Kanzleiordungen*; he might just
as well have put them with his 'Constitutiones', which they resemble
save that many of the constitutions were merely ineffective while
the reforms were still-born.[55]

Of all these gestures the most surprising is that of Alexander VI.
His devotion to reform was a convulsive reaction to the murder of
his son the duke of Gandia in June 1497, in the interval before the
pope a year later transferred his ambitions to a secular career for
Cesare Borgia, released from being a cardinal in August 1498. The
grief-stricken pope appointed a very powerful commission, com-
prising six cardinals, two bishops, two priests and two deacons.
Their papers have survived, rather moving in their way, a typical
collection of somewhat messy working documents, submissions by
officials, notes by the members of the commission, drafts of reports,
copies of earlier attempts at reform, the earlier drafts, such as Sixtus
IV's *Quoniam regnantium cura* brought out and dusted.[56] The affair
has usefully been discussed by Léonce Célier.[57] What strikes one is
the hunt for precedents, not least among election capitulations and
from the drafts already mentioned of previous bulls. These cardinals,
and the high curial officials advising them, were sober and serious
men, far from desiring revolutionary changes and they proposed
none. The draft bull begins by the pope referring to his early impulses to reform and blames the French invasions for their postponement. The projected reform then turns to the trivial details of the
official adjustments which by now had in practice come to be equated
with reform. Pastor promised an edition of the whole document,
but did not produce it, I think. Tangl gives the sections covering
the chancery and the other non-financial departments of the curia.[58]
It is important that nothing was proposed to be done about the
reverenda camera apostolica, although much evidence was submitted
on it.[59] It is, of course, even more important that absolutely no attention whatever is paid to expectatives, commendams, compositions,
sale of offices, and all the corrupt and debilitating devices which
were now so regularly depended on as sources of income, as sources of
papal influence, especially in Italy itself. Even if the bull had been
published and the curia had had its way, virtually nothing would
have changed.

One might conclude that reform of such a kind would hardly have
stilled ciriticism among the clerical and lay rank and file of the

church. Indeed by introducing fresh financial stringency it might have irritated men further by a papacy which was not only venal but also efficient. These three draft bulls are, goodness knows, mild enough but the innocuousness is due to Pius, Sixtus and Alexander being unwilling to disturb the accustomed pattern of curial administration, unwilling to stand up to the upper ranks of their own bureaucracy. The possessor of the keys, the vicar of Christ, whose plenitude of power was so often invoked by the clergy below him, was in practice paralysed by the machinery of his own government.

Perhaps this chapter should conclude with a brief description of the plenitude of power, to which orthodox reformers like Giustiniani and Quirini attached such importance. Undoubtedly it could do much for good as well as for evil. For example any northern scholar must admire the facility by which monasteries were transferred by papal fiat from one order to another, and sometimes to a third; and the same transformations can happen to an individual. Consider Ludovico Barbo (d. 1443), who became a regular canon of S. Giorgio in Alga and then a Benedictine monk of Sa Giustina at Padua.[60] We hear much about the bad effects of papal graces. This was one of the good effects, and there were many more. What is generally less well understood is that the papal sovereignty was anything but conclusive. The pope might undo what his predecessor had done. And even when all popes wanted the same thing they sometimes failed to make their wills prevail.

This can be neatly illustrated from the history of Dominican reform. Neatly, but not briefly. It would take too long to present even a summary that was complete, even though some salient facts in the story have been told,[61] but the message of papal vacillation is too important to omit. The questions at issue derived from the ambiguous nature of the relations between the reformed houses and the rest of the province. Raymond of Capua in November 1390 had envisaged the establishment of a reformed house in each province (under the Provincial) while existing Observant communities would come under the vicar-general, all under the ultimate authority of the minister-general. When Boniface IX confirmed this arrangement in January 1391 the reference to the vicar-general was omitted, and a series of battles was fought during the next century to secure the advantages from the intentions behind Boniface's bull or from its literal terms. Popes issued documents giving the edge now to one party and now to the other. Boniface gave his support to the reformer Dominici in 1399 but then withdrew it, under pressure from the Provincials, the next year. Similar upheavals occurred in 1417, 1421,

1426, 1428. In 1436 a vicariate gave independence to the reformers – for six months. Nicholas V supported reform, but issued contradictory documents under the influence of the French minister-general. Pius II's sympathies lay with the Observants but in 1470 Paul II was persuaded to overthrow all reforming legislation. These are the highlights of a tangled story which begins in 1391 and was not over a century later. In the sixteenth century the two sides were still wrangling, still getting popes to upset earlier papal decisions.

Much the same sort of capricious papal intervention can be observed when a devout bishop or patron tried to reform a church or convent: the abbot *ad vitam* appealed against displacement and a brief enjoined the bishop to hold his hand – there was then need for the bishop to explain to the curia the true facts of the case. Decades could go by before the final decision.

As for the practical effects of even moderately consistent papal policy the fate of the Lateran Canons in Rome is worth pondering. It will be recalled that this order of reformed canons-regular, based on a convent near Lucca, was intimately connected with the group of Augustinians at S. Giorgio in Alga at Venice.[62] The Venetian Eugenius IV decided to invoke the new order for the reform of the papal basilica of St John Lateran, whose secular canons were in a sad state. As noted above, the canons-regular were far from anxious to deplete their numbers by sending a missionary band to Rome in 1431. When the pope was re-established in the city, he issued a bull which confirmed the new Congregation in its privileges and ordered the secular canons to hand over the Lateran and its endowments. The fun – 50 years of it – then began. The seculars in possession of the Lateran prevaricated, whipped up local hostility to the 'foreigners', demanded that only Romans should enjoy Roman benefices, and staged a wild rumpus in May 1440 when the old canons and the new fought over the Corpus Christi procession. It needed the castellan from S. Angelo with troops to give possession to the reformers who had been ousted by the mob. After this Eugenius allowed them to depart. In 1443 and 1446 the pope tried again without much effect. Under Nicholas V for a time the Lateran Canons (as they were now officially called) actually seem to have controlled the Lateran. In 1452 the reformed canons, trying to conduct the ceremonies surrounding the emperor Frederick III's visit, were rudely interrupted by the old unreformed chapter. The unregenerate seculars refused to hand over endowment income. The old canons had their rivals expelled in 1455 by Calixtus III – the Spaniard who was ever an enemy of innovation. The Venetian Paul II, who as

Cardinal Barbo had been protector of the Congregation, restored them to the Lateran in 1464; there were various attempts made to placate the seculars with pensions and canonries,[63] but on Paul's death the old seculars forcibly ejected the reformed canons and Sixtus finally agreed to their eviction. In this account the swing of the pendulum has been lengthened; the goings and comings were frequent and violent in the long and tortuous story. But enough has surely been said to answer the question: who had the whip hand in these Roman transactions? Certainly not the popes who, on their own doorstep, were compelled to cede to local pressure from a handful of well-heeled clergy. However, the pope enabled the Lateran Canons to build a Roman house, the little church of Sa Maria della Pace, where twenty years later (1500–4) Bramante built them an enchanting cloister. Now the church is shut and the cloisters are rented appartments.

With these feeble exercises of the *plenitudo potestatis* and self-defeating attempts at reform, we should perhaps link some of the crazier manifestations of contemporary religiosity. Some of these were very divisive, and led to violent debates between the friars in particular: such was the bitter dispute between Franciscans and Dominicans over the Holy Blood, Bleeding Hosts and related issues, which did nothing but bring discredit on all concerned. The cult of the liquefaction of the blood of S. Gennaro at Naples seems to have reached its apogee in the mid-fifteenth century. From such absurdities not all was loss. The feast of Corpus Christi was enhanced; and in the Vatican Stanze we have the magnificent painting by Raphael of the Miracle of the Mass at Bolsena.

6

THE ITALIAN RENAISSANCE
AND THE CLERGY OF ITALY IN THE
FIFTEENTH CENTURY

The sketch given above of the Italian church and clergy was intended initially as a preparation for an examination of some of the problems posed by the emergence in Italy of novel artistic, educational and moral programmes in the decades at the end of the fourteenth and the beginning of the fifteenth century. The intention was to find answers to the questions: what did the Italian clergy make of the Renaissance? What did the Renaissance make of the clergy in Italy?

The debate about religion and its relations with the Renaissance

These are not new questions as such. Indeed the old writers were convinced that there was a simple answer, though they were not entirely agreed on what the answer was. For Burckhardt the Renaissance was the exciting if painful moment when modern man was born.[1] And modern man was a creature of little faith; there was a strain of scepticism about the Italian humanists and their patrons which was to grow in the centuries ahead. Only a few years later Pastor took up the same theme and accepted Burckhardt's thesis – subtly expressed as it had been – treating it as a confirmation of the existence of a 'pagan' renaissance. Alongside this Pastor drew his reader's attention to the Christian renaissance – in which the artists and scholars of the *quattrocento* were displayed devoting their talents to the service of God, or at any rate to the service of the clergy. Pastor counted saints as a clue to the spirituality of Renaissance Italians; he counted sculptures and church architecture to establish a core of decent artistic sentiment in the wickedness of the fifteenth century; he quoted from Müntz the calculation that 'the proportion of religious to classical pictures stands at about twenty to one'.[2] Now it is easy to ridicule Pastor and his dogmatic certainties and it is impossible to dismiss the carefully qualified essay of Burckhardt. But Pastor was trying to tackle, with objectivity, exactly the question which deserves to be put to that distant age – for distant it is, although both Burckhardt and Pastor regarded it as part of the world they lived in.

One matter may be rapidly disposed of. No one can any longer accept unquestioningly the existence of that paganism which Pastor and Burckhardt saw lurking in every *putto*, in every solemn and unsmiling nude, in every classical motif; their excited reactions are still redolent of the Café Greco in its heyday, and of the northerners in Rome from Goethe onwards – Protestant or Catholic – liberated by distance from home and by the lovely wines of the Castelli, by the handsome women and the grand perspectives of the piazza, the arches and the domes. Some few sceptics there were in Renaissance Italy, but were there more than in the France of the twelfth and thirteenth centuries? It may well be doubted. And no one can regard humanist writing as atheistical. We are again face to face with Trent, and in this case with a tradition too of the development of seventeenth- and eighteenth-century 'philosophy' in northern Europe.[3] The scholars and artists of the century before the Reformation were at one with the clergy: to confess and communicate once a year was what was socially required – and what was legally required too. Excess, such as daily mass, could not be enforced for all priests, and communion as frequently as four times a year was indulged in only by a few holy women and men: a suspiciously holy lot, undependable and sometimes given to weird imaginings. The vast majority accepted Bible, services, priests, and even popes, with unquestioning fidelity but a minimum of excitement. Many people must have known about the goings on of Alexander VI: are prostitutes more discreet than other mortals?[4] No one seems to have been especially shocked, just as everyone – given a mood of social or political excitement – seems to have found entirely appropriate the wild glosses of a Joachimite kind, prophecies of joy, but chiefly prophecies of disaster.[5]

In juxtaposing Burckhardt and Pastor I am aware of the sharpness, the over-simplified nature, of the comparison. There are, indeed, knotty questions to be faced, for there were a few clergy who elected to see danger to religion in the heady intellectualism of their day. Might one take as one's anchor that distinction drawn by S. Antonino: 'Scholarship should devote itself to what is righteous and proper according to reason, accepting the manner, the time and the end in view. This is studiousness: all else is idle curiosity' (haec . . . vocatur *studiositas*, alias vocatur *curiositas*). This distinction is at least as old as Bonaventure. Criticism of both learning as such is, of course, older than that. 'Vanity of vanities, saith the Preacher, . . . all is vanity. . . . Of making many books there is no end; and much study is a weariness of the flesh. Fear God, and keep his commandments: for this is the whole duty of man' (Ecclesiastes i. 2, xii. 12–13). Such condemnations echo down the ages – in Damian, in Francis, in Thomas à Kempis. Yet these sentiments are expressed in books (though this is not true of St Francis). The very argument that human learning is empty, that only leading a good life matters, has to be expressed in books or at any rate in words and if the words are eloquent they are more effective. Besides in the Bible itself are the reflections of the ethical, metaphysical and literary conventions of the Hellenistic world. 'I am debtor to the Greeks and to the Barbarians; both to the wise and the unwise', St Paul wrote to the Romans (i. 14) The debate continued through the Middle Ages[6] but the Renaissance gave it a new urgency and, once again, this was because by the fourteenth century literacy was widespread among the laity, not least in Italy. In the Middle Ages the propriety of studying the classics was a question debated of and between the clergy who, in the process of learning the Latin needed for reading the Scriptures and the liturgy, inevitably encountered pagan writers if only in scraps or in 'moralised' versions. Now the issue, while still felt more urgently by conscientious men of religion, affected a much wider public. The Bible in translation, widespread learning, were these not signs of grace?

But a century before such views were advanced in a sermon by Bernardino Tomitano da Feltre (d. 1494), the answer to the availability of so much knowledge given by Giovanni Dominici was very different. The very title of his celebrated *Lucula noctis* was biblical: 'the light shineth in darkness, and the darkness comprehendeth it not' (John i. 5). In a sense the debate goes on today, its arguments affected by the methods of physical science, the Enlightenment, Marxism, existential thought. But at no point was it tenser, at no moment did the outcome seem more important to scholars and men of letters, than in the fifteenth century. The scholars and men of letters were overwhelmingly clergy and overwhelmingly Italians.[7]

Dominici's influence was profound because it was reiterating an old criticism of the cultivation of letters, of concerning oneself with 'fables' and pagan 'poetry'. Boccaccio's *De genealogia deorum* had defended poetry (among its other contributions to Renaissance attitudes) and his defence was the usual one, most recently advanced by Musatto: that the Bible is poetical and thus poetry has an inbuilt divinity, exercising an influence to virtue rather than vice: that the poet turns his back on the solid gaining of wealth. In the diction of the *Vates* the word of Truth might have to be distilled; and of course there was poetry that aimed mostly to entertain or hurt. But in broad terms poetry was an inspiring study for a worthy man. This was the doctrine that had inspired Petrarch to write the *Africa* and to long to read Homer in the original, and it was to justify the humanist grammar school curriculum in its first century, although all too soon the schoolmaster had forgotten why he had to take his pupils through the *Aeneid* or the *Metamorphoses*. To this humanist programme Dominici in the *Lucula noctis* replied (his target was Coluccio Salutati, rather than Boccaccio) that the danger outweighed any advantages. If ancient writers had sometimes glimpsed the truth, that was not what they were trying to do; and he emphasised St Paul's damning juxtaposition of 'philosophy and vain deceit' (Col. ii. 8) and of the beguilement of enticing words (Col. ii. 4). 'It is more worthwhile for Christians to plough the land than to study the books of the gentiles'. Man's end was God not love of wisdom (philosophy) or fables and poetry.[8] Dominici's own reading list in the *Governo di cura familiare* shows the limits of his tolerance of ancient literature: Cato, Aesop, Boethius, S. Augustine (in Prosper of Aquitaine's extracts), Prudentius, Hugh of St Victor, Theodulus's versification of the Bible. It is the sort of catalogue of books prescribed by Colet for the new St Paul's School.[8]

It has recently been argued that this debate was dying out by the mid-century.[9] When Ermolao Barbaro, bishop of Treviso and later of Verona (d. 1471), attacked the poets in essay-letters addressed to a friar, Bartolomeo di Lendinara, he included the calm argument that in antiquity no one took the poet seriously, i.e. no one thought of appointing him to public office; it was absurd to equate even Vergil and Horace with the theologians. In point of fact not all poets were condemned by the bishop. What he recommended was selective reading, and Horace and Vergil would have been allowed to pass. Barbaro was a lawyer by academic training and no mean scholar himself, so that his so-called *Orationes contra poetas* (*c.* 1405–9) deserve to be taken seriously.[10] That these arguments were answered by another clergyman, indeed a regular, Timoteo Maffei a reformed Lateran Canon, with a piece entitled *In sanctam rusticitatem*, does not seem to me to prove that men of the church were ceasing to be troubled about the matter.[11] At much this time Archbishop Antonino of Florence, friendly though he was to many humanists, took a very firm line against poetry and fables in his *Summa*, although his best biographer concludes that he was 'ni un adversaire ni un partisan de l'humanisme',[12] and this doubtless applied to many other pastors and men of religion. But there remained many who were qualified judges and who were unconvinced. Here again the 'Libellus' of Giustiniani and Quirini of 1511 may be adduced. These Camaldolese hermits, with their well-to-do Venetian patrician background, are vehement in their denunciation of the new learning. Their diatribe is too long to be quoted in full.[13] But what it boils down to is that, having convicted the clergy of ignorance and lack of grammar, they go on to bewail the way the learned embrace the lies of the poets and the impiety of the philosophers, and of the way new literature had led to the neglect of the Scriptures and especially the gospels. As already mentioned, their work often has a hint of Erasmus about it and not least in the paradoxical way in which good Latin is employed to denounce the humanities.[14]

The fifteenth and early sixteenth centuries have a fair number of humanists who are clergy, regular and secular, by profession. Some are of high quality both as writers and as men of devout inclination. Ambrogio Traversari, who has recently appeared above as a reformer of the monks of Camaldoli, was undoubtedly such a man and has subsequently been beatified. So also was the Franciscan Alberto Berdini da Sarteano, a pupil of Guarino and an Observant who wrote very good Latin.[15] The friar, later cardinal, Giles of Viterbo is another outstanding figure both as a scholar and a reformer of the Augustinian friars.[16] Later still Gasparo Contarini was a member of the devout group at Venice which, as we have seen, was so extraordinarily influential. He in the end became a cardinal, but earlier wrote *De officio viri boni ac probi episcopi* about 1516; this impressive work seems to have been based on the episcopal activities of Pietro Barozzi, who had the see of Padua from 1487–1507.[17] These men are all, in some sense, Erasmians *avant la lettre*. Were they typical? Alongside them we should place the trite commonplaces of the friar Andrea Biglia (d. 1435), historian of Milan, critic of S. Bernardino, propagandist for the Augustinian tradition that Augustine himself organised the Augustinians in Tuscany.[18] Another mediocre figure, despite his good Latin, was Ermolao Barbaro (d. 1493), better at getting on in the world of the church than inspiring it.[19] His contemporary, the Lateran Canon Matteo Bosso of Verona, is to be judged (according to himself) by his sermons rather than by his writings which display, it seems, little fervour or originality; he assiduously assembled his own *epistolario*, which does not seem to have had much influence.[20]

Many sermons have survived, the liveliest beyond doubt those in the vernacular by Bernardino da Siena and Bernardino da Feltre.[21] But Latin sermons, addressed to monks and other religious bodies, undoubtedly could be important and in an age when more and more clergy were educated in the humanities it might be prudent for a preacher to master the rules of ancient oratory.[22] Timoteo Maffei, the Lateran Canon already mentioned, was a great preacher, much admired in his own order for his gifts.[23] And how important contemporaries regarded sacred oratory may be seen in the choice of preachers before the pope. These men were chosen or approved by the papal theologian, the *magister palatii*, and might be laymen although they were usually clergy and often friars. The sermons were regularly preached – about eighteen times a year (Sundays in Advent and Lent and certain other great feast days throughout the year, especially those associated with Christmas and Easter). Many have perished, but a fair number have survived, including printed copies (doubtless for style as such, but also as models of piety for less eloquent preachers who then as now found fragrance in other men's flowers). Such solemn liturgical occasions usually produced short sermons, overwhelmingly based on the scriptures with these themes emerging again and again: the Incarnation; the Unity and Trinity of the Godhead; and divine providence. In particular the first theme attracted many speakers, who stressed the redemption of man rather than the Passion of Jesus, and so underlined the 'dignity of man'.[24]

How elevated and even poetical such effusions could become may be seen in the letter (really a sermon addressed to Julius II) written to a Roman magistrate. It is a long paean of praise for the rôle of Rome and the pope in man's Redemption.

Hear, O ye Romans. Hear, O seven hills. And above all hearest thou, most holy Father. Thou, I repeat, thou great Julius. . . . Lo, the spirit speaks: Christ is the head of Heaven, Rome is the head of the earth. . . You are mine, mine I say, O seven Roman hills! Hail, happy bride (of Christ)! Hail, holy hills! Hail, Aventine. . .

And thou, O Tiber, washing the walls of my Vatican, thou shalt be a vessel for holy use. . .

And so on the rhapsody goes, with discreet references to Julius's ancestry and influence (*robur*).[25]

Nor can we dismiss as mere literary exercises the sermons and the passionate appeals such as Giles of Viterbo's, both in the letter just quoted nor in his address to the Fifth Lateran Council.[26] On the surface it would also seem that Leo X paid attention to the 'Libellus' of Giustiniani and Quirini. It has been plausibly argued that the bull

Apostolici regiminis of 1513 was not aimed so much at the 'Pomponazzi school' speculating on the immorality of the soul, as at an over-ready adoption of the standards of profane literature in education. That this went counter to the traditions by now taken for granted by many of the pope's humanist friends shows that Giustiniani and Quirini had friends in high places.[27]

There is, in short, something equivocal about the influence of the humanities on religion. One is reminded of the dramatic consequences of sermons in the vernacular, in the enthusiastic adoption of 'reform' by a city, in the competition to have the best and most popular Lenten preachers. The results were short-lived, and perhaps the same is true of the effects of the humanities on *quattrocento* religion. Professor Alberigo has no doubt that they did have an effect and added an inspiration to Catholic Reform. He is, of course, referring specifically to the Council of Trent[28] and by the mid-sixteenth century we are rapidly approaching a time when *all* educated men had been educated in the new grammar, whether Protestant or Roman Catholic. Unquestionably the traditions of the Roman communion were conservative, and the pervasive study of the classics did nothing to alter that: the *Vulgate* was frozen as an official text of the Scriptures; the services of the church were conducted in Latin. But Protestants handled their vernacular Bibles gingerly, at any rate after the 1520s, while one has only to read the prose of Edward VI's *Prayer Books* to realise that the ingenious translators were not only steeped in the old liturgy but in the even older classical literature of Rome. Cultural unities were maintained and even perhaps increased over Europe as a whole; religious unities did not finally collapse until the First Vatican Council (1869–70) finally recognised the pitifully powerless pope as a spiritual autocrat.

Modern ecumenical thought has encouraged scholars to put the question: was there an Italian *devotio moderna*? It may be suspected that this is also partly because writers dealing with northern intellectual history have sometimes associated the *devotio moderna* with the 'classical revival', despite the denunciations of book learning by the monk Thomas à Kempis, despite Erasmus's contempt for the school at Deventer run by the Brethren of the Common Life, where he was educated, despite the total absence of any influences one could label *devotio moderna* behind the greatest northern humanist, Thomas More. The fullest answer to the question as put above comes to the conclusion that there was no *devotio moderna* in Italy, save in the restricted Venetian circles of Ludovico Barbo and Lorenzo Giustiniani, the former bishop of Treviso from 1437–43, the latter the first patriarch of Venice (1451–56).[29] But the argument, despite its negative result, turns largely on the Italian editions of the *Imitatio Christi* (12 in Latin before 1500 and 11 in Italian),[30] though much other interesting material is thrown up on the way by the author from whom these facts are derived: eucharistic piety is not common, silent prayers very rare.[31] Other studies have speculated on the failure of Italians to produce a movement comparable to that of the North and partly accounted for it by the influence of the new stress on the humanities; mysticism failed to become organic and positive.[32] What, of course, is so strikingly different at first sight is the tendency of piety – much of it of Venetian origin – to be monopolised by the well-to-do and the well-educated. Where in Italy are the *béguinages*? Perhaps there were developments along these lines which have been overlooked, such as the few *case sante* in Rome, sometimes containing Dominican or Franciscan tertiaries, sometimes just groups of poor women, widows, *zitelle* (old maids).[33] But the *béguinage* or its equivalent owes next to nothing to the church as such; nor is it a kind of prelude to Reformation. Thus it seems somewhat useless to regard the possession of the *Imitation*, or some of Gerson's works (he was often regarded as the author of the *Imitation*), as a bridge between the new learning and the old piety.

The Italian clergy and intellectual innovation

There is no need here to repeat the account given above of the state of the lower clergy as a whole. With the rarest exceptions parish clergy were ill-educated and ignorant, quite uninterested in the ideas and practices we summarise in the word Renaissance, and, one imagines, quite indifferent to them. This is not to say that a few simple *chiericati*, with first tonsure merely or in minor orders, or a handful of real priests, were not scholars; many men in the curia, even sometimes bishops and cardinals, were in this position. In any case, the medieval manner of supporting learning with church endowments was found in Italy as elsewhere and did not die out for centuries. But in the bigger centres one has the impression that the members of the *haute bourgeoisie* coveted benefices for the immediate income they afforded – for the stupid members of the family rather than the clever men or ambitious ones. An aspiring man of letters of humble origins was more likely to secure support by becoming a secretary or by tutoring, unwelcome though that might be. The religious orders it is true sometimes afforded opportunities for the scholar and writer as we have seen; we can instance the Augustinian

Luigi Marsili, or the Camaldolese Ambrogio Traversari. Yet both
these men were, as Lauro Martines has shown, scions of ancient and
important families.[34] The Florentines behaved very like Venetian
patricians, save that the Venetians turned earlier and more effectively
to the church, producing whole dynasties of monks who became
bishops (Ludovico Barbo), bishops who became cardinals (Francesco
Condulmer, Marco Barbo), cardinals who became popes (Gregory
XII, Eugenius IV, Paul II); all these men were related to each
other.

With the episcopate we enter a group larger and much better
documented than the lower clergy. Although there are gaps and uncertainties in the record, we have a mass of information about a
mass of men.[35] Their numbers are reassuringly large. For reasons
which have been touched on (above pp. 19–21) there were somewhat
more frequent appointments to Italian sees than to those of northern
Europe. In the fifteenth century there must have been something
over 2,000 nominations to sees on the mainland of Italy. I do not
mean that quite so large a number of men became bishops: some of
these nominations resulted in a translation of one bishop to another
see: the point has been made that a fair number of bishops contrived
to swap their sees, to exchange their *infulae*, as Ughelli would have
put it; some men rattled through senior positions like successful
American professors. And of course, as we have seen, in a large
number of cases these prelates never saw their flocks; or saw them
only by proxy; or saw them once, at a *joyeuse entrée*, all cavalcade
and civic protocol, where in the procession shuffled members of the
chapter, suspicious that their comfortable customs might conflict
with the prerogatives of the bishop as they had often in earlier and
more rigorous days.

Nevertheless these men were the cream of the Italian clergy and
among them we find the best educated as well as those who were to
go highest in the church. What cautious remarks may be made about
their quality and about the quality of their education? The figures
about to be quoted are derived from a review of provisions to thirty
sees in the fifteenth century: eighteen of these in south Italy (of which
seven were immediately subject to the Holy See, that is, they did
not form part of any province), six sees in the centre (all immediately
subject) and six sees in the north (Milan and five of its suffragans).[36]
These numbers reflect in proportion the overall disposition of bishoprics in the peninsula. Of the total of 126 individuals named, only
fifty claimed in the 'Obligationes et solutiones', from which the information mostly comes, to be graduates.[37] Of these for every one

theologian there were four graduates in law. The law was dominantly canon law, although a significant number (a quarter of all the lawyers) were *doctores utriusque juris* – a familiar feature of the later medieval scene in Italy. Surprisingly, a third of the twenty Franciscans claimed a theological qualification and only one of the nine Dominicans; if we assume that all Dominicans had a thorough grounding our theologians would be increased a little. The late arrival in Italy of theology as an academic subject is, of course, well known, and it would be interesting to try to find out how many of the minority of theologians had in fact received their training in non-Italian centres. With the lawyers we are not likely to err in supposing them to be graduates of Italian universities. Law in Italy was a senior degree and, while no one would pretend that commentaries on the *Decretum* or the *Sext* constituted a highly cultural training,[38] the earlier basic study of logic, grammar and style undoubtedly did so. So we may guess that at least a quarter of the Italian prelates were tolerably well-educated men, a few of them – the D.U.J.s – very well educated. And we should also remember that there were many men who had attended or been educated by a well-known master who had no degree to show for it, though they may have been better equipped to understand the changes in literature and art than were the products of the old educational machinery. Of the six minor humanists whom one can identify in this sample of bishops one was certainly a graduate – Piero del Monte, described as D.Arts and D.U.J. in his provision to the see of Brescia in 1442.[39]

But then of our 126 bishops how many are significant figures in any sense? Two only, I believe, and of them only one is celebrated enough to have reached the text books – Cardinal Giulio Cesarini (who is listed here as bishop of Grosseto, 1439). The other is Nardini (archbishop of Milan, 1461), who has been discussed earlier not as the curialist emissary of Pius II to Germany, but as the cardinal who founded the seminary in Rome whose desolate hulk still stands in the via di Parione. Both these men became cardinals and both had some abiding influence on the life of their own day. Both were old-fashioned in their cultural attitudes and (it so happens) both were reformers of the clergy. But then it would be unrealistic to think that the aim of clerical reform was likely always to go along with humanist values in fifteenth-century Italy. A very great reformer like Capranica, whose seminary, as we have observed, also survives in Rome was, to judge from his library as well as from his career, not much interested in classical literature and learning as a preparation for life.[40]

This pitiful attempt at quantification lends support, I believe, to the view that in general the Italian prelates were not much interested in promoting either the old learning or the new. One might perhaps go on to add that they were not remarkable in any direction: six very minor humanists, two prominent administrators and reformers (who both became cardinals) is a small haul of merit out of the 120-odd bishops I have isolated. True, one *beatus* with a local cult was remembered in Ughelli's day.[41] But even that is not very notable by Italian standards. Vespasiano da Bisticci could find only a score of Italian bishops to insert in his lives of worthies and some of them are dull and insignificant men.

When we raise our eyes to the cardinals and the popes there is evidence sometimes of a conscious interest in the new art and the new learning. There are some conspicuous 'humanist' pontiffs – Nicholas V, Pius II, Sixtus IV and the Medici popes of the early sixteenth century. And yet one is perplexed to know what exactly they were about. Nicholas V does seem to have had a genuine love of all the features of cultural innovation, a new art and architecture, a new literature and learning. With others one is less secure. Pius II's appetite for public display is not in doubt. Besides the processions he loved to encourage in Rome, his transformation of Corsignano into a Renaissance museum piece is a remarkable indication of his sympathy with novelty. So is his own vast literary output, as vainglorious as Pienza itself, though destined to be more influential. It is precisely this quality of self-advertisement, reflected (it will be recalled) in the proliferation of monumental inscriptions,[42] which detracts from the patronage of Sixtus IV and his successors. There is a vulgarity about some of their gestures which does something to diminish the genius of the best of their servants. Can one imagine the bulldozing effect which the monument to Julius II would have had if it had ever been completed to the earlier designs? As for the cardinals, there were some great patrons of culture, well attuned to the rhythms of a new age. But overall how dismal a crew they are from the point of view of education and enlightenment. Let us again make Vespasiano our yardstick. In his lifetime popes created some 147 cardinals, 75 being foreigners.[43] The Florentine bookseller can find only six of these Italians to commemorate and an equal number of foreigners – hardly evidence of the intellectual richness of the cream of the cream.

Of course it is obvious that a good parish priest scarcely needs to be a good scholar. Popes and princes chose prelates in the fifteenth century, as always before and since, primarily because they were well-connected or efficient or sometimes both, but seldom because they were distinguished as patrons or practitioners of art or literature. In Professor Martines's list of humanists in Florence, 1390–1460, his fifty profiles include only half a dozen clergymen; in the 600-strong élite which Peter Burke has identified for study in *Renaissance Italy 1420–1540*[44] he finds seventy-eight, though the number drops to a mere forty-four when we look at his categories of 'writers' and 'humanists' representing only about a quarter of the names in his lists of men strictly comparable to those of Martines. They are more or less comparable too with the figures arrived at by Carlo Dionisotti in his essay on clergy and laity[45] in which, of a group of about a hundred writers who flourished in the first half of the sixteenth century, something like half were clergy of one sort or another, though mainly in minor orders, holding benefices without cure of souls, often living a life very similar to the laity.

The question of a choice of a lay or clerical career was growing more acute in Italy at the time when it was tending to diminish somewhat elsewhere. If the figures quoted can be relied on as a rough guide, they show a steady progression among writers from predominantly lay to the predominantly clerical. The explanation for this given by Professor Dionisotti – that although during the period of the councils and the Great Schism uncertainties in the church made a lay career more secure, while after 1417 and the establishment of the papacy in Rome a clerical career became more advantageous – may perhaps not be the whole answer, for several families of curialists did not seem to seek promotion in the church. Such was the family of Flavio Biondo of Forlì, scholar and curialist, whose sons followed him in papal service.[46] Another celebrated curial dynasty was that of the Maffei of Verona, a protean clan. Gherardo di Giovanni was a papal notary in the curia in 1432 and reached the rank of secretary. By then he had four sons; of the three surviving, two were *scrittori*, but married, the other went into the office of the penitentiary and, after obtaining canonries and *commendams*, became bishop of Aquino in 1516; he was later translated to Cavaillon by Clement VII.[47] Another climber was Jacopo Gherardi of Volterra, the celebrated diarist Volaterrano (not to be confused with the Raffaelo Maffei, also called Volaterrano, who wrote the *Commentarii urbis*). Gherardi was a favourite of Cardinal Ammanati, became a papal secretary after the cardinal's death and, it was assumed, would have become a cardinal had Sixtus IV lived longer. As it was he was amply beneficed, got a bishopric (Segni) towards the end of his life, and was then translated to Aquino by Leo X in 1513 –

he was the predecessor of the Mario Maffei referred to above.[48] Other examples of families of curialists married or clerical could be instanced, for example the Cortese family; Paolo Cortese's work *De cardinalatu* is one of the best available accounts of how cardinals at the curia were expected to live.[49]

Nevertheless, there was undoubtedly tension between those curialists who had a future of promotion through the ranks of the hierarchy and those debarred by matrimony. It is indeed plausibly suggested by Delaruelle and his colleagues in their survey of the church at this time that such pressures account for the childish indecencies of a work like Poggio Bracciolini's *Facetiae*, an authentic account, it seems all too probable, of the after-work relaxation of the papal secretaries, boozing at the 'Bugiale'. 'Par ces ragots les laics se revanchent des humiliations que leur ont fait subir des cardinaux sans culture, ragots qui vont courir la ville et alimenter les *lazzi* de Madame Lucrèce et de Pasquin'.[50] In view of the close connection between humanists and the curia it is a matter of some surprise that no fifteenth-century Italian writer seems to have made out a case for adequate promotion and pay in a lay bureaucracy; although of course the education of the laity for responsible secular government was part of the new humanist programme, and many laymen had penetrated to high positions in the service of the princes of the peninsula. Exactly such a man (and he was to be followed by others, including the author of the *Facetiae*) became chancellor of Florence in the person of Coluccio Salutati, who retained the office till his death in 1406. Salutati, twice married, was greatly admired as a Latin stylist in the new manner. Yet despite his own career, when asked by a monk to produce a reasoned defence of the life of religion, he wrote a substantial work, *De seculo et religione*, in which he reiterated with much vehemence and every appearance of sincerity the traditional justifications of withdrawal from the world. True, one of Coluccio's letters survives in which he discourages a friend from entering a monastery. The whole question of the chancellor's conflicting views and the apparent contradiction between some of his principles and all of his life, has occasioned much learned debate. But we are here dealing, I believe, with commonplaces of debate, void of material significance.[51] The same observation applies to the empty oratory of Ermolao Barbaro's *De coelibatu*. Nor is there any coming to grips with the question which must have agitated so many contemporaries in Gian Antonio Campana's essay 'On the dignity of matrimony'. There we find Pauline precepts elegantly presented in classical diction; interesting though it is as an idealised picture of

Italian marriage among the well-to-do in the late fifteenth century, it has little to offer that is original in outlook. Campana, of very humble background, became a favourite of Pius II and ultimately bishop of Cotrone (1462), whence the following year he was translated to Teramo. He was celebrated for his wit and his life of Pius II, but not much more. He must clearly have opted with some deliberation for the clerical life and clerical promotion.[52]

One could, however, have it both ways, or at least postpone the decision whether to remain a *chierico conjugato* of a minor kind (and dozens of the curial clerks and many others besides were in minor orders) until the main chance to higher things offered itself. It was possible to have a hasty marriage annulled in favour of a career as a papal servant. This was how Adriano Castellesi acted after he regretted his marriage to Brigida Inghirami; he had been so ill (he claimed) that the marriage was not consummated, and he then had a vision (so a critic alleges) that he would be pope if he took orders. Innocent VIII wrote an accommodating directive to the bishop of Volterra ordering him to dissolve the marriage of his (the pope's) familiar, and Adriano, of obscure origins, began his meteoric rise, largely paid for (said another critic) by his bleeding white the Church of England. At any rate, even though he died in disgrace and obscurity, he accumulated enough money to buy a cardinal's hat in 1503 and to build a fine Renaissance palace, still standing in the Borgo which he gave, before it was completed, to his patron Henry VIII of England.[53] This man had, in any worldly sense, chosen well. We do not know when he was born (it was at Corneto, nowadays Tarquinia) or when he died (probably near Venice and by the sword, around 1522). But he accumulated an enormous fortune. Another occasion worth recalling is that moment when Francesco Guicciardini's uncle, a bastard called Rinieri who was bishop of Cortona, died in 1504. Should Francesco go into the church.[54] If he had he would surely have become a cardinal instead of a disillusioned lay servant of the popes who came to hate the clergy as the cause of Italy's miseries, and who said he would have become a Lutheran save for self-interest.[55]

There is little doubt that in maintaining a clerical bureaucracy into the sixteenth century and later, the papacy cut itself off from contemporary trends in Europe. There the laity was steadily taking over from the fifteenth century onwards. This had its own problems, since office was treated as property. But then often, by *resignationes in favorem* and the other devices already mentioned, office had also become property in Rome. Culturally royal secretaries in England

and France were no different from their opposite numbers in Rome. But when they were laymen they were freer agents and had a greater incentive to exercise power and influence since they could transmit their gains to their direct heirs.[56] This was more difficult, it seems, with the wealthiest cardinals, top members of the curia. Their wealth was stupendous – quite beyond computation, since one cannot know how much of their income was filched from them by agents. But there is no doubt of the staggering accumulation of benefices by even bigger fry than Cardinal Adriano Castellesi. Cardinal Francesco Gonzaga (d. 1483) and Cardinal Marco Barbo (d. 1491) both had a fabulous collection of *commendams*; so had Giovanni Battista Zeno (d. 1501) and Ascanio Sforza (d. 1505), and so had Raffaelo Riario (d. 1521), perhaps the richest of the lot in this period. [57] But wealth paradoxically breeds beggary if it is used to keep up appearances and above all to build – to repair the titular church, to construct great palaces, to maintain a huge establishment of servants[58] and above all if it is derived from church offices and not directly from land. Many cardinals were poor, but the very rich in effect built rather for Rome than for their families. The Palazzo Venezia, as it is now called, was the palace of Cardinal Pietro Barbaro, who later resided there as Paul II: it remained a papal residence until it became the home of the Venetian ambassador to Rome in 1564. The colossal palace of Riario became the Cancelleria.[59]

The re-building in Rome and in Renaissance Italy cannot be dealt with adequately here and it has in any case attracted a large and modern literature.[60] But of all the builders the popes and their richer colleagues (rich and in debt at the same time as they might be) were among the most impressive. Scarcely a church that was not rebuilt or redecorated in the new manner, and of the palaces the greatest was that raised by successive popes at the Vatican.[61] St Peter's itself was not to be completed for generations, and the Borgo did not take the form that Pope Nicholas V had hoped for it. But the basic scheme had been set, from Porta del Popolo and its radiating streets, to the Campidoglio designed by Michelangelo, for the first great planned city in Europe. And the basis of the plan was essentially antique. *Ut poesis architectura*, if the adaptation be allowed. In their building the popes and other patrons were, of course, at first following Florentine models, and following also in the tracks of the other princelings of Italy. But they had the city to play with and could and did proceed on a larger scale than other contemporary governments in the peninsula. There seems little doubt that the new artistic and architectural manner was adopted by the smaller courts of Italy, including the papal court, before it penetrated Naples, Milan, Venice or the countries of northern Europe.

Art has, indeed, been advanced often as an indicator of Renaissance pressures on Italian cultural life, and in particular on the attitude of the popes and other clergy, unquestionably the biggest group of patrons. Pastor, as I have remarked above, first tried to enlist the numbers of religious paintings, sculptures and ecclesiastical buildings as evidence of active Christian principles in the *quattrocento*. For paintings he took over from Müntz the statement that for every Renaissance painting of this period with a pagan subject there were twenty with a religious subject.[62] Basing himself on the work of Errera, Peter Burke has recently shown that of dated pictures the percentage of secular subjects rose from 5 per cent in the 1480s to 22 per cent in the 1530s.[63] That there is broad agreement here is evident; it is also obvious that religious paintings, preserved in churches and monasteries, have a better chance of surviving than secular works painted for patrons who tended themselves to be laity. But the analysis by subject leaves out of account the style in which the painting was done. In many ways Michelangelo's God the Father on the ceiling of the Sistine Chapel seems to me related closely in spirit to Raphael's Plato in the 'School of Athens', or even to his Galatea. Michelangelo's art is profoundly religious; it also profoundly differs from church decoration in the Middle Ages. He and his predecessors and successors were surely doing something which cannot have failed to affect religious sensibility, though it is impossible to know exactly what the effects were.

Pastor's list of buildings and sculpture is a much more curious affair.[64] He simply ignores not only the question of style but any church that he finds offensive, like the Malatesta Temple at Rimini.[65] Nor does he explain the relationship of new churches to old: one might guess that for every church being built or extended or lavishly decorated in Renaissance Italy at least one other was crumbling into ruins. And sometimes the two processes coincided, as in the building at Pienza. Finally, the financing of church building remains overall extremely obscure. For Milan, Florence and one or two big cathedrals we have accounts running over a long period.[66] For most individual Renaissance churches we know nothing; but the Italian church in the fourteenth to sixteenth centuries was, it seems, getting progressively poorer,[67] perhaps because it was building so much.

It may be suspected that in art and architecture the Italian clergy were often at the mercy of lay patrons, and that in general neither laymen nor clergy were pursuing a deliberately innovating policy in literature and the arts until the sixteenth century. A great deal of the old survived, marked by or mingling with the new. At Pienza one can admire Pius II's cope – fine old-fashioned *opus anglicanum*; and his cathedral in its overall structure is an old-fashioned building. At Rimini Alberti's temple only partially clothes the old church which is its core. Both at Rimini and Pienza it is in the detailed decoration that one is buffeted by the wind of change. Much the same is true of Cardinal Branda's buildings at Castiglione Olona in northern Italy.

These physical changes in Rome and other large towns, which must have struck ordinary men and women, must also have struck ordinary clergy. With these should perhaps be linked papal encouragement of display in the form of public ceremonial, a question already touched on above (pp. 40–1, 45–6). The most famous occasion for this in Rome was the *possesso*, when the pope, with the whole curia in due (and sometimes angrily disputed) order, made his way solemnly to take possession of his basilica at the Lateran, the Roman's church *par excellence*, a grander example of those ceremonies attending the entry of a bishop into his diocese, on which we have already remarked.[68] This ceremony was not new; something like it occurred whenever the pope entered a town; but it was lovingly cultivated by the papacy established in Rome, which, from the mid-fifteenth century, they governed ever more securely. The details are carefully recorded by papal masters of ceremonies, like Burckard, and one such has been described above.[69] The colourful scenes were repeated, with less solemnity perhaps, during Jubilee visits to the principal churches.[70] It may be added that papal preparations for the enormous numbers of visitors during the Holy Years led to embellishments and improvements of the facilities of the city and its physical appearance, from Sixtus IV onwards; the Holy Year, in fact, was an important factor in the phasing of the reconstruction of Rome already mentioned.[71]

Nor must we forget the classical motif that often accompanied other papal display. One must recall, since he is so careful to do so himself, the solemnities of the reception into Rome of the head of St Andrew by Pius II and the gaieties – faintly 'pagan' in quality? – he encouraged at Pienza,[72] and which took form under Paul II in the carnival – also faintly 'pagan' – which he sponsored from 1465, so it has been argued, as an alternative to the grosser public amusements of Rome;[73] this occasion, and its races, were to give the Corso its name.

The Italian clergy in the early sixteenth century

There is no need to recapitulate the evidence brought forward in earlier chapters, but some general reflections may suitably conclude this brief survey.

As a whole, and not least because of the mountainous terrain, the parochial clergy of rural Italy were of extremely poor quality, intellectually and morally. In the cities, for a variety of reasons, and notably because of the absence of the bishop, local authorities, communal or princely, interfered with the clergy often to the detriment of the discipline of chapters of cathedrals and the establishments of convents of men and women religious. Among the laity there is hardly any evidence of anti-Christian sentiment, though there is massive evidence of ignorance and inertia, hardly balanced (one might guess) by the spasmodic responses to Bernardino or Savonarola and other great preachers, nor by the existence of many charitable and other confraternities among the better-off. If there is little outright heresy, there was not much evidence of profound piety among the poor, though the mystique of Mary remained untouched and many new liturgical devotions appealed to all classes, such as the rosary and the pax (above p. 69).

As for the effects of the Renaissance on the clergy in the end they had no alternative but to conform to the new manner. The lower clergy, not least because they were often elected by their parishioners, or employed by lay-controlled guilds and confraternities, were very much the subservient creatures of the secular culture around them. Few would have followed the argument over 'poetry' or 'paganism'; fewer still would find the basic form of Renaissance architecture – in towns, especially Rome, where the forms of the ancient basilica had never lost their dominance – at all shocking, whatever they thought about the detailed decoration. We would like to know what simple clergymen thought of the new religious art as it developed from Masaccio down to Raphael and Michelangelo. From its rapid diffusion in churches and convents big and little one can only assume its mixture of charm and realism met with clerical approval. In any case the leader of the clergy, the cardinals and above all the pope, if they gave no lead worth the name in church reform, did give a lead in the literary, moral and artistic developments which, from their base in Tuscany, had spread through Italy in the second half of the fifteenth century and which, by 1500, had their focal point in Rome. The popes, it has been said, were anxious to replace a spiritual leadership in Christendom by a cultural leadership in

Europe. Rome was already the capital of grace and prayer. Now it was to be the capital of pomp and culture.[74] That this was offensive to northern reformers like Erasmus and Luther is one of the sadly comical aspects of a situation in which the papacy could seldom distinguish its long-term and its short-term interests.

We must, however, be most cautious in attributing too great a degree of coherence in papal and curial leadership in such changes. Neither Martin V nor Eugenius IV were in any real sense sympathetic to new cultural developments. If Nicholas V certainly was, then Calixtus III most certainly was not. Pius II is a puzzling figure, and if Pienza and Siena saw his relatively modest buildings, Rome certainly owes little permanent to him. Thereafter the popes are carried along increasingly on a cultural wave on which they were content to be borne: Paul II with his gems and medals, Sixtus IV with the library, and all of them with the Vatican palaces. Inside the palace was established the library which is one of the great glories of the Vatican,[75] and inside the palace the archives continued to accumulate, increasingly if unsystematically written in the *corsiva cancelleresca* which was so greatly to influence the style of European handwriting and printing.[76]

When Rome began to recover after the Sack of 1527 and when with the mid-sixteenth century Italy settled down to a period of relative peace, the clergy gradually emerge, in all fundamental points, similar to those of the rest of Europe. Those that were educated were familiar with the basic Latin classics and the Bible; and so were their lay contemporaries in both Protestant and Catholic lands. After the Council of Trent the spread of seminaries slowly, very slowly, reached most of the larger Italian episcopal towns and an instructed priest became far less rare. The process may have been slower in Italy than in northern Europe: it is a matter worth investigating. Certainly the hierarchy in Italy set its face against some of the more exciting intellectual developments of the later sixteenth and seventeenth centuries. It was at this stage that Italy, which from 1350 had been the intellectual leader of Europe, ceded pride of place again to France. That this was the result solely of papal or clerical attitudes it would be absurd to argue. That these played a large part in the intellectual stagnation of a peninsula exhausted by war cannot be doubted. Nor can the historian of Europe deny that the general position of the Italianised church in the century prior to Luther made it singularly unfit to meet the challenge of the reformers.

ITALIAN SEES 1400–1500

The following list more or less follows the order found in the traditional *Provinciales*, but corrects errors in those in Eubel and other reference books. The assessment for common services is given in florins in brackets behind each see. The list is based on sees in existence in 1400; changes down to 1500 are recorded. Only sees in the area of modern mainland Italy are given, save for those in Istria (above p. x). In the list modern names are given, but in the index Latin names are also given when they are markedly different. Metropolitan sees are printed in italics. Those sees immediately subject to the pope, i.e. not in a province, are termed i.s.

It had been hoped to illustrate the following list with a map or maps but investigation showed this to be extremely difficult and expensive. Happily the reader with a magnifying-glass can turn to plate 26 by Th. Menke in K. Spruner and Th. Menke, *Historische Handatlas*, 3rd ed. (Gotha 1880); it is better for the early and central Middle Ages than for our period. There are also now the magnificent plates accompanying the various volumes of the *Rationes decimarum Italiae* published in the Vatican series, 'Studi e teste', nos. 58, 60, 69, 84, 96–7, 98, 128, 148, 161–2 (Città del Vaticano 1932–52); these cover in effect the dioceses of mainland Italy with the exception of Lombardy and Piedmont but are basically concerned with the thirteenth and fourteenth centuries, so that changes recorded in the following lists are not depicted. Sicily and Sardinia are included in nos. 112–13 of the same series (1944–5).

Central Italy

1. Cardinal bishop of Ostia and Velletri
2. Cardinal bishop of Porto
3. Cardinal bishop of Palestrina
4. Cardinal bishop of Tusculum
5. Cardinal bishop of Sabina
6. Cardinal bishop of Albano

Province of Rome (all i.s. save those subjected to new provinces of Florence and Siena; see below *Tuscany*)

7. Tivoli (100)

8. Segni (40)
9. Anagni (300)
10. Alatri (66⅔)
11. Veroli (50)
12. Ferentino (100)
13. Terracina (200)
14. Grosseto (1000); suffragan to Siena, 1459.
15. Bagnoregio (100); 10 Feb. – 17 Oct. 1449, united with Viterbo.
16. Montefiascone (100, 200 after union); 1435, united with Corneto re-erected.
17. Viterbo (300); see Bagnoregio above.
18. Nepi (70); united with Sutri, 1435.
19. Sutri (50, 136⅓ after union); see Nepi above.
20. Orte (40); united with Città Castellana, 1439.
21. Città Castellana (50, 90 after union); see Orte above.

Umbria

22. Rieti (300)
23. Narni (200)
24. Terni (68)
25. Amelia (100)
26. Castro (100)
27. Perugia (600)
28. Città di Castello (250)
29. Assisi (200)
30. Foligno (100)
31. Gubbio (400)
32. Nocera (330)
33. Orvieto (300)
34. Todi (300)
35. Spoleto (1000)

March of Ancona

36. Ancona; (300) united with Umana, 1422.
37. Umana (120, 520 after union); see Ancona above.
38. Osimo (200)
39. Recanati and Macerata (150)
40. Ascoli Piceno (300)
41. Camerino (200)
42. Jesi (300)
43. Cagli (100)
44. Montefeltro (100)
45. Urbino (300)
46. Fermo (600)

47. Fossombrone (200)
48. Sinigaglia (400)
49. Fano (300)
50. Pesaro (300)
51. Cesena (180)
52. Rimini (400)

Tuscany

53. Cortona (433⅓)
54. Arezzo (600)
55. Chiusi (400); suffragan of Siena, 1459.
56. Sovanna (300); suffragan of Siena, 1459.
57. *Siena* (600); erected into metropolitan church, 1459, with suffragans Chiusi, Sovanna, Grosseto and Massa Maritima.
58. Fiesole (200); suffragan of Florence, 1420.
59. *Florence* (1500); erected into metropolitan church, 1420, with suffragans Pistoia and Fiesole.
60. Pienza and Montalcino (100); erected 1463.
61. Pistoia (400); suffragan of Florence 1420.
62. Lucca (2000)
63. Volterra (500)
64. *Pisa* (800); suffragans Massa Maritima until 1420, and three bishoprics in Corsica.
65. Massa Marittima (300); suffragan to Pisa until 1420, then to Florence.

South Italy

66. *Benevento* (750); with the following suffragans:
67. Sant' Agata de' Goti (180)
68. Alife (100)
69. Ariano (33⅓)
70. Ascolo Puglia (66⅔)
71. Avellino (50); united with Frigento, 1492.
72. Bojano (100)
73. Bovino (50)
74. Città (50); united with Lucera, 1439–50.
75. Dragonara (33⅓)
76. Fiorentino (60)
77. Frigento (50); united with Avellino, 1492.
78. Guardialfiera (66⅔)
79. Larino (100)
80. Lesina (66⅔); united with Benevento, 1459–73.
81. Lucera (200); see Città above; united with Tortiboli, 1425, but separate bishops for rest of century.
82. Monte Corvino (33⅓); united with Volturara 1434.

83. Monte Marano (33⅓)
84. Termoli (100)
85. Telese (140)
86. Trivento (150); made i.s. 1474.
87. Tortiboli (33⅓); united with Lucera, 1425; but see Lucera above.
88. Trevico (100)
89. Volturara (50); united with Monte Corvino, 1434.
    and the following adjacent sees i.s.:
90. Teramo (300)
91. L'Aquila (100)
92. Marsi (100)
93. Penne and Atri (400)
94. Chieti (500)
95. Valva-Sulmona (170)

96. *Capua* (2000); with the following suffragans:
97. Cajazzo (130)
98. Carinola (50)
99. Calvi (100)
100. Caserta (216)
101. Isernia (50)
102. Sessa (200)
103. Teano (250)
104. Venafro (70)
    and the following adjacent see i.s.:
105. Sora (100)
106. Gaeta (250)
107. Aquino (120)
108. Fondi (200)

109. *Naples* (2000); with the following suffragans:
110. Acerra (58)
111. Ischia (50)
112. Nola (400)
113. Pozzuoli (130)
    and the following see adjacent i.s.:
114. Aversa (400)

115. *Salerno* (1500); with the following suffragans:
116. Acerno (70)
117. Capaccio (600)
118. Nocera Inferiore (200)
119. Marsico Nuovo (100)
120. Nusco (50)
121. Policastro (84)
122. Sarno (66⅔)
    and the following adjacent sees i.s.:

123. Ravello (130)
124. Cava (1000); reduced to its status as a Benedictine monastery, 1465.

125. *Sorrento* (150)
    and the following adjacent sees i.s.:
126. Vico Equense (33⅓)
127. Massa Lubrense (33⅓)
128. Castellamare (60)

129. *Amalfi* (150); with the following suffragans:
130. Capri (40)
131. Lettere (33⅓)
132. Minori (33⅓)
133. Scala (60)

134. *Manfredonia* (500); with the following suffragan:
135. Vieste (66⅔)
    and the following adjacent sees i.s.:
136. Troja (200)
137. Melfi (350)
138. Monopoli (250)
139. Rapolla (150)

140. *Trani* (1000); united with Salpe (prov. Bari); with the following
    suffragans:
141. Andria (50)
142. Bisceglie (80)
143. Montepeloso (66⅔); erected 1460 out of part of Andria.

144. *Bari* (1500); with the following suffragans (including Cattaro or
    Kotor in Dalmatia, not listed):
145. Bitetto (33⅓)
146. Bitonto (250)
147. Canna (33⅓)
148. Conversano (33⅓)
149. Giovinazzo (36)
150. Lavello (70)
151. Molfetta (76); i.s. from 1484.
152. Minervino (40)
153. Polignano (50)
154. Ruvo (33⅓)
155. Salpe (30); united with *Trani*, 1425.

156. *Otranto* (400); with the following suffragans:
157. Alessano (40)
158. Castro (100)

159. Gallipoli (33⅓)
160. Lecce (100)
161. Ugento (130)
    and the following adjacent see i.s.:
162. Nardò (60); erected from Benedictine abbey, 1413.

163. *Brindisi* (600); with the following suffragan:
164. Ostuni (50)

165. *Taranto* (400); with the following suffragans:
166. Castellaneta (125)
167. Motula (60)

168. *Acerenza* (300); with the following suffragans:
169. Anglona (100)
170. Gravina (100)
171. Potenza (100)
172. Tricarico (300)
173. Venosa (100)

174. *Conza* (200); with the following suffragans:
175. Sant' Angelo de' Lombardi (100)
176. Bisaccia (100)
177. Lacedonia (100)
178. Monteverde (33⅓)
179. Muro (66⅔)
180. Satriano (50)

181. *Santa Severina* (160); with the following suffragans:
182. Belcastro (50)
183. Cerenza (33⅓)
184. Isole (33⅓)
185. San Leone (nil); from 1449 reduced to simple church; later titular bishopric.
186. Strongoli (33⅓)
187. Umbriatico (33⅓)

188. *Rossano* (25) with no suffragans, but with the following sees adjacent and i.s.:
189. Bisignano (70)
190. San Marco (50)

191. *Cosenza* (600); with the following suffragan:
192. Martirano (33⅓)

193. *Reggio–Calabria* (600); with the following suffragans:

194. Bova (33⅓)
195. Cassano (100)
196. Catanzaro (50)
197. Cotrone (50)
198. Gerace (66⅔); united with Oppido, 1462.
199. Nicastro (100)
200. Nicotera (275)
201. Oppido (33⅓); united with Gerace, 1462.
202. Squillace (166⅔)
203. Tropea (33⅓)
    and the following adjacent see i.s.:
204. Mileto (200)

North Italy

205. *Genoa* (1000); with the following suffragans, including three sees in Corsica not listed:
206. Albenga (800)
207. Bobbio (200)
208. Brugnato (133⅓)
209. Noli (100)
    and the following adjacent see i.s.:
210. Luni and Sarzana (2000)

211. Aosta (250); prov. *Tarentaise* (see above p. 27).
212. *Milan* (3000)
213. Alba (250)
214. Alessandria (200); detached from Aqui and re-erected, 1405.
215. Aqui (126); see Alessandria above.
216. Asti (600)
217. Brescia (700)
218. Casale (133⅓); erected 1474.
219. Cremona (500)
220. Ivrea (300)
221. Lodi (150)
222. Mondovì (200)
223. Novara (600)
224. Bergamo (700)
225. Savona (125)
226. Turin (333⅓)
227. Tortona (800)
228. Vercelli (1200)
229. Ventimiglia (102)
    and the following adjacent sees i.s.:
230. Pavia (400)
231. Piacenza (500)

232. *Aquileia*, patriarchate (10,000); with the following suffragans, including Laibach or Lubliana not listed:
233. Cittanova d'Istria (100)
234. Belluno and Feltre (1600); separated 1462; see Feltre below.
235. Ceneda (100)
236. Concordia (400)
237. Como (800)
238. Capodistria (100)
239. Feltre (800); separated from Belluno in 1462.
240. Mantua (400)
241. Padua (2000)
242. Parenzo (100)
243. Pedena (100)
244. Pola (150)
245. Trieste (300)
246. Treviso (450)
247. Trent (2000)
248. Verona (900)
249. Vicenza (1000)

250. *Grado* (250), see Asolo below; after 1451 *Venice*, when united with Castello and with Jesolo, 1466, (1000), with the following suffragans:
251. Caorle (40)
252. Castello (650); united with *Venice*, 1451.
253. Asolo (100); united with Grado, 1440.
254. Chioggia (68)
255. Jesolo (33⅓)
256. Torcello (200)

257. *Ravenna* (4000); with the following suffragans:
258. Adria (200)
259. Bologna (1000)
260. Bertinoro (350)
261. Cervia (200)
262. Comacchio (100)
263. Forlì (150)
264. Imola (350)
265. Modena (150)
266. Parma (2000)
267. Reggio-Emilia (800)
268. Sarsina (50)
269. Faenza (400)
     and the following adjacent see i.s.:
270. Ferrara (1300).

Note. References for unions, new erections, etc. have been taken from

Eubel and Ughelli; Eubel's figures for common services have been checked against Hoberg's. Not all authorities agree on the status of certain bishoprics, the most complicated case being in the province of Ravenna. Ughelli gives Ferrara under Ravenna and denies it was free (ii. 515). In Hoberg's *Provinciale* Ferrara and Piacenza are given as i.s., adjacent Ravenna. The bishoprics used in the calculations above pp. 44 and 99–101, are those numbered in the above list: 9, 10, 12, 14–15, 20, 84–95, 156–60, 162, 212–17.

Index to list of Italian bishoprics

These do not always correspond with the present location of sees which have sometimes been removed to a less ruinous site, sometimes supressed. Latin forms are only given when they differ markedly from the Italian. To facilitate consultation of Eubel prefixes Sa, San' etc. are ignored.

Acerenza, 168

Acerno, 116

Acerra, 110

Adria, 258

Aemonen., 233

Aequen., 126

Sant' Agata de' Goti, 67

Alatri, 10

Alba, 213

Albano, 6

Albenga, 206

Alessandria, 214

Alessano, 157

Alife, 68

Amalfi, 129

Amelia, 25

Anagni, 9

Ancona, 36

Andria, 141

Sant' Angelo de' Lombardi, 175

Anglona, 169

Aosta, 211

Aprutinen., 90

Aquapendente, 26

Aqui, 215

Aquileia, 232

Aquino, 107

Arezzo, 54

Ariano, 69

Ascoli Piceno, 40

Ascolo Puglia, 70

Asolo, 253

Assisi, 29

Asti, 216

Astunen., 164

Auximan., 38

Avellino, 71

Aversa, 114

Bagnoregio, 15

Bari, 144

Belcastro, 182

Belluno, 234

Benevento, 66

Bergamo, 224

Bertinoro, 260

Bisaccia, 176

Bisceglie, 142

Bisgnano, 189

Bitetto, 145

Bivinen., 73

Bitonto, 146

Bobbio, 207

Bojano, 72

Bologna, 259

Bova, 194

Bovino, 73

Brescia, 217

Bretinorien., 260

Brindisi, 163

Brixien., 217
Brugnato, 208

Cagli, 43
Caietan., 97
Cajazzo, 97
Calinen., 98
Calvi, 99
Camerino, 41
Canna, 147
Caorle, 251
Capaccio, 117
Capodistria, 238
Capralen., 251
Capri, 130
Capua, 96
Caputaqua, 117
Carinola, 98
Casale, 218
Caserta, 100
Cassano, 195
Castellamare, 128
Castellaneta, 166
Castello, 252
Castro (Aquapendente), 26
Castro (suff. Otranto), 158
Catanzaro, 196
Cava, 124
Ceneda, 235
Cerenza, 183
Cervia, 261
Cesena, 51
Chieti, 94
Chioggia, 254
Chiusi, 55
Città, 74
Città di Castello, 28
Cittanova d'Istria, 233
Cività Castellana, 21
Civitanova dell'Estuario, 254
Civitaten., 74
Civitatis novae, 253
Comacchio, 262
Como, 237
Concordia, 236
Conversano, 148

Conza, 174
Cortona, 53
Cosenza, 191
Cotrone, 197
Cremona, 219
Cuman., 237
Cupersanen., 148
Cusentin., 191

Dragonara, 75

Equilin., 255

Faenza, 269
Fano, 49
Faventin., 269
Feltre, 239
Ferentino, 12
Feretran., 44
Fermo, 46
Ferrara, 270
Fiesole, 58
Fiorentino, 76
Florence, 59
Foligno, 30
Fondi, 108
Forlì, 263
Fossombrone, 47
Frequentin., 77
Frigento, 77

Gaeta, 106
Gallipoli, 159
Genoa, 205
Gerace, 198
Gerentin., 183
Giovinazzo, 149
Grado, 250
Gravina, 170
Grosseto, 14
Guardialfiera, 78
Gubbio, 31

Hydruntin., 156

Imola, 264
Insulan., 184

Interamnen., 24
Iporien., 220
Ischia, 111
Isernia, 101
Isole, 184
Ivrea, 220

Jesi, 42
Jesolo, 255
Justinopolitan, 238

Lacedonia, 177
Laquedonen., 177
L'Aquila, 91
Larino, 79
Lauden., 221
Lavello, 150
Lecce, 160
San Leone, 185
Lesina, 80
Lettere, 131
Leucaden., 157
Licien., 160
Lodi, 221
Lubren., 127
Lucca, 62
Lucera, 81
Luceria Christianorum, 118
Luni and Sarzana, 210

Manfredonia, 134
Mantua, 240
San Marco, 190
Marsi, 92
Marsico Nuovo, 119
Martirano, 192
Massa Lubrense, 127
Massa Marittima, 65
Melfi, 137
Milan, 212
Mileto, 204
Minervino, 152
Minori, 132
Modena, 265
Molfetta, 151
Mondovì, 222

Monopoli, 138
Monte Corvino, 82
Monte Marano, 83
Montefeltro, 44
Montefiascone, 16
Montepeloso, 143
Monteverde, 178
Montisregalis, 222
Motula, 167
Muro, 179

Naples, 109
Nardò, 162
Narni, 23
Naulen., 209
Neocastren., 199
Nepi, 18
Neritonen, 162
Nicastro, 199
Nicotera, 200
Nocera, 32
Nocera Inferiore, 118
Nola, 112
Noli, 209
Novara, 223
Nusco, 120

Ogentin., 161
Oppido, 201
Orte, 20
Orvieto, 33
Osimo, 38
Ostia and Velletri, 1
Ostuni, 164
Otranto, 156

Padua, 241
Palestrina, 3
Parenzo, 242
Parma, 266
Pavia, 230
Pedena, 243
Penne and Atri, 93
Pergamen., 224
Perugia, 27
Pesaro, 50

Piacenza, 231
Pienza and Montalcino, 60
Pisa, 64
Pistoia, 61
Pola, 244
Policastro, 121
Polignano, 153
Porto, 2
Potenza, 171
Pozzuoli, 113
Praeneste, 3

Rapolla, 139
Ravello, 123
Ravenna, 257
Recanati and Macerata, 39
Reggio–Calabria, 193
Reggio–Emilia, 267
Rieti, 22
Rimini, 52
Rossano, 188
Ruben., 154
Ruvo, 154

Sabina, 5
Salerno, 115
Salpe, 155
Saonen., 225
Sarno, 122
Sarsina, 268
Satriano, 180
Savona, 225
Scala, 133
Segni, 8
Sessa, 102
Santa Severina, 181
Siena, 57
Sinigaglia, 48
Sipontin., 134
Sora, 105
Sorrento, 125
Sovanna, 56
Spoleto, 35
Squillace, 202
Stabien., 128
Strongoli, 186

Suessan., 102
Sutri, 19

Taranto, 165
Teano, 103
Telese, 85
Teramo, 90
Tergestin., 245
Termoli, 84
Terni, 24
Terracina, 13
Tervesin., 246
Theatin., 94
Thermulan., 84
Tifernum, 28
Tivoli, 7
Todi, 34
Torcello, 256
Tortiboli, 87
Tortona, 227
Trani, 140
Trent, 247
Trevico, 88
Treviso, 246
Tricarico, 172
Trieste, 245
Trivento, 86
Troja, 136
Tropea, 203
Turin, 226
Tusculum, 4

Umana, 37
Umbriatico, 187
Ugento, 161
Urbevetan., 45
Urbino, 45

Valva–Sulmona, 95
Venafro, 104
Venice, 250
Venosa, 173
Ventimiglia, 229
Vercelli, 228
Veroli, 11
Verona, 248

Vestan. 135

Vican., 88

Vicenza, 249

Vico Equense, 126

Vieste, 135

Vigilien., 142

Vigintimilien, 229

Viterbo, 17

Volterra, 63

Volturara, 89

APPENDIX II
POPES 1378–1534

Urban VI 8 April 1378–15 Oct. 1389
    Clement VII 20 Sept. 1378–16 Sept. 1394
        Benedict XIII 28 Sept. 1394–deposed 26 July 1417
Boniface IX (Naples/Tomacelli) 2 Nov. 1389–1 Oct. 1404
Innocent VII (Sulmona/Migliorati) 17 Oct. 1404–6 Nov. 1406
Gregory XII (Venice/Correr) 30 Nov. 1406–resigned 4 July 1415
    Alexander V (Candy/Filargo) 26 June 1409–3 May 1410
    John XXIII (Naples/Cossa) 17 May 1410–deposed 29 May 1415
Martin V (Rome/Colonna) 11 Nov. 1417–20 Feb. 1431
Eugenius IV (Venice/Condulmer) 3 March 1431–23 Feb. 1447
    Felix V (Savoy) 5 Nov. 1439–resigned 7 April 1449
Nicholas V (Sarzana/Parentucelli) 6 March 1447–24 March 1455
Calixtus III (Spain/Borja) 8 April 1455–6 Aug. 1458
Pius II (Siena/Piccolomini) 19 Aug. 1458–15 Aug. 1464
Paul II (Venice/Barbo) 30 Aug. 1464–26 July 1471
Sixtus IV (Savona/Rovere) 9 Aug. 1471–12 Aug. 1484
Innocent VIII (Genoa/Cibo) 29 Aug. 1484–25 July 1492
Alexander VI (Spain/Borgia) 11 Aug. 1492–18 Aug. 1503
Pius III (Siena/Piccolomini) 22 Sept. 1503–18 Oct. 1503
Julius II (Savona/Rovere) 21 Oct. 1503–21 Feb. 1513
Leo X (Florence/Medici) 11 March 1513–1 Dec. 1521
Adrian VI (Utrecht/Dedel) 9 Jan. 1522–14 Sept. 1523
Clement VII (Florence/Medici) 18 Nov. 1523–25 Sept. 1534

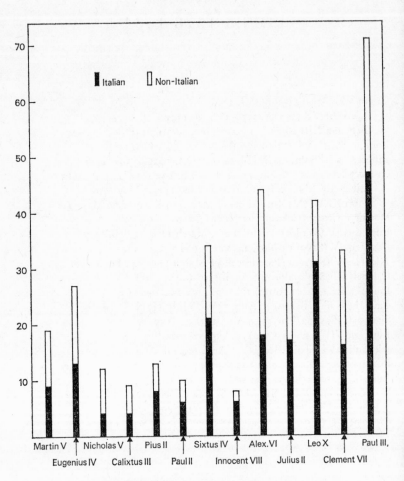

Promotions of cardinals 1417–1549
Two pontificates omitted: Pius III – 1503 (no promotions);
Adrian VI – 1522–3 (one non-Italian promotion)

APPENDIX IV

ITALIAN CHURCH ARCHIVES
(NOT INCLUDING PAPAL RECORDS)

In collecting material for this book I have had so much trouble in finding out the state of ecclesiastical archives in the peninsula that it seemed worth while to set out such general information as I have assembled even at the risk of error or omission.

A. Documentation

There is a complete collection of papal and curial instructions from the sixteenth century onwards in *Enchiridion archivorum ecclesiasticorum. Documenta potiora Sanctae Sedis de archivio ecclesiastico a concilio Tridentino usque ad nostros dies*, eds. Dom. S. Duca and Simeon A. S. Familia, O. C. D. (Città del Vaticano 1966). A brief account of the history of ecclesiastical archives is given by Professor G. Battelli in *Enciclopedia cattolica*, s.n. 'Archivio'.

B. In addition to the older publications referred to in chapter 1 above, parts of which are the more valuable now in view of the serious damage occasioned by the Second World War, there are a number of reliable books which I have referred to in the notes. Two series are worth searching for volumes of value: the Studi e teste published by the Vatican Library; and, somewhat surprisingly, the Publicazioni degli Archivi di Stato.

C. The damage of the last war was mitigated somewhat by the energetic efforts of Vatican officials before fighting started; after fighting began the same officials managed to get a good deal of co-operation from both groups of combatants. Nevertheless losses were inevitable in a campaign which traversed the entire country. The results may be studied in two accounts: the final report of the Allied Commission for Monuments, Works of Art, and Archives, issued in Rome in 1946; and two short articles by Giulio Battelli, who, as professor of Archival Studies at the Vatican (begun systematically in 1923) had largely been responsible for security measures, *R.S.C.I.*, 1 (1947), 113-16, 306-8. In the second of these articles there is a summary statement of damage. The worst affected records were parochial (and therefore affecting very little the history of the later Middle Ages). The following episcopal or chapter archives were, it seems, either totally destroyed or extremely seriously damaged:

Veneto: Treviso

Liguria: Genoa

Emilia: Rimini, Faenza, Fidenza*, Ferrara

Tuscany: Grosseto

Marches: Ancona, Urbania*

Lazio: Alatri, Aquino, Pontecorvo*, Terracina, Civita Vecchia*, Nepi–Sutri

Abruzzi and Molise: Isernia, Venafro

Campania: Benevento, Avellino, Capua, Cava dei Tirreni*

Calabria: Catanzaro

* Not bishoprics in the fifteenth century.

NOTES

Common Abbreviations (For details see list of references)

A.S.V.   Archivio Segreto Vaticano
B.V.   Bibliotheca Vaticana
D.B.I.   *Dizionario biografico degli Italiani*
E.   Eubel, *Hierarchia Catholica*, i–iii
Hefele–Leclercq *Histoire des conciles*
Moroni   *Dizionario*
Pastor   *History of the Popes* (English version unless otherwise
                indicated)
RR.II.SS   'New' Muratori
R.S.C.I.   *Rivista di storia della chiesa in Italia*
Tangl   *Kanzleiordnungen*
U. or Ughelli   *Italia sacra*, quoted in columns

Chapter 1 *The problems of Italian church history*

1. The fullest account in print of his history of the popes is by B. Gaida, in his edition of the *Liber de Vita Christi ac omnium pontificum*, RR.II.SS (Città di Castello 1912–32). See also the unpublished thesis (M.Litt.) by Richard Palermino (Edinburgh 1973).

2. See my essay in *Proceedings of the British Academy*, xlv (1959).

3. Gaida, introduction p. xv.

4. I do not mean that he was writing institutional history, in which regard he is in fact very disappointing.

5. Onofrio Panvinio (1530–68) made extensive collections, some of which are in B.V. Cod. Lat. 12124 (originally in A.S.V. Arm. xi. 40–2). For Ughelli's and Wadding's part in this see Cod. Reg. Lat. 379, and A. Wilmart's full analysis in *Cod. Reg. Lat.* ii (Città del Vaticano 1945), 397–9.

6. Alfonso Chacon, d. 1599.

7. Cf. Pius II's remarkable *tour d'horizon* with the Milanese envoy Carretto, 12 March 1462, in L. von Pastor, *Ungedruckte Akten zur Geschichte der Päpste*, i (Freiburg 1904), p. 153; but the pope had in fact treated Italy state by state and not as a unit. There was, of course,

an 'Italian nation' represented at the Council of Constance and, to a more limited extent, at the Council of Basel. Cf. H. Leclercq in *Dictionnaire d'Archéologie Chrétienne*, VII. 1612–1841, esp. cols. 1629, 1652–3, and below p. 10.

8. For another approach to this question, and for further elaboration of what follows, see my forthcoming paper on Ughelli and church historians.

9. See my paper on Ughelli. Moroni is worth reading on Ughelli, despite mistakes.

10. Recently reprinted by Forni at Bologna (1972–4).

11. For the period of overlap the vernacular work of Giuseppe Cappelletti, *Le chiese d'Italia*, 21 vols. (1844–71) is heavily dependent on Ughelli. For a scathing assessment of Cappelletti and some other general works, see P. Burchi (ed.), *Bibliotheca ecclesiarum Italiae*, I, parte prima, *Comacchio, Cesena, Brescello* (Rome 1965), introduction.

12. It will be evident that I make much use of Eubel. For vols. I–III I use the revised second edition (Münster 1913–23).

13. The work edited by Burchi referred to in n. 11 above is of uneven quality and has not progressed beyond the first volume. Much valuable work has been done in recent decades on the history of many northern and central sees for the period before A.D. 1300.

14. 'New light on post-Tridentine Italy: a note on recent Counter-Reformation scholarship', *Catholic History Review*, LVI (1970), 291–319; cf. *id.*, 'What is Catholic historiography?', *ibid.*, LXI (1975), 169–190; see too the severe criticism of G. Alberigo, *I vescovi italiani al Concilio di Trento* (Florence 1959), pp. 22–3, and the 'premessa' in G. Miccoli, 'La storia religiosa', in G. Einaudi (ed.), *Storia d'Italia*, 2 (Turin 1974), pp. 431–47.

15. B. Ferrari, *La soppressione della facoltà di teologia nelle università dello stato* (Brescia 1968); see also the interesting review of this in *R.S.C.I.*, XXIV (1970), 229–32 by G. Martina, S.J. Even before formal suppression the theological faculties which survived were in a moribund condition. An admirable book on recent church–state relations in Italy is A. C. Jemolo, *Chiesa e stato in Italia negli ultimi centi anni* (Turin 1952).

16. B.V., Cod. Barberini Lat. 3242, fo. 349.

17. The first attempted central depository of diocesan archives was ordered by Sixtus V in 1587, when the bishop of Trivento was appointed archivist. C. C. Calzolari, 'L'archivio arcivescovile toscana', *Rassegna storica toscana*, III (1957), 127–81; Pastor, XXI. 451–2n.

18. See *Archiva ecclesiae*, II (1959) reporting a conference on the question in 1958 together with subsequent papal initiatives.

19. Arnaldo D'Addario, reviewing *L'archivio arcivescovlie di Siena. Inventario* (1970) in *Archivio storico italiano*, CXXVIII (1970), 103–10.

20. R. Bevacqua, *Un grido di allarme e di speranza. Gli archivi ecclesiastici calabresi* (Reggio–Calabria 1969). Cf. the quieter account given by Pietro Burchi of the state of the episcopal archive at Cesena ('bordering on chaos') before 1957, *Storia delle parrochie di Cesena*, II (Cesena 1962); or the dreadful state of capitular archives at Genoa prior to reform: D. Puncuh in *Bolletino ligustico*, VIII (1956), 13–20.

21. In this instance Teramo: Michele Monaco, 'Due eminenti prelati della diocesi Aprutina...Simone de Lellis ed Antonio Fatati', *Abruzzo*, XII (1974), 55–72 at p. 70.

22. Princeton 1968. And see his article in *Traditio*, XVI (1960), 241–4 where the nine volumes of episcopal *acta* consist of both protocol books of notaries and a sort of register of collations, visitations etc. As he says, there may be more material of this kind elsewhere.

23. For details see below p.10 and appendix 1. It must also be remembered that besides notarial archives many papers are in communal and provincial archives – e.g. the papers of *conventi soppressi* in Florence and Venice.

24. 'Note in margine: uno studio sulla partecipazione dei vescovi italiani al primo periodo del Concilio di Trent', *Problemi di vita religiosa in Italia nel cinquecento* (*Italia sacra* II) pp. 61–72.

25. See *Enchiridion archivorum ecclesiasticorum* (Città del Vaticano 1966).

26. C. C. Calzolari, 'L'archivio'.

27. Vincenzo Maria Egidi, 'Il "diplomatico" dell'archivio capitolare di Cosenza', *Calabria nobilissima*, IX (1955), 8–25, where a summary catalogue goes down to 1548.

28. Burchi, 'Storia delle parrochie'. And see appendix IV.

29. Cf. G. Le Bras, *Études de sociologie religieuse*, 2 vols. (Paris 1955–6) esp. I. 101, 199–200.

30. C. Piana, 'Il diaconato di Fra Girolamo Savonarola', *Archivum Fratrum Praedicatorum*, XXXIV (1964), 343–8.

31. H. O. Evennett, ed. J. Bossy, *The Spirit of the Counter-Reformation* (Cambridge 1968) and cf. J. Bossy, 'The Counter-Reformation and the people of Catholic Europe', *Past and Present*, XLVII (1970), 51–70.

32. L. Prosdocimi, *Il diritto ecclesiastico nello stato di Milano dall'inizio della signoria viscontea al periodo Tridentino* (*sec. XIII–XVI*), (Milan 1941). E.g. pp. 51–77 where princely control of preferment to benefices is referred to as 'la tradizione lombardica'! A rather different kind of irritation is induced by the all too common Italian habit of labouring the obvious as, e.g. when Noemi Meoni finds it necessary to waste nearly four precious pages of her article on pastoral visitations at Cortona, *Archivio Storico italiano*, CXXIX (1971), p. 183 explaining the canonical prescriptions for such visitations! The *R.S.C.I.*, it is to be feared, contains a great deal of padding of this kind. Alas, these faults communicate themselves sometimes to foreign scholars at work in Italy: see the devastating review by Julius Kirshner in *Speculum*,

XLVIII (1973), 593–7, of the volume edited by Trexler, below chap. 4 n. 7.

33. The thirteen books of the *Commentaries* of Pius II, to be read in their entirety, must be read in the (very badly annotated and indexed) English translation by Florence Alden Gragg, ed. Leona C. Gabel, 'Smith College Studies in History', vols. XXII, XXV, XXX, XXXV, XLIII (Northampton, Mass. 1937–57) since the Latin original, first printed in 1584, was severely censored by Giovanni Antonio Campano, the pope's favourite, in the interests of discretion. The two ladies responsible for this translation of the complete MS. (B.V. Reginensis 1995) proposed originally also to edit the Latin text; in the event they produced an abbreviated English version *Memoirs of a Renaissance Pope* (London 1960). There is now an Italian translation *I commentari*, ed. Giuseppe Bernetti, which has reached book x in 4 volumes (Siena 1972–4) piquantly enough in a series called 'I classici cristiani'. This has one or two interesting observations in the introductions to each volume but is otherwise lacking in scholarly annotation, and marred by unctuousity of approach. Of the original Latin we have an edition by F. Gaeta of book I only (L'Aquila 1966). See the other autobiographical work, also called 'Commentaries', by Pius II *De gestis concilii Basiliensis Commentariorum libri ii*, ed. and trans. Denys Hay and W. K. Smith (Oxford 1967).

34. Of which the best remains that by Cecilia M. Ady *Pope Pius II* (London 1913); this in general supersedes the big study by Georg Voigt, *Enea Silvio de' Piccolomini als Papst Pius II*, 3 vols. (Berlin 1856–63).

35. Above, n. 25.

36. See *Archiva ecclesiae*, above n. 18 and also for what follows.

37. Reference may be made here to the Istituto per lo Studio di Religione at Bologna which also has a recently formed but admirable collection.

38. Cf. Jemolo.

39. Catherine E. Boyd, *Tithes and Parishes in Medieval Italy: The Historical Roots of a Modern Problem* (Ithaca, N.Y. 1952).

Chapter 2. Diocesan and parochial organisation

1. Tangl, pp. 6–32, dated by him as thirteenth to fourteenth centuries, but by A. Clergeac, *La curie et les bénéfices concistoriaux* (Paris 1911), pp. 86–7 as 1354; It is, however, almost inconceivable that lists of bishoprics did not exist much earlier, cf. the reference to a *Provinciale* in W. E. Lunt, *Papal Revenues in the Middle Ages*, 2 vols. (New York 1934); II. 501 (December 1316), and, not much later, pp. 505, 506. For one of the many early published lists I have consulted *Practica cancellariae apostolicae* (Rome 1503). The *Provinciale* there printed, fos. 1–40vo, is vitiated by gross misprints, substantial omissions (e.g. 12 sees in the south of Italy) and it completely ignores

unions and suppressions made in the fourteenth and fifteenth centuries as well as new sees and metropolitans; I speak only of its defects regarding Italian provinces. It is, in short, an extremely corrupt version of a *Provinciale* of *c.* 1300. Even well-informed Italians were confused about the number. Biondo in the *Italia illustrata* reckons 264 but Leandro Alberti regards this an an underestimate, *Descrittione di tutta Italia* (Bologna 1550), p. vii.

2. Excluding Cattaro (Kotor) in Dalmatia, although a suffragan of Bari, Lubliana (prov. of Aquileia), the three Corsican suffragans of Pisa, but including Aosta although in province of Tarentaise. That is, sees within the boundaries of modern Italy, not counting the islands. As explained in the preface, I have however continued to count the bishoprics of fifteenth-century Aquileia (other than Lubliana) in my totals.

3. For comparative purposes one may note that there are now some 302 sees in Italy, not counting Sicily and Sardinia.

4. Giovanni Battista de Luca, *Il vescovo pratico* (Rome 1675), pp. 13–23. He indignantly rejects the argument that the numbers (which were by his day of course even more disproportionate) were designed to counter-balance the combined powers of the bishops of other nations. The cardinal in effect refuses an exact computation ('un conto esatto e minuto'), p. 16!

5. Cf. Hay, 'Flavio Biondo'.

6. Eubel gives the figures but less accurately than Mgr H. Hoberg, *Taxae pro communibus servitiis...1295-1455* (Città del Vaticano 1949); see appendix 1 above. It must be stressed that it is episcopal income which is estimated for tax, not the wealth of the town.

7. On these questions see Jean Favier, 'Temporels ecclésiastiques: le poids de la fiscalité pontificale au XIVe siecle', *Le journal des savants*; jan.–mars 1964, pp. 102–27 (his examples all being from the north; and *id.*, *Les finances pontificales à l'époque du grand schisme d' occident* (Paris 1966), pp. 391–4. For concordats and common services see A. Mercati, *Raccolta di concordati*, (Rome 1954), 1, pp. 144–58. The Dragonara case, U., vIII. 282. The elect of Nicastro in 1411 offered to pay his tax in kind, E., 1. 362. Some north Italian sees were also very poor, e.g. Adria, Comacchio.

8. Trivento, prov. Benevento. While Tommaso Carafa was bishop (1473–1498) the see was made immediately subject on the grounds that that had once been its status and that the pope was also acceding to the request of Ferrante. Ughelli prints the bull of 1474, 1. 1330–1.

9. Raoul Morçay, *Saint Antonin: fondateur du couvent de Saint Marc, archevêque de Florence 1389-1459*, (Paris 1914), pp. 154–9; S. Orlandi, *S. Antonino*, 2 vols. (Florence 1960), 11. 202–3. Metropolitan visitations were getting less frequent in northern Europe in the later Middle Ages.

10. U., vIII. 3–13; Moroni, s.n. 'Benevento'.

11. A. Hamilton Thompson, *The English Clergy and their Organisation in the later Middle Ages* (Oxford 1947) pp. 1–39; and G. Mollat's contribution to F. Lot and R. Fawtier, *Histoire des institutions françaises au moyen âge*, III (Paris 1962), esp. pp. 407–37.

12. Although Moroni, s.n. 'Vescovi', says that the chapters at Asti and Mondovì long retained the right to elect, and at Mondovì some capitular elections certainly occurred in the fifteenth and sixteenth centuries: Gioachino Grassi, *Memorie istoriche della chiesa vescovile di Monteregale*, 2 vols. (Turin 1789), 1.9, 54, 59, 61.

13. Paolo de Töth, *Il beato cardinale Niccolò Albergati e i suoi tempi 1375–1444* (Aquapendente 1934), pp. 117–27; U., II. 31.

14. In 1510 (again during the Schism) the chapter at Chiusi asked for a *congé d'élire* from the magistrates at Siena, U., III. 642–3.

15. C. Cenci, 'Senato veneto – "Probae" ai benefizi ecclesiastici', *Spicilegium Bonaventurianum*, III (1968), p. 389.

16. U., I. 1175–7.

17. *Ibid.*, 1030–1 and 599–60.

18. See further below chapter 3.

19. The Dieci sequestrated all Zeno's benefices, 5 September 1471. See also G. Soranzo, 'Giovanni Battista Zeno, cardinale di S. Maria in Portico', *R.S.C.I.*, XVI (1962) 249–74. (Ghirado's name is variously given as Gherardo, Gerardo, Girardo; cf. U., V. 1305, E., II. 21, 264).

20. This paragraph is mainly based on the interesting paper by C. Cenci, above n. 15, pp. 313–454.

21. The Senate often asked the pope to wait if members got wind of a change in territories or even learnt that a prelate was old or ailing, Cenci, 'Senato veneto', p. 401.

22. *Ibid.*, p. 352.

23. *Ibid.*, pp. 373–4.

24. Luigi Fumi, 'Chiesa e Stato nel dominio di Francesco I Sforza' *Archivio storico lombardo*, LI (1924), 54.

25. *Ibid.*, pp. 26–9; P. Gentile, 'Finanze e parlamenti nel Regno di Napoli dal 1450 al 1457', *Archivio storico per le provincie napoletane*, XXXVIII (1913), 185–231.

26. Gentile, pp. 213–14 and notes.

27. Morçay, *Saint Antonin*, pp. 107–21; the Florentine preference for one of the five, Donato di Medici, was indicated. On Scarampo, see Pio Paschini, 'Ludovico, cardinale camerlengo', *Lateranum* new series., V (1) (Rome 1939).

28. For details and documentation, U., III. 166–8; Pius II, *Commentaries*, pp. 163–4; Pastor, IV. 294–6; cf. N. Rubinstein, *The Government of Florence under the Medici, 1434 to 1494* (Oxford 1966), p. 166. It is itself significant that Professor Rubinstein can afford, apart from the Neroni episode, to omit any reference to the bishops of Florence.

29. This was, of course, a very odd story – Gaetani, Colonna, Orsini and

other Roman barons. For the later developments cf. F. Chabod, *Lo stato e la vita religiosa a Milano nell' epoca di Carlo V*, ed. E. Sestan (Turin 1971).

30. From its inception (below n. 34) the A.S.V. series Resignationes frequently includes examples of *permutacio* below the level of the episcopate. For Italian cases e.g. vol. 1, fos 6vo, 18vo, 19vo etc.; in the Obligationes et Solutiones, vol. 72, fo. 37 illustrates abbeys being exchanged. See further below on resignations with the financial adjustments they often involved.

31. These may be controlled by consulting Eubel and the A.S.V. series Obligationes et Solutiones. E.g. for the Belley–Mondovì case see vol. 70, fos. 219, 244, 244vo; for Orvieto–Penne and Atri vol. 76., fos. 123, 124vo, and also vol. 72, fo 88vo, and vol. 66, fo 68vo. A glance at this series shows that there are more Italian cases of exchanges than those listed in the text above; there are also a few from other areas, for instance a French example Angers–Perigueux in 1470, vol. 82, fo. 57vo; I have only observed one case from Ireland – between bishops of Elfin and Emly in 1449, vol. 72, fo. 63vo. The most staggering example of exchanges I have noted is 1482 Verdun–Ventimiglia, Amalfi–Verdun, Ventimiglia–Amalfi: Obligationes et Solutiones, vol. 82, fos. 134, 145, 145vo; not, I think, with any effect. The series of Obligationes et Solutiones is extremely hard to use systematically, since the acts it records were not always entered contemporaneously but were registered often long after the transaction, or on loose sheets bound up out of chronological order. See further below n. 35 on the series Resignationes.

32. Pier Giovanni Caron, *La rinuncia all'ufficio ecclesiastico nella storia del diritto canonico* (Milan 1946), pp. 349–50.

33. Cf. Jean Delumeau, *Vie économique et sociale de Rome dans la seconde moitié du XVᵉ siècle*, 2 vols. (Paris 1959) II. 773; 'Rome compte beaucoup de courtiers...'

34. On this see Favier, *Finances*, p. 374–5. Hence the protests at the Council of Constance, Hefele–Leclercq, VII. 536–8, etc. Paolo Sarpi, 'Trattato delle materie beneficiare' in *Scritti giurisdizionalistici*, ed. G. Gambarisi (Bari 1955), p. 94 shrewdly observes that conciliar legislation was not 'received' in Italy.

35. The Resignationes, soon with blank sheets and disordered chronology, and a fair number of gaps as they survive in A.S.V., begin in 1458. From vol. 2 they disintegrate badly and are only pulled together partially in vol. 15 where the verso of the unnumbered folio at the beginning is cancelled and so with other blanks, thus observing the rules laid down by Leo X (24 September 1513) to avoid fraudulent dating.

36. The whole of this question of *resignationes* in favour of named parties is admirably discussed in Clergeac, *Bénéfices concistoriaux*, likewise 'regress' and reservation of pensions. 'Regress' was the

privilege of resuming the prelacy which had been resigned (i.e. in effect its revenues).

37. *Ibid.*, pp. 50f; P. Tacchi-Venturi, S. J., *Storia della compagna di Gesu in Italia* I. i, parte prima, 2nd ed. (Rome 1951), pp. 27–30 for some startling 'hereditary' bishoprics, mainly from the sixteenth century.

38. A patient search of Gams or Eubel throws up many cases.

39. Often to be inferred from the dates in Eubel and plentifully confirmed in the Acta Cameralia in A.S.V.

40. E.g. Bergamo, where Lorenzo Gabriele was provided on 13 October 1484. His proctor took possession on 8 May 1485; the bishop entered the town on 13 July 1485. U., IV. 485.

41. Many vicars in spirituals were able men with legal training. See below p. 57 on visitations.

42. *I vescovi italiani*, above chap. I, n. 14.

43. U., IV. 485 (cf. n. 40 above). For the tensions in the chapter at Florence which even Antonino found it hard to compose, see Morçay, *Saint Antonin*, pp. 141–2.

44. Cf. Philibert Schmitz O.S.B. *Histoire de l'ordre de Saint-Benoît*, III (Maredsous 1948), pp. 64, 81–92, 157–74.

45. On this see A. Hamilton Thompson, 'Diocesan organisation in the Middle Ages: archdeacons and rural deans', *Proceedings of the British Academy*, XXIX (1943), 153–94, based on a careful reading of Ughelli. 285 sees with details show that 141 had chapters headed by archdeacons; in a further 63 archdeacons are lower in dignity, but in 50 they come second in precedence. In the north of Italy prominence is often given to a provost.

46. U., II. 515.

47. U., IV. 521.

48. U., I. 976–9. (Foundation bull of 1369). Another recent foundation, Mondovì, had archdeacon, provost, archpriest, cantor, and ten canons with prebends. Grassi, *Memorie istoriche della chiesa di Monteregale*, p. 285.

49. Re-established by the will of Archbishop Giovanni, d. 1453, on condition that it was in the gift of the Visconti. U., IV. 256–7.

50. Carlo Castiglioni, 'Gli ordinari della metropolitana attraverso i secoli', *Memorie storiche diocesa di Milano*, I (1954), 11–56; Carlo Marcora, 'Carlo da Forlì, arcivescovo di Milano', *ibid.*, II (1955) at pp. 260–1.

51. See below pp. 35–6, 56–7.

52. E.g. Grosseto, a bull of Innocent VIII (1484) ordering the appointment of eight supernumerary canons who would attend services. U., III., 682. Earlier Sixtus IV (1479) had tried to achieve residence by augmenting the canons' *mensa*; U., *loc. cit.*

53. G. Forchielli, *La pieve rurale* (Bologna 1938), p. 224; C. Chimenton, *Formazione dei chierici in Treviso prima del concilio di Trento*, 2nd ed. (Treviso 1945), pp. 47–52.

54. A brief but clear account by G. Forchielli in *Enciclopedia italiana*, XXVII (1935), s.n. 'pieve'.

55. Paolo Sambin, *L'ordinamento parrochiale di Padova ned medio evo* (Padua 1941). That relics of the old order survived is shown in this admirable work, pp. 71–6, where a synodal regulation of 1927 abolished the custom of only baptising in urban parish churches from Saturday of Holy Week to a week after Easter Day.

56. See Sambin, 'Studi di storia ecclesiastica medioevale', *Deputazione di storia patria per le Venezie: miscellanea*, IX (1) (Venice 1954) 53–60; Franco Molinari, 'Visite e sinodi pretridentini a Piacenza', *Italia sacra* II (1960), 248–9; Natale Caturegli, 'Le condizione della chiesa di Pisa nella seconda metà del secolo xv', *Bolletino storico pisano*, XIX (1950), 34–5; cf. Pietro Burchi, *Storia delle parrochie di Cesena*, p. 121 for an example of an oratory being erected into a parish church.

57. Caturegli.

58. Sambin, 'Studi di storia ecclesiastica', pp. 1–15.

59. B. Cecchetti, *La repubblica di Venezia e la corte di Rome nei rapporti della religione*, 2 vols. (Venice 1874), I. 165–6; Verona area: Forchielli, pp. 185–203, on the *jus eligendi* of clergy and people; Pisa: Caturegli, pp. 57–9; Florence: Gene Brucker, *Renaissance Florence* (New York 1969) p. 187, an excellent account of the election of a priest for the parish of S. Piero Buonconsiglio, in which 26 parishioners participated in 1388. Milan: *Visite pastorale di Milano (1423–1859)*, inventario ed. A. Palestra (Rome–Florence 1971), pp. 565–6; Genoa: Puncuh, *Carteggio*, p. 81 (San Remo 1422); Chieri: L. Giordano, *La chiesa di S. Giorgio e la elezione popolare del parroco* (Turin 1896); Emilia: A. Sorbelli, *La parrochia dell' Appenino emiliano nel medio evo* (Bologna 1910), esp. pp. 30–5, 73–83. The only general study I have encountered, D. Kurze, *Pfarrerwahlen im Mittelalter*, (Cologne–Graz 1966) has little to say regarding Italy or the later Middle Ages.

60. Forchielli, pp. 116–17.

61. Maria Billi, 'Origine e sviluppo delle parrochie di Verona', *Archivio veneto*, ser. 5, XXIX (1941), 59.

62. Burchi, *Storia delle parrochie di Cesena, passim*.

63. Cf. Bossy, 'The Counter-Reformation and Catholic Europe', 56–7.

64. An extremely interesting article by Enrico Cattaneo, 'Il battistero in Italia dopo il Mille', *Italia sacra*, xv (1970), 171–95. This is mainly on the central Middle Ages; the author draws attention to the house behind the baptistery at Parma (*domus baptizatorum*) where registers of baptisms are kept dating from 1 January 1459.

Chapter 3. The Schism in Italy

1. A.S.V., Resignationes 2, fo. 12vo, 1 July 1482: a pension of 300 ducats to Dominus Johannes Jacobus de Sclafenatis, papal cubicularius, from Carolus de Seyssel of Grenoble, apostolic protonotary and papal

familiar, who had just been provided to the preceptory of St Anthony at Chambéry. This is typical of several of the entries in this series.

2. I treat the second Borgia pope, Alexander VI, as an Italian.

3. Cf. the 'republicanism' of S. Antonino in Florence: Brucker, *Renaissance Florence*, p. 202.

4. See the relevant section of Eubel, I.

5. Below appendix III.

6. K. Eubel, 'Die Provisiones praelatorum während des grossen Schismas', *Römische Quartalschrift*, VII (1893), 405–46; *id.* 'Die provisiones praelatorum durch Gregor XII nach Mitte Mai 1408', *Römische Quartalschrift*, X (1896), 99–131 and *ibid.*, pp. 508–9, 'Welches Vehrfahren wurde im grossen Schisma beobachtet, wenn ein der einen Obedienz geweihter Bishof zur andern übertrat?'. Cf. the remarks of P. Brezzi, 'Lo scisma d'occidente come problema italiana', *Archivio delle deputazione romana di storia patria*, LXVII (1944), 391–450, whose study is, however, mainly a political narrative.

7. The following account simplifies a very tangled story and is derived from G. de Renaldis, *Memorie storiche dei tre ultimi secoli del patriarcato d'Aquileia* (Udine 1888), pp. 9–20; E. Piva, 'Venezia e lo schisma', *Nuovo archivio veneto*, XIII (1897); cf. Hefele–Leclerq, VII. i. 49, 55, 63n.

8. A friar who preached against deserting Gregory XII was imprisoned for six months and banned from the *dominio* for life: Piva, p. 153.

9. John XXIII made him a cardinal in 1411.

10. U., IV. 805–8, cf. I. 449; Eubel, I, *sub titolis*.

11. G. Rossi 'Un vescovo scismatico della chiesa ventimigliese', *Archivio storico italiano*, ser. 5, XII (1893), 139–48.

12. Punuch, *Il carteggio*, *passim*. For complications in Naples see lists of rival archbishops in Domenico Ambrasi, 'La vita religiosa', in *Storia di Napoli*, III (Naples 1969) pp. 558–9.

13. E., I. 99n.

14. E., I. 95n.; U., I. 366.

15. U., I. 626; Guiseppe Mirri, *I vescovi di Cortona*, revised by Guido Mirri (Cortona 1972), pp. 82–114. Note ordination 7 June 1438 of many foreigners, perhaps in connection with the Council of Basel, p. 85.

16. U., III. 642. The Council of Basel also nominated a rival patriarch of Aquileia.

17. Pastor, I. 264–5.

18. Hefele–Leclerq, VII. i. 65–6.

19. Eubel, 'Welches Verfahren wurde. . .', pp. 508–9.

20. Rossi, above n. 11, pp. 145–7.

21. See Moroni, s.n.; Caron, *La rinuncia*, pp. 304–5, 337, says that a bishop who renounced could be called 'formerly bishop of x' or 'a bishop in the universal church'.

22. Above pp. 13–16.
23. See the admirable survey by Jean Guiraud, *L'état pontifical après le Grand Schisme* (Paris 1896); Peter Partner, *The Papal States under Martin V* (London 1958); Katherine Walsh, 'Papstum, Kurie und Kirchenstaat im späteren Mittelalten; neue Beiträge zu ihrer Geschichte', *Römische historische Mitteilungen*, xvi (1974), 205–30; for the Malatesta story, besides Pius II's *Commentaries*, see now Philip J. Jones, *The Malatesta of Rimini and the Papal States* (Cambridge 1974). I give one further example. The doge of Genoa in 1440, having heard that the bishop of Albenga was on his last legs, ordered the chapter there to elect a Doria and the podestà to see that this was done: Valeria Polonio, 'Crisi e riforme nella chiesa genovese', *Miscellanea di studi storici*, i (Genoa 1969), p. 27n. the bishop did not die. Note the confusions in U., iv. 920.
24. Below pp. 60–1. On dioceses and state boundaries cf. Delio Cantimori, *Prospettive di storia ereticale* (Bari 1960), p. 59.
25. Brian Tierney, *Foundations of the Conciliar Theory*, (Cambridge 1968).
26. Cf. K. J. Scarisbrick, 'Clerical taxation in England 1485–1547', *Journal of Ecclesiastical History*, xi (1960), 41–54.
27. E.g. Venice and Sixtus IV and Julius II: G. Dalla Santa, 'L'apellazione della repubblica di Venezia dalle scommuniche di Sisto IV e Giulio II', *Nuovo archivio veneto*, xxxiv (1899), 216–42; 'Il vero testo', *ibid*; xxxviii, (1900), 348–61.
28. B. Guillemain, *La cour pontificale d'Avignon* (Paris 1962) pp. 188, 192–5.
29. Cf. Pastor, i. 260–2.
30. Pastor, ii. 7.
31. *Ibid.*, 319–20.
32. Cf. Paschini, 'Ludovico, cardinal camerlengo'.
33. Pastor, iv. 58.
34. *Ibid.*, iv. 464n.; M. Mallett, *The Borgias* (London 1969), p. 310n. 21.
35. Mallett, p. 76.
36. Ady, *Pius II*, pp. 242–50, 263–6.
37. Pastor, iv. 119–20, 200n. And cf. above pp. 13–14.
38. Cf. E., ii. 16–20 and notes; and Pastor, iv. 409–13.
39. See the genealogical tables in Mallett's book.
40. Cf. Roberto Palmarocchi, 'Lorenzo de' Medici e la nomina cardinalizia di Giovanni', *Archivio storico ital.*, cx (1952), 38–54. Innocent first offered the hat to Lorenzo himself.
41. Cf. Pastor, vi. 218–22 for Julius II's promotions.
42. For one of the exceptions, see David Chambers, *Cardinal Bainbridge in the court of Rome 1509–14* (Oxford 1965).
43. Paul III (1539–49) had created 47 Italian cardinals and 24 non-Italian, a total of 71. Cf. appendix iii.

44. E.g. at the conclave of 1522, with its overwhelming Italian composition, and its astonishing result (the Fleming, Adrian VI) nine non-Italians did not appear. Cf. Pastor, IX. 14.

45. 'This disorderly and corrupt conclave was joined during its prolonged session (50 days) by three French cardinals and one Italian, all late arrivals'. Numbers present are not without their difficulties; see Pastor, IX. 259n. There is a list (omitting Bourbon) in A. Ciaconius, *Vitae et gesta summorum pontificum* (Rome 1601), pp. 1091–2.

46. Favier, *Les finances*, pp. 690–1.

47. P. Partner 'The "Budget" of the Roman Church', in *Italian Renaissance Studies* ed. Jacob (London 1960); A. Gottlob, *Aus der Camera apostolica des 15 Jahrhunderts* (Innsbruck 1889) p. 253–5.

48. W. von Hofmann, *Forschungen zur Geschichte der kurialen Behörden*, 2 vols. (Rome 1914).

49. For what follows see P. Partner 'The "Budget" of the Roman Church', pp. 566–78.

50. Partner, p. 263.

51. Partner, p. 269, and now in full in Michele Monaco, *La situazione della reverenda camera apostolica nell' anno 1525* (Rome 1960) and *id.*, 'Le finanze pontificie al tempo di Clemente VII', *Studi romani*, VI (1958), 278–96.

52. An admirably clear statement in Delumeau, *Vie économique*, pp. 751–8.

53. Cf. Favier, *Les finances*, pp. 689–90.

54. Gottlob, p. 257.

55. D. Redig de Campos, *I palazzi vaticani* (Rome 1967) p. 94; Cf. D. L. Galbreath, *Papal Heraldry* (Cambridge 1930).

56. V. Forcella, *Iscrizione delle chiese e d'altri edifici di Roma dal secolo XI fino ai giorni nostri*, 14 vols. (Rome 1869–84) esp. vols. VI, XII. Cf. The London University M.Phil thesis (1973) of H. J. Marchant, 'Papal Inscriptions in Rome 1417–1527'.

57. In general W. E. Lunt, *Papal Revenues in the Middle Ages*; G. Mollat, 'Contributions à l'histoire du Sacré Collège de Clément V à Eugene IV', *Revue d'histoire ecclésiastique*, XLVI (1951) 22–122, 566–94. And further below p. 43.

58. A.S.V. Resignationes 1, fo. 19, (9, April 1460); 'Gratis pro palafrenario domini nostri papae'; *ibid.* 2, fo. 33vo: 'gratis per fratrem domini Gregori Cubiculari'; Obligationes at Solutiones 85, fo. 35: 'Remissioni pro electo Interamnense, nepote pontificis. Gratis etc'; Formatori 8, fo. 155vo: 'gratis pro nepote notarii camerae'.

59. Hefele-Leclerq, VII. i. 422 and refs.

60. Von Hofmann, n. 48 above.

61. Guillemain, n. 28 above.

62. This again had been part of some of the Constance Concordats, Hefele–Leclercq, VII. i. 562.

63. Pastor, I. 242–3n.

64. Guillemain, p. 443.
65. Delumeau, II. 768–82.
66. Von Hofmann, II. 173–4.
67. *Ibid.*, II. 174.
68. Cf. above p. oo and n. 57; David Chambers, 'The economic predicament of Renaissance cardinals', *Studies in Medieval and Renaissance History*, III (1966), 289–313; A. V. Antonovics, 'A late XV century division register of the College of Cardinals', *Papers of the British School at Rome*, XXXV (1967), 87–101.
69. On the other hand Leo X borrowed at 40 per cent at a critical moment: Delumeau, II. 783, quoting Pastor.
70. Moroni, s.n. 'Vacabilia'; cf. M. Monaco, 'Il primo debito pubblico ponteficio: il Monte della Fede (1526)', *Studi romani*, VIII (1960), 553–69.
71. Some references are given in my paper in *Itinerarium Italicum*, essays presented to P. O. Kristeller, ed. Oberman and Brady (Leyden 1975) at pp. 356–7.
72. Biondo's two sons, also in papal service, were both married: Flavio Biondo, *Scritti inediti*, ed. B. Nogara (Città del Vaticano 1927) pp. clxxix–clxxxi. On the tensions between lay and clerical in administrative careers, see further below p. 102.
73. Domenico de' Domenichi, *Liber de dignitate episcopali* (Rome 1757), dedication to Pius II, p. 45 and part iii, pp. 133–346; Cf. Moroni, s.n. 'Vescovo' para. III.
74. Johannes Burckardus, *Liber notarum*, ed. Celani, 2 vols. RR.II.SS. (Città di Castello, 1907–1942, indices not completed) I. 64–5.
75. A pontifical of 1451 made for Giovanni Barozzi, bishop of Bergamo, 1449–64 and later patriarch of Venice: Mark Dykmans, S. J., 'D'Avigon a Rome. Martin V et le cortège apostolique', *Bulletin de l'institut historique belge de Rome*, XXXIX (1968), 202–309, with two colour plates showing Martin V's 'possesso'. On processions, a subject worthy of much more study, cf. Pastor, v. 89–95; Herbert Thurston, S. J., *The Holy Year of Jubilee* (London 1900) with an illustration of a seventeenth-century cavalcade at p. 60; Vincenzo Forcella, *Tornei e giostre, ingressi e trionfali e feste carnavelesche in Roma, sotto Paolo III* (Rome 1885) – a slight piece but with some contemporary documents.
76. Burckardus, I. 97–100. Details of public concistories are given in Eubel, appendix I, Annotationes ad part I.
77. Cf. Carlo Castiglioni, 'Gli ordinari'.
78. *Les papes d'Avignon*, pp. 9–11.
79. The phrase is Delaruelle's in 'La pietà popolare alla fine del medio evo', X° Congresso internazionale di scienze storiche (Rome 1955), *Relazione*, III (Florence 1955) p. 521.
80. *Commentaries, passim.*
81. Pastor, *Ungedruckte Akten*, p. 167 (15 March 1462).

82. Cf. E. Cerchiari, *Capellani papae et apostolicae sedis auditores causarum...seu sacra romana rota*, 4 vols. (Rome 1919–21), pp. 163–4. In the summer of 1462 the Rota was in Rome although the pope was not. Cf. Pastor, VI. 262n.

83. Pastor, VI. 471. On these cultural developments see further below pp. 105–9.

Chapter 4. The state of the clergy and laity in fifteenth-century Italy

1. 'Under secular and papal leadership the formalization of church archives grew apace.' See R. L. Poole, *Lectures in the History of the Papal Chancery...to Innocent III* (Cambridge 1915); C. R. Cheney, *English Bishops' Registers 1100–1250* (Manchester 1950), esp. p. 132. Professor Cheney kindly allowed me to consult him on this matter.

2. P. Sambin, 'Chierici ordinati a Padova alla fine del trecento', *R.S.C.I.*, II (1948), 381–402; cf. *id.*, 'Altri chierici ordinati a Padova nella seconda metà del secolo XIV', *R.S.C.I.*, VI (1952) 386–407 for fuller lists for 1350–2, 1357–94. Piana, 'Il diaconato di Savonarola', pp. 343–8 (Bologna 1477); Orlandi, *S. Antonino*, II. 155–80 (Florence 1420–45) and II. 325–40 (Florence 1447–59) – though only Dominicans are identified; Pietro Posenato, 'Chierici ordinati a Padova dal 1396 al 1419', *Fonti e ricerche di storia ecclesiastica padovana*, II (1969), 11–106, as summarised in *R.S.C.I.*, XXIV (1970) 675; Mirri, *I vescovi di Cortona*, p. 85 (1438).

3. C. Piana, 'Promozioni di religiosi agli ordini sacri a Bologna', *Spicilegium Bonaventurianum*, III (1968), 1–312 (1341–508 with some gaps esp. 1349–64 and 1419–4 and covering *all* religious): R. Maiocchi and N. Casacca, *Codex diplomaticus ordinis E. S. Augustini Papiae*, II (Pavia 1966) pp. 131–366 *passim* (Augustinian friars 1464–80, 1487–1500 with some gaps). Cf. next note, T. Kaeppeli's lists; and note that regulars are often very numerous in general ordinations, as in P. Sambin's list above n. 2.

4. A.S.V. Formatori on which I hope to publish more; see Ludwig Schmitz, 'Die Libri formatorum der Camera Apostolica', *Römische Quartalschrift*, VIII (1894) 451–72; Tommaso Kaeppeli, O. P., 'Domenicani promossi agli ordini sacri presso la curia romana 1426–1501', *Archivum fratrum praedicatorum*, XXXIV (1964), 155–89. The Formatori record general ordinations, consecrations of bishops and similar acts and were registered because a fee was exigible in the case of orders lower than those of priest.

5. Bologna: Töth, *Albergati*, I. 153–208; Brescia: P. Geurrini, 'Per la storia dell'organizzazione ecclesiastica della diocese di Brescia nel medio evo', *Brixia sacra*, XIV (1923), 174–96; Cortona: N. Meoni, 'Visite pastorale', esp. 190–226 (the earliest in Tuscany go back to 1337); Florence and Fiesole: cf. E. Conti, *I catasti agrari della repubblica fiorentina* I (Rome 1966), p. 87n.; Milan: Marco Magistretti, 'Visite

pastorale del secolo XV nella diocesi di Milano', *Ambrosius* (1955), 196–214 and cf. C. Marcora, 'Frate Gabriele Sforza', *Memorie storiche della diocesi di Milano*, I (1954), 296–329 and 'Carlo da Forlì', *ibid.*, II (1955), 321–2; Padua: G. de Sandre Gasparini in *Italia sacra*, XVI (1970), on Pietro Barozzi, who was bishop from 1487 to 1507, and his life in *D.B.I.* VI, pp. 510–12 by F. Gaeta; Piacenza: Molinari, 'Visite e sinodi pretridentini a Piacenza', 241–79; Pisa: Caturegli, 'La condizione della chiesa di Pisa', pp. 17–124; Siena: G. Catoni and S. Finestri, *L'archivio arcivescovile di Siena* (Rome 1970), pp. 14–15.

6. I have failed to find a copy of F. Coradini, *La visita pastorale del 1424 nel casentino del vescovo Francesco da Montepulciano* (Anghiari n.d.). For S. Antonino's metropolitan visitation, Morçay, *Saint Antonin*, pp. 156–9, and Orlandi, *S. Antonino*, II. 202–3. Some material from records of general chapters will be considered below. Of rather different interest are: A. Dini-Traversari, *Ambrogio Traversari e i suoi tempi* (Florence 1912), appendix (separately paged) giving the *Hodoeporicon*, much used by G. G. Coulton, *Five Centuries of Religion*, IV (Cambridge 1950), 246–310; Brucker, *Renaissance Florence*, pp. 190–1 (Vallombrosan convents); T. Leccisotti, 'Le visite pastorale...nell' abbazia di Montecassino', *Italia sacra*, II (1960) 215–24; *Le 'Liber visitationis' d'Athanase Chalkéopoulos (1457–8). Contribution à l'histoire du monarchisme grec en Italie meridionale*, ed. M. H. Laurent and A. Gouillou (Città del Vaticano, 1960).

7. References as for n. 5 above: for Bologna see Töth, pp. 163–4, 261–4; Brescia: Guerrini, XIV. 174–96; Cortona: Mirri, p 128; Piacenza: Molinari, pp. 262–9; Florence (provincial): Morçay, p. 154; Sabina: H. Albano, *Constitutiones synodales Sabinae diocesis* (Urbino 1737), pp. 296–8; F. S. Dondi d'Orologio, *Dissertazione nona sopra l'istoria ecclesiastica padovana* (Padua 1817). The fullest modern collections are Richard C. Trexler, *Synodal Law in Florence and Fiesole* (Città del Vaticano 1971), on which see the review by Julius Kirshner, *Speculum*, XLVIII (1973), 593–7; and (for Genoa) *Synodi diocesanae et provinciales* (Genoa 1933), which I have failed to find. Silvino Da Nardo, O. F. M. Cap., prints a list of published canons prior to 1534 as an appendix to his *Sinodi diocesani italiani. Catalogo bibliografico degli atti a stampa 1534–1878*, (Milan 1962); but it is manifestly incomplete, i.e. it does not include those in Dondi d'Orologio, above.

8. For what follows see the old but admirable work of the Oratorian, Louis Thomassin, *Ancienne et nouvelle discipline de l'eglise* 4 vols. (Paris 1678–81), esp. II. 161–7 on age for ordinations; and III. 130 for what he calls (uncomfortably) seminaries, which he realises did not really exist in the interval between the university becoming a training ground for ambitious administrators in the thirteenth century, and the Council of Trent; and the admirable and painstaking work of G. Pellicia, *La preparazione ed ammissione dei chierici ai santi ordini*

nella Roma del secolo XVI (Rome 1946), on which I greatly depend in what immediately follows. The importance of a 'title' or benefice is stressed heavily by Giustiniani and Quirini in their 'Libellus' of 1511: see below p. 84n. 46.

9. E.g. it is taken for granted by Hamilton Thompson in his *English Clergy*.

10. Hastings Rashdall, *The Universities of Europe in the Middle Ages*, ed. Powicke and Emden, 3 vols. (Oxford 1936), 1. 279n. For Italian universities *ibid.*, 1 (Salerno, Bologna), 11 (the rest).

11. There was hardly any theology at the Sapienza until after 1513. But on the Roman university D. S. Chambers has now demonstrated that it was somewhat more active than used to be supposed: 'Studium Urbis...The University of Rome in the fifteenth century', in Clough (ed.), *Cultural Aspects of the Italian Renaissance* (Manchester 1976) pp. 68–110.

12. Luciano Bertoni, 'Il "collegio" dei teologi dell'università di Siena', *R.S.C.I.*, xxii (1968), 1–56 and at p. 7n. a list of the half-dozen universities where some theology was taught by the fifteenth century.

13. Caturegli, p. 54.

14. Forchielli, *Pieve rurale* p. 224; see further below p. 57.

15. Castiglioni, 'Gli ordinari', p. 23.

16. Below p. 81.

17. Cf. P. Heath, *English Parish Clergy on the Eve of the Reformation* (London 1969), pp. 16–18.

18. P. Mazzuchelli, *Osservazioni intorno al saggio storico critico sopra il rito Ambrosiano* (Milan 1828), pp. 377–8. For Antonino's practice see Orlandi, ii. 215–7.

19. Orlandi, ii. 335, 340.

20. C. Piana, 'Promozioni di religiosi', *passim*. There are gaps in the series, as noted above, n. 3.

21. Maiocchi and Casacca, ii. 131–366 *passim*.

22. Marc Venard, 'Recherches sur le recrutement sacerdotal dans la province d'Avignon', *Annales*, xxiii (1968), 987–1016. The legate also had more extensive powers of dispensing from canonical requirements, including the need for letters dimissory, p. 998.

23. Posenato, 'Chierici ordinati a Padova', pp. 11–106 at p. 17.

24. Piana, 'Il diaconato di Fra Girolamo'. At Padua (previous note) 200 out of 677 were financed by their families.

25. Cf. n. 4 above.

26. S. Antonino abolished charges for ordination. They had been: subdiaconate 1 fl. 13s., diaconate 2 fl 4s., priesthood 3 fl. 6s. Orlandi, ii. 215–17. It should be noted that occasionally the Formatori record the issue of free testimonials: for the poor, 'gratis pro paupere': as well, of course, for the rich and well-connected curialists. For payments at Padua see Posenato *passim*.

27. A.S.V. Formatori 4, fo. 2vo: 'Mandatum affigendum Valuis Castri Sanctiangeli, Sancti Celsi, et Campiflorum pro ordinibus celebrandis', 17.9.1464.
28. Formatori, 1, fos. 49–51 – 2, fo. 116vo.
29. J. Toussaert, *Le sentiment religieux* (Paris 1963); P. Adam, *La vie paroissiale en France au XIVe siècle* (Paris 1964).
30. Cf. Heath, *The English Parish Clergy*; Margaret Bowker, *Secular clergy in the diocese of Lincoln, 1485–1520* (Cambridge 1968). For the regulars, Dom David Knowles, *The Religious Orders in England*, vols. II and III (Cambridge 1955, 1959).
31. Töth, pp. 153–8.
32. Morçay, pp. 156–9; Orlandi, 1. 75.
33. There is debate about the effects of Florentine occupation. See Michael Mallett, *The Florentine Galleys in the Fifteenth Century* (Oxford 1967).
34. Caturegli, pp. 34–9.
35. Molinari, 'Visite e sinodi', pp. 241–79.
36. It will be appreciated that the sort of information given above could be adduced for a fair number of other centres.
37. For references see notes 31, 32, 34, 35, above; and cf. below p. 57.
38. Forchielli, *Pieve rurale*, p. 224.
39. Töth, *Albergati*, 1. 209–45; Sambin, 'Studi di storia ecclesiastica mediovale', pp. 90–7.
40. Caturegli, pp. 81–4.
41. References above n. 6.
42. Chalkéopoulos, above n. 6.
43. The most important and best documented upheavals occurred (almost from the beginning) in the Franciscan order: for a synoptic view with admirable bibliographies, see J. R. H. Moorman, *A History of the Franciscan Order from its Origins to 1517* (Oxford 1968), and the Edinburgh (1974) Ph.D. thesis of Dr Duncan Nimmo on the Observants, to be published by the Capuchin Historical Institute. For the Dominicans, who proceeded by 'congregations', the key name is Raymond of Capua at the end of the XIV century: see R. Creytens, O. P. and A. D'Amato, O. P., 'Les actes capitulaires de la congrégation dominicaine de Lombardi', *Archivum Fratrum Praedicatorum* XXXI (1961), 213–306, especially pp. 213–44 for origins; there are many other scattered articles. The Austin Hermit reform: see G. Raponi, O.S.A., 'Il cardinale agostiniano Alessandro Olivia di Sassoferato (1407–63)', *Analecta augustiniana*, XXV (1962), 89–143, XXVI (1963) 194–293, and Katherine Walsh, 'The observant congregations of the Augustine friars in Italy *c.* 1385–*c.* 1465, (Ph.D thesis, Oxford 1972). Carmelites: Ludovico Saggi, *La congregazione mantovana dei carmelitani*, (Rome 1954).
44. A. M. Galuzzi, O. M., *Origini dell'ordine dei minimi*, (Rome 1967).
45. Melchior A. Pobladura, O.F.M. Cap., *Historia generalis ordinis*

fratrum minorum capuccinorum, 1. (1525–1619) (Rome 1947) pp. 21–54; Father Cuthbert, O.F.M.C., *The Capuchins. A Contribution to the History of the Counter-Reformation*, 2 vols. (London 1928), 1. 17–147.

46. Creytens and D'Amato, cited above n. 43, give an excellent short account. Cf. below, p. 74.

47. Cesare Cenci, O.F.M., 'I Gonzaga e i fratri minori dal 1365 al 1430', *Archivum Franciscarum Historicum*, LVIII (1965), 3–47, 201–79, and this was to lead to a comical piece of legislation by the Lombard congregation in 1516: friars were to have no manner of role as bearers of political letters, and 'tam in conventu quam extra, non nisi bona de principibus loquantur...' Creytens and D'Amato, 'Actes capitulaires', p. 228.

48. Below p. 82.

49. Cesare Cenci, 'Antonio da Pereto, Ministro generale O.F.M., e i capitoli generali di Roma (1411) e di Mantova (1418)', *Archivum Franciscanum Historicum*, LV (1962), 468–500; the separate bedrooms were to be allowed to the old, the ill, the *sacrae theologie magister*, and any minister present or past.

50. Moorman, pp. 502–3, etc.

51. As the second half of the article of Fathers Creytens and D'Amato, pp. 244–307.

52. Brucker, p. 193: the figures refer to respectable houses and husbands – 1,000 florins for the latter, 100 for the former. Provisions of dowries became a notable aspect of charity in the later Middle Ages. Cf. Brucker, p. 210; Sorbelli, *Commune rurale*, pp. 186–7; Pullan, *Rich and Poor in Renaissance Venice* (Oxford 1971), pp. 163–9.

53. G. Priuli, *I Diarii*, ed. A. Segre and R. Cessi, RR.II.SS (Città di Castello – Bologna 1912–41) 4 vols. (of which vol. 3 has never appeared), IV. 33–5, s.a. 1509. In general, Pio Paschini, 'I monasteri feminili in Italia nel'500', in *Italia sacra*, II (1960), 31–61.

54. Was sodomy more popular or more easily tolerated by the early sixteenth century? In 1407, 15 nobles and 18 *popolari* were executed for it. See C. Cenci, 'Fra Francesco di Lendinara e la storia della provincia di S. Antonio tra la fine del secolo XIV e l'inizio del secolo XV', *Archivum Franciscanum Historicum*, IV (1962), 103–92 at p. 140 n. 2. This arose because seven Franciscans were denounced anonymously for having (?) practised idolatry, sodomy, seduced Poor Clares; in the end they were rehabilitated. This was in Venice.

55. M. Morpurgo-Castelnuovo, 'Il cardinale Domenico Capranica', *Arch. della soc. romana di storia patria*, LII (1929), 1–146 at pp. 83–4; Valeria Polonio, 'Crisi e reforme', p. 274 n. Messina: Coulton, IV. 321–2.

56. Cf. Caturegli, pp. 84–8 (on the convent of S. Matteo where the girls came from good Pisan families).

57. Cf. D. Herlihy, 'Veillir à Florence au quattrocento', *Annales*, XXIV (1969), 1338–52.

58. Brucker, *Renaissance Florence*, pp. 192–3.
59. Dini-Traversari, pp. 149ff.
60. Aretino claimed that his work had a reforming intention. It is so repulsive that, taken in connection with the details above (and much more could be adduced), one wonders if he had not a higher moral purpose than his readers usually credit him with.
61. For the 'Libellus' of the two Venetians see below chapter 5 and n. 46.
62. See refs to S. Antonino in n. 6 above; Caturegli, pp. 40–51.
63. Tacchi-Venturi, p. 327.
64. *Inter alia* see now P. O. Kristeller, 'Le mythe de l'athéisme de la Renaissance...', *Bibliothèque d'humanisme et de la Renaissance*, xxx (1975),337–48.
65. Brucker, *Renaissance Florence*, p. 176.
66. Brucker, pp. 176–7, 290 citing Elio Conti. Tuscany was, compared with Lombardy, an area where endowment of the church had not been as lavish as elsewhere. The late Professor Federico Chabod told me once that he was sure that the church today was better off in its Italian properties than it had ever been in the Middle Ages – but this was in the mid-fifties!
67. Cf. Marjorie Reeves, *The Influence of Prophecy in the later Middle Ages: a Study of Joachism* (Oxford 1969).
68. And its history now attracts much interest. See, e.g., the good survey by Giovanni Gonnet, *Le confessioni di fede Valdesi prima della riforma* (Turin 1967).
69. The literature is now extensive. The most general work remains G. M. Monti, *Le confraternite medioevali dell'alta e media Italia*, 2 vols (Venice 1927), which doubtless has mistakes (as P. Sambin notes, 'Studi di storia ecclesiastica', p. 105) but it is a remarkably useful study; for another even older view see Pastor, v. 35–6. Among recent works see *Il movimento dei disciplinati nel settimo centenario dal suo inizio* (Perugia 1960), Deputazione di storia patria per l'Umbria, appendice al *Bolletino* n. 9 (Perugia 1962), especially contributions by Delaruelle and Alberigo. For an even wider social background see Jacques Heers, *L'Occident aux XIV° et XIV° siècles: Aspects economique et sociaux* (Paris 1963), esp. pp. 305–13; for some later developments, G. G. Meerseman, 'La riforma delle confraternite laicali in Italia prima del concilio di Trento', *Italia sacra*, II (1960), 17–30, and John Bossy, 'The Counter-Reformation' pp. 58–60 ('an artificial kin-group'). For an elaborate representative of local studies see Lia Sbriziolo, 'Le confraternite veneziane di devozione – saggia bibliografica e premesse storiografiche', *R.S.C.I.*, xxi (1967), 167–97, 502, 542.
70. Delaruelle and Alberigo (as in previous note); Lia Sbriziolo, 'Note su Giovanni Dominici', *R.S.C.I.*, xxiv (1970), 4–30 and esp. bibliog. p. 10n. Dominici was banned from Venetian territory for five years;

for Florentine reactions in 1399 see Brucker, *Renaissance Florence*, pp. 204–5.

71. Castiglioni, 32–7, 313–18.

72. Illustrated authoritatively for Venice in Pullan. See further below pp. 79–80 on confraternities or companies of Divine Love.

73. See Mariano Da Alatri, O.F.M. Cap., 'La carità christiana a Roma – il medio evo', *Roma Cristiana*, x (Bologna 1968), pp. 123–87.

74. Da Alatri, pp. 161–183; cf. A. Maroni Lumbroso and A. Martini, *Le confraternite romane nelle loro chiese* (Rome 1963), where it appears that the high point was reached in the sixteenth century, with 85 new confraternities. Luther's admiration for Italian hospitals should be remembered.

75. '...homini del mondo e abbiamo governo de robba e famiglia, non possiamo stare semper occupati nel servitio de Dio come li religiosi', Alberigo as in note 69 above, pp. 176–9.

76. The two best examples are the complete sermons of S. Bernardino da Siena in *Opera omnia*, ed. P.P. Colegii S. Bonaventurae, 7 vols. (Florence 1950–9), and *Sermoni del beato Bernardino Tomitano da Feltre, nella redazione di fra Bernardino Bulgarino da Brescia, minore observante*, ed. P. Carlo Varischi, O.F.M. Cap., 3 vols. (Milan 1964). There are attractive English works on Bernardino da Siena by E. Ferrers Howell, *S. Bernardino of Siena*, (London 1913) and Iris Origo, *The World of San Bernardino*, (London 1963); two recent essays on Bernardino da Feltre are by Gino Barbieri, *Il beato Bernardino da Feltre nella storia sociale del Rinascimento* (Milan 1962) and Nello Vian, 'Il beato Bernardino da Feltre in edizioni e studi recenti', *R.S.C.I.*, xxiv (1970), 193–203. For the connection of Bernardino da Feltre with Monti di Pietà, see further below p. 68. On preaching in Italy at this time in general cf. Pastor, v. 175ff.

77. P. Villari, *La storia di Girolamo Savonarola e de' i suoi tempi*, 2 vols., (Florence 1859–61); Roberto Ridolfi, *Life of G. S.*, trans. Grayson (London 1959); Romeo de Maio, *Savonarola e la curia romana* (Rome 1969); Donald Weinstein, *Savonarola and Florence* (Princeton 1970).

78. Zelina Zafarana, 'Per la storia religiosa di Firenze nel quattrocento: una raccolta privata di prediche', *Studi medievali*, ser. 3, ix (1968) 1017–1113; the author considers the influence of religion on the collector's life to have been great but strictly limited and without extending spiritual sensibility, p. 1027. On sermons, local pilgrimages and lay devotion cf. Brucker, pp. 201–12, and in general pre-Reformation material in A. D'Addario, *Aspetti della contrariforme a Firenze*, (Rome 1972).

79. Herbert Holzapfel, O.F.M., *Die Anfänge der Montes Pietatis, 1462–1515* (Munich 1903), and the table on p. 136 (that this needs revision is evident from the careful article by V. Meneghin, 'Il "Mons

Euganeus" di Giovanni Barozzi', *Fonti e ricerche di storia ecclesiastica padovana*, II (1969), 11–106); Cf. Philip Roth, *The Jews in
Renaissance Italy* (New York 1959). R. de Roover, *Money Banking
and Credit in Medieval Bruges*, (Cambridge, Mass. 1948), is the
best account of the economics of the pawn-shop at this time. For
Venice see Pullan, index, s.v. Monti di Pietà and p. 456 for the
reaction there to Bernardino da Feltre.

80. Cf. below p. 154 n.18.

81. Cf. above p. 24.

82. S. Tramontin and others, *Culto dei Santi a Venezia* (Venice 1965), the
best example being the plague saint S. Rocco, preceded by a confraternity, 1477–8, and imported from Lombardy; his body was
obtained in dubious ways in 1485. Ughelli, v. 1179–81, enumerates
49 saints whose bodies are in Venice.

83. The Capitano del Mar was ordered in 1426 to get the head of S.
Giorgio preserved in the island of Aegina by persuasion and he was
directed not to use force ('per vim nihil tentari debeat'). Tramontin,
Culto, pp. 186–8 (A. Niero).

84. Paolo Prodi, 'The structure and organisation of the church in
Renaissance Venice: suggestions for research', in J. R. Hale (ed.)
Renaissance Venice (London 1973), pp. 413–14.

85. Ambrasi, 'La vita religiosa', pp. 549–60.

86. Richard C. Trexler, 'Sacred Images in Florentine Religion', *Studies
in the Renaissance*, XIX (1972), 7–41.

87. Amply treated in *Catholic Encyclopedia* and similar reference
works.

88. As in n. 87; see also Delaruelle *et al.*, *L'Église au temps du grand
schisme*, II. 690–1 for mass movements precipitated by the concept
of peace.

89. Thurston, *Jubilee*, pp. 247–56; in principle these were given by the
pope and Nicholas V anathematised persons selling them.

90. Cf. Evennett, *Spirit*, p. 39.

91. Above p. 64.

92. The basic work remains the thorough study of Alessandro D'Ancona,
Le Origini del teatro italiano, 2nd ed., 2 vols. (Turin 1891); the
second volume consists of texts and appendices. My colleague
Professor Peter Brand has drawn my attention to a recent anthology,
Sacre rappresentazioni del quattrocento, ed. Luigi Banfi (Turin
1963), which is entirely restricted to Florentine material, much the
richest and best studied area of this theatrical development of the
liturgy. In Italy the feast of Corpus Christi was less important as a
focal point of religious drama than it became in the North, although
it was not without a distinct influence.

93. Ferrers Howell, pp. 218–19.

94. F. Biccelari, O.F.M., 'Un francescano umanista, il beato Alberto da
Sarteano (1395–1450)', *Studi Francescani*, X (1938), 28 quoting a

letter of Poggio; Carlo Marcora, 'Carlo da Forlì arcivescovo di Milano (1457–1461)', pp. 247–52, quoting Erasmus, *De ratione concionandi*.

95. At Florence confraternities came under civic control in 1418; Brucker, *Renaissance Florence*, p. 208; for the state and confraternities in Venice see Pullan, *passim*.

96. The fullest study is by Romano Guarnieri, 'Il movimento del libero spirito', *Archivio italiano per la storia della pietà*, IV (1965), 355–650 with an edition of the *Mirouer*; see the same author's article in M. Viller *et al.* (eds.), *Dictionnaire de spiritualité*, V (1964), cols. 1242–68.

Chapter 5. The quality of Italian religious life. Reform

1. Above p. 24.

2. Moorman, *A History of the Franciscan Order*, p. 508.

3. E. Dupré-Theseider, 'Sul "dialogo contro i fraticelli" di S. Giacomo della Marca', *Italia sacra*, XVI (1970), 577–611 where it is clear that the remaining handful were more or less polished off by the Inquisition and Paul II. On the latter, see M. Miglio, 'Vidi thiaram Pauli papae secundi', *Bulletino dell' istituto storico italiano per il medio evo*, LXXXI (1969), 273–96, who attributes it (I am sure rightly) to Cardinal Jouffroy; but there is more to be got out of this interesting dialogue between a cardinal and a *fraticello* than Paul's pomp; see B. V. Ottoboniano Latino 793 and note, fo. 36, the cardinal's argument that St Thomas of Canterbury died for the sake of the possessions of his church.

4. 'Les actes capitulaires', where the historical survey is on pp. 213–244. See above p. 60.

5. Walsh, 'The Observant Congregations of the Augustine Canons'; for the later story see the Ph.D. thesis (Cambridge 1958) by F. X. Martin, O.E.S.A. on Egidio da Viterbo, a prior-general (1506–18) with an Observant background. For Egidio see further below pp. 95–7.

6. 'Congregation' in this sense is used to refer to a group of houses following common practices and with arrangements for chapters tec. See below p. 77.

7. Saggi, *La congregazione mantovana dei Carmelitani, cit.* Vicars-general for the reformed houses were first made in the following year, *ibid.*, p. 83.

8. See the admirable study by Clergeac, already referred to.

9. Dini-Traversari, p. 179 (quoting Mehus nos. 25, 136).

10. For what follows see Coulton, *Five Centuries of Religion*, IV, chap. xxiii; I. Tassi O.S.B., *Ludovico Barbo (1381–1443)* (Rome 1952); L. Pesce, *Ludovico Barbo*, 2 vols. (Padua 1969).

11. Tassi, p. 129.

12. Dr Katherine Walsh is surely right to discuss as illusory a general observantine 'movement' in the decades around 1400.

13. De Maio, *Savonarola*, pp. 25–36.

14. For what follows see N. Widloecher, *La congregazione dei canonici regolari lateranensi: periodo di formazione (1402–1483)* (Gubbio 1929). For some stimulating discussion of early sixteenth-century developments, Philip McNair, *Peter Martyr in Italy: an Anatomy of Apostacy* (Oxford 1967).

15. This is the theme of Professor McNair's book.

16. Galuzzi, *Origini dell'ordine dei minimi*; useful background information in F. Russo, *Storia dell'arcidiocesi di Cosenza*, (Naples n.d., c. 1956). The spread of Minims and Capuchins outside Italy was, of course, on a much more restricted scale (especially that of the Minims) than the original Franciscan movement, one reason being the upheavals of the Reformation. Cf. H. O. Evennett in *New Cambridge Modern History*, II (Cambridge 1958) chap. ix, 'The new orders'.

17. Suppressed (with the Geronimites of Fiesole) in 1668.

18. Cf. refs. above chap. 4, n. 69.

19. Alberigo, 'Contributi alla storia delle confraternite', pp. 193–4.

20. See the older account in Monti, who notes, I. 306–7, that at the twenty-second session of the Council of Trent confraternities were firmly put under episcopal control. For much of what follows I have used V. Meneghin O.F.M., 'Due compagnie sul modello del "Divino Amore" fondate da Francescani a Feltre e Verona 1499, 1503', *Archivum Fratrum Historicum*, LXII (1969), 518–64. A. Cistellini, *Figure della riforma pretridentina* (Brescia 1948), pp. 269–91 prints some documents from Brescia; Pio Paschini, *La beneficenza in Italia e le compagnie del Divino Amore nei primi decenni del cinquecento. Note storiche* (Rome 1925); M. Da Alatri, O.F.M. Cap., 'La carità cristiana a Roma', pp. 123–87.

21. The most general study is Pierre Michaud-Quantin, *Sommes de casuistiques et manuels de confessions au moyen âge, XII–XIV siècles* (Louvain 1962); for Antonino see p. 73 ff. and cf. R. Creytens, 'Les cas de conscience soumis à S. Antonin de Florence par Dominique de Catalogne O.P.', *Archivum Fratrum Praedicatorum*, XXVIII (1958), 149–220, where one is sometimes struck by the triviality of the problems and by the reliance on canon law rather than common sense for the saint's replies. For the literature on preparing for death and related iconographical material, see the admirable book by Alberto Tenenti, *Il senso della morte e l'amore della vita nel Rinascimento* (Turin 1957).

22. The first edition of the Bible in Italian was in 1471 at Venice; there were many devotional works: Cf. Alberigo, 'Contributi alla storia delle confraternite', pp. 209–14.

23. Gaetano da Thiene, Luigi Lippomano, Gian Pietro Carafa and Giacomo Sadoleto.

24. The above is based on Morpurgo-Castelnuovo, 'Il Cardinale Domenico Capranica', p. 87; the article does not seem trustworthy in detailed matters.

25. Above p. 22.

26. Morpurgo-Castelnuovo, pp. 92–116, where some of the revision of the foundation rules are discussed. The *Almae Collegii Capranicensis Constitutiones* (Rome 1705), is a rare volume and I have to thank M. Jean Prinet of the Bibliothèque Nationale at Paris for securing me a photocopy.

27. The best account of the Nardini foundation I have seen is in Moroni, xii.

28. *Five Centuries of Religion*, iv. *passim*.

29. De Maio neatly refers (p. 28) to 'i piccoli cesaropapismi degli stati italiani'.

30. Cenci, 'I Gonzaga', pp. 3–47, 201–79. The demands of the Gonzaga were brutally put forward and unctuously received – provided the friars were Mantuans. Cf. 17–19 the letter of a Mantuan provincial minister on his election: 'si qua pro vobis possum, vestrum est mandare et meum obedire'; an offending guardian might be removed from office, pp. 201–2. Francesco Gonzaga's protest (1391) that 'his' chaplains were being distracted by conventual business, pp. 208–10. Similar material in Cenci, 'Antonio da Pereto', pp. 468–500.

31. Cf. A. D'Amato, 'Vicende dell'osservanza nella congregazione Domenicana in Lombardia negli anni 1469–72', *Archivum Fratrum Praedicatorum*, xv (1945), 52–101, where Borso d'Este's support is inspired by purely political motives.

32. *Id.*, 'Sull introduzione della riforma Domenicana nel Napolitano per opera della Congregazione Lombarda 1489–1501', *ibid.*, xxvi (1956), 249–75; The Regno was one of the few areas where the Dominican Observance was a relative failure.

33. Prosdocimi, *Il diritto ecclesiastico*, p. 82 n. 9.

34. Alberigo, *I vescovi italiani al concilio di Trento*.

35. J. Haller and others (eds.) *Concilium Basiliense. Studien und Quellen zur Geschichte des Konzils von Basel*, 7 vols, Basel 1896–1926, viii pp. 143–7, in 1434; Cf. p. 22 of introduction and pp. 33–8 (early 1432).

36. Prosdocimi, p. 90. Eugenius was, of course, under military pressure from Milan in 1433, when Sforza and Fortebraccio occupied part of the Papal States, to accept the demands of the Fathers at Basel.

37. Aeneas Sylvius Piccolomini (Pius II), *De Gesto concilli Basiliensis Commentario*, pp. 210–13 and nn.

38. *Ibid.*, pp. 210–12.

39. *Scritti giurisdizionalistici*, p. 94.

40. Fumi, 'Chiesa e stato nel dominio di Francesco I Sforza', pp. 26–7.

41. *Ibid.*, pp. 58–9.

42. *Ibid.*, p. 26.

43. G. B. de Luca, *Il cardinale della S. R. Chiesa pratico*, (Rome 1680), p. 103.

44. N. H. Minnich, 'The participants at the fifth Lateran Council,' *Archivium historiae pontificae*, XII (1974), 158–206.

45. *Id.* 'Concepts of reform proposed at the fifth Lateran Council,' *ibid.*, VII (1969), 163–251; for Egidio da Viterbo's sermon at the opening session see the works already cited by J. O'Malley, who discusses Egidio's reforming ideas in 'Man's dignity, God's love, and the destiny of Rome', *Viator*, III (1972), 389–416.

46. Paulus Justinianus et Petrus Quirinus, eremiti Camaldulenses, 'Libellus ad Leonem X.P.M.' (1513), in J. B. Mittarelli and A. Costadoni *Annales Camaldulenses*, IX (Venice 1773), cols. 612–719. This is paraphrased, with biographies of the authors, in Silvio Tramontin, 'Un programma di riforma della Chiesa per il concilio lateranense V', *Venezia e i concilii* (Venice 1972) (='Quaderni del Laurentianum', I); cf. J. Leclerq, *Un humaniste érémite. Le bienheureux Paul Giustiniani*, (Rome 1951).

47. 'Libellus' col. 708.

48. Roberto Weiss, *Un Umanista Veneziano, Papa Paolo II*, (Venice 1957). And cf. Miglio's article cited above n. 3.

49. For the Venetian background in the sixteenth century see Pullan, *Rich and Poor*, already cited; W. Bouwsma, *Venice and the Defence of Republican Liberty: Renaissance Values in the Age of the Counter-Reformation* (Berkeley 1968); G. and M. Cozzi eds., *Paolo Sarpi, Opere* (Milan 1969), introduction.

50. In general Pastor, v. 173–4; L. Célier, 'L'Idée de réforme à la cour pontificale du concile de Bâle au concile du Lateran', *Revue des questions historiques*, LXXXVI (1909) 418–35; Massimo Marcocchi, *La riforma cattolica: documenti e testimonianze*, I, (Brescia 1967), chapter viii.

51. Plan of Cusa in J. M. Duex, *Nikolaus von Kusa*, (Regensburg 1847), II. 451ff.; Domenichi's proposals (Tractatus de reformatione curiae romanae) in B. V. Vat. Lat. 5869 and other MSS, the author's original being in the Biblioteca Barberini; an incunable of 1495 published at Brescia. For the draft bull see B. V. Vat. Lat. 12192 fos. 1–36, and other MSS.; for extracts see Tangl, pp. 372ff. and Pastor, III. 397ff. It is now printed in full by R. Haubst, 'Der Reformentwurf Pius der Zweiter', *Römische Quartalschrift*, XLIX (1954), 188–242 at pp. 205–242.

52. Printed Rome, 1757. In part VI he stresses heavily the argument that the authority of bishops was directly derived from the apostles, a well-known position of the Fathers at Basel as Pius II must have recognised.

53. Charles Lefebvre, 'Le tribunal de la Rote Romaine et sa procédure au temps de Pio II', in *Enea Silvio Piccolomini Papa Pio II. Atti del*

convegno per il quinto centenario, ed. D. Maffei (Siena 1968), pp. 199–211.

54. For a revised date of draft, see new Italian trans. of Pastor, by Angelo Mercati and Pio Cenci, II (Rome 1961), p. 722n.
55. Tangl, pp. 362ff, 379; cf. Pastor, IV. 467.
56. B.V., Vat. Lat. 3883, 3884. The first volume contains the most interesting material and is strictly contemporaneous with Alexander VI's conversion; the second, which contains a good deal of conciliar material from Basel (fos. 1–26vo), was assembled temp. Julius II, presumably towards the end of the pontificate (cf. fo. 10 where Carafa is dead, and fo. 52vo where Julius is alive).
57. 'Alexandre VI et la réforme de l'église', *Mélanges d'archéologie et d'histoire*, XXVII (1907), 65–124.
58. Pastor, v. 558f.; Tangl, p. 404. Célier, 'Alexandre VI', prints it, pp. 119ff.
59. B.V. Lat. 3883, fos. 53–86^{v}.
60. See the works of Pesce and Tassi already cited.
61. Above pp. 60–1. Creytens and D'Amato, there cited, remain the authorities followed.
62. Above pp. 77–8, and the narrative in Widloecher.
63. Cf. A.S.V., Resignationes, vol. 2, fo. 32 (14 December 1468): Bartolomeo de Siciliano, canon of the Lateran, resigns this on being given canonry in St Peter's; and so *ibid.* with Stefano de Canovis (8 February 1469).

Chapter 6. The Renaissance and the clergy of Italy in the fifteenth century

1. *Civilization of the Renaissance in Italy*, many eds. and trans. after first German ed. of 1860. Burckhardt was, of course, inheriting a long tradition in this regard: cf. W. K. Ferguson, *The Renaissance in Historical Thought* (Cambridge, Mass. 1948).
2. Pastor, v. 80. A more sophisticated calculation by Peter Burke, based on the work of Errera, has recently shown that of dated pictures the percentage of secular subjects rose from 5 per cent in the 1480s to 25 in the 1530s, *Renaissance Italy 1420–1540* (London 1972), p. 39.
3. Cf. P. O. Kristeller, 'Paganism and Christianity', in *Renaissance Thought*, I (New York 1961); *id.*, 'Le mythe de l'athéisme'.
4. The prostitutes of Rome were notorious, especially those in the Borgo. Giustiniani and Quirini in their 'Libellus' write (col. 706): 'Horret animus cogitare sacratum palatium tuum [i.e. Leo X's] meretricibus circumdata ita, ut neque Tu e domo pedem efferre possis, neque alius sedem tuam adire, cui mille meretricum una spectacula non sint intuenda'. There is no doubt that they frequented the papal palace from time to time during Alexander VI's pontificate, not so much for direct papal enjoyment as part of the general dissolute gaiety

which the pope indulged in; this is all amply documented in, e.g. Burckard's *Liber notarum*, and seems beyond dispute.

5. Savonarola's prophetic utterances are more celebrated than others; see D. Weinstein, *Savonarola and Florence*. For the main influence on this activity see Reeves, *The Influence of Prophecy*.

6. G. G. Meerseman, '"In libris gentilium non studeant." L'étude des classiques interdite aux clercs au moyen âge?' *Italia medioevale e humanistica*, I (1958), for a clear, brief exposé.

7. Cf. B. Bernardino Tomitano da Feltre: 'Quid vult dicere tanta habuntia librorum quibus omnis villa et doma est plena? Olim erat prohibitum ut nunquam Biblia esset in vulgari redacta, et tamen nunc est impresa in vulgari. Quid vult dicere hoc, nisi quod Deus, istis temporibus infelicissimis et obscuratis, tantum lumen fecit ut nemo possit excusari. Nunquam finit tantum lumen in mundo, chè omnis scriptura est ad hunc finem ut faciat hominem virtuosiorem, ut dicit Aristoles...No fu mai veduto tanti libri...' *Sermoni, cit.,* I. 249. Barbieri, *Il Beato Bernardino da Feltre* notes, pp. 19–20, that S. Bernardino da Feltre quoted Livy as an advocate of honest poverty against corrupt wealth. The matter is discussed in more detail than is possible here in a number of books: Vladimir Zabughin, *Storia del Rinascimento cristiano* (Milan 1924); Charles Trinkaus, *In Our Image and Likeness*, 2 vols (London 1970); Evenett, *Spirit of Catholic Reformation*; the work of C. Angeleri, *Il problema religiosa del rinascimento* (Florence 1952), is an over-schematic (and by now very out of date) bibliography.

8. G. Boccaccio, *Genealogia deorum gentilium libri*, ed. V. Romano, 2 vols. (Bari 1951). G. Dominici, *Lucula noctis*, ed. E. Hunt (Notre Dame 1940); Pino Da Prati, *Giovanni Dominici e l'umanesimo* (Naples 1965), esp. pp. 145–201. Useful extracts from the *Governo* in Claudio Varese, ed., *Prosatori volgari del quattrocento* (Milan 1955), pp. 24–40.

9. A succinct statement of this point of view is P. O. Kristeller, 'The contribution of religious orders to Renaissance thought and learning', *American Benedictine Review*, XXI (1970), 1–55, esp. pp. 14–16.

10. See the interesting discussion in V. Zabughin, *Vergilio nel Rinascimento, italiano*, 2 vols. (Bologna 1921), I, pp. 120–2; E. Bigi, *D.B.I.*, VI (1968), 95–6 with bibliography.

11. This is Kristeller's point in the article cited above, n. 9.

12. Morçay, p. 303.

13. 'Libellus', cols. 675–6. They are, of course, also thinking of the undergrowth of modern commentary and gloss surrounding the theological works taught in universities. Later they refer to 'hunc Parisiensium cavilliosiorem disciplinam' (cols. 677–8).

14. Above pp. 92–3.

15. Above n. 9. For Sarteano see B. Alberti [Berdini] da Sartheana,

Opera omnia, ed. F. Harold O.F.M. and Patrick Duffy (Rome 1688), a well-edited book; not much further is to be found in Biccelari, 'Un francescano umanista', pp. 22–48.

16. Above p. 74. Cf. below p. 96.

17. Gigliola Fragnita, 'Cultura umanistica e riforma religiosa: il "de officio. . .episcopi" di Gasparo Contarini', *Studi veneziani*, XI (1969), 75–189.

18. R. Arbesmann, O.S.A., 'Andrea Biglia, Augustinian friar and humanist (d. 1435)', *Analecta Augustiniana*, XXVIII (1965), 154–218. B. de Gaiffier, 'Le mémoire d'André Biglia sur la predication de S. Bernardin de Sienne', *Annalecta Bollandiana*, LIII (1935), 348–358, discusses Biglia's second treatise attacking Bernardino's cult of the Name of Jesus as leading to idolatry.

19. *Umanesimo europeo e umanesimo veneziano*, ed. V. Branca, (Venice 1964); V. Branca's contribution, 'E. Barbaro e l'umanesimo veneziano', pp. 192–212; Pio Paschini, 'Tre illustri prelati del Rinascimento', *Lateranum*, new ser., XXIII (Rome 1957), 11–42; V. Branca has recently edited the *De coelibatu, de officio legati* (Florence 1969).

20. G. Soranzo, *Matteo Bosso di Verona 1427–1502. I suoi scritti e il suo epistolario* (Padua 1965).

21. Bernardino da Siena's sermons, *Opera omnia*; for Bernardino da Feltre see above n. 7.

22. Pastor, I. 33.

23. Widloecher, pp. 317–20. In 1454 he was in danger of becoming archbishop of Milan: Carlo Marcora, 'Frate Gabriele Sforza', pp. 236ff. Cf. the garbled account in U., IV. 258–63 which shows Maffei's zeal to be in the class of great preachers like Bernardino da Siena and Vincent Ferrer.

24. This account is based on John W. O'Malley, S. J., 'Preaching for the Pope', *The Pursuit of Holiness in late Medieval and Renaissance Religion*, ed. Charles Trinkaus and Heiko Oberman (Leiden 1974), pp. 408–43. Father O'Malley is engaged on further study of this type of literature.

25. Translated from the edition by John W. O'Malley, 'Man's dignity, God's love, and the destiny of Rome, a text of Giles of Viterbo', *Viator* III (1972), 389–416, at pp. 411–13. *Robur* = 1. Oak tree (the coat of arms of the della Rovere family); 2. Strength, force.

26. O'Malley, *Giles of Viterbo* (Leiden 1968), pp. 155–6.

27. Felix Gilbert, 'Cristianesimo, umanesimo e la bolla "apostlolici regiminis" del 1513', *Rivista storica italiana*, LXXIX (1967), 976–90. Professor Gilbert also points out that Giuliano de' Medici was sympathetic to the ideas of the Venetian reformers and that the bull was issued early in Leo X's pontificate, before the pope had committed himself to display and pomp.

28. 'Humanism, which had impregnated all lively thought everywhere

in the peninsula for more than a century, had promoted a notable spiritual advance', *I vescovi italiani*, p. 464.

29. Massimo Petrocchi, *Una 'devotio moderna' nel quattrocento italiano? ed altri studi*, (Florence 1961).

30. *Ibid.*, p. 16 and n.

31. *Ibid.*, pp. 23–40. Much use is made in this interesting paper of Italian incunables devoted to piety.

32. R. Cessi, 'Paolinismo preluterano', *Rendiconti dei Lincei*, classe di scienze morali, ser. viii, xii (1959), 3–30.

33. Da Alatri, 'La carità cristiana a Roma', pp. 175–6.

34. *The Social World of the Florentine Humanists 1390–1460* (London 1963), pp. 306–8, 311–12.

35. See above chapter 1.

36. The Sees in question are those referred to above, p. 118.

37. The Obligationes et Solutiones record the operations involved in the payment of common services. The number of graduates was certainly higher than this, for it was difficult for a curialist to reach a bishopric (and a fair number of curialists did so) who was not a lawyer, although this fact is not always recorded.

38. Cf. Vespasiano da Bisticci's contempt for Calixtus III: 'well might it be said of him, as is said of the legists, that a mere legist or canonist, without any other learning, is a man quite deficient in general knowledge'. This is (trans. Waters) from the life of Cosmas, bishop of Vich: *Vite de uomini illustri del secolo XV*, ed. P. d'Ancona and E. Aeschlimann (Milan 1951), pp. 166–7.

39. For Piero del Monte see, *inter alia*, Roberto Weiss, *Humanism in England during the Fifteenth Century*, rev. ed. (Oxford 1957) *passim* but esp. p. 24 and n. The other 'humanists' in this random selection were: Colantonio di Valignano (Chieti 1445), Gianantonio Campano (Teramo 1463), P. Palagorio (Telese 1487), A. Gerardino (Volturara 1496), A. Celadoni (Gallipoli 1494).

40. A. V. Antovics, 'The library of Cardinal Domenico Capranica', in *Cultural Aspects*, q.v., pp. 141–59.

41. Alerino de Rambaldis (Alba 1419). See U., iv. 290, E., ii. 84n, but not Pastor, v. 84!

42. Cf. above pp. 40–1.

43. I here treat the later Borgias (i.e. after Calixtus III) as foreigners, which in many ways they were not; they are dealt with as Italians in the cardinals created after 1458 (above pp. 34–7 and below appendix iii). For a sparkling picture of early Renaissance Rome see Delaruelle *et al.*, *L'église au temps du grand schisme*, ii, pp. 1140–56.

44. p. 62; Martines, as above n. 34.

45. 'Chierici e laici' *Geografia e storia della letteratura italiana* (Turin 1967), pp. 47–73. And cf. below p. 104.

46. Flavio Biondo, *Scritti inediti*, introduction *passim*.

47. Pio Paschini, 'Una familia di curiali: i Maffei di Volterra', *R.S.C.I.*,

VII (1953), 344–76. A relative, Giuliano O.F.M., became successively bishop of Bertinoro and archbishop of Ragusa; he too worked in the penitentiary.

48. *Diario*, ed. E. Carusi, RR.II.SS. (Città di Castello 1904–11), introduction pp. xii–xviii. Another humanist who, like Gherardi, had been tutor in the Medici household, was the bishop of Arezzo, Gentile Becchi, on whom see the article by Cecil Grayson in *D.B.I.*, VII (1965), and now the same authors, 'Poesie latine di Gentile Becchi in un codice Bodleiano', *Studi offerti a Roberto Ridolfi* (Florence 1973), pp. 285–303.

49. Pio Paschini, 'Una familia di curiali nella Roma del quattrocento: i Cortesi', *R.S.C.I.*, x (1957), 1–48.

50. *L'église au temps du grand schisme*, p. 1144 n.

51. Salutati's *De seculo et religione*, ed. B. L. Ullman (Florence 1957); a full discussion by Ullman in his *The Humanism of Caluccio Salutati* (Padua 1963), pp. 26–30.

52. Barbaro, *De coelibatu, de officii legati*, ed. V. Branca (Florence 1969); Campana, 'De dignitate matrimonii', *Opera omnia* (Venice 1495), fos. d[v]^{vo}–cii^{vo}. It was addressed to Francesco Massimo, a Roman. On Campana, besides works (such as Miss Ady's) on Pius II, see F. R. Hausmann in *D.B.I.*, XVII (1974) with up-to-date bibliography.

53. A. Ferrajoli, 'Ill matrimonio di Adriano Castellesi e il suo annullamento', *Archivio della società romana di storia patria*, XLII (1919), 295–306, prints the documents and the criticism that he came to a bad end because he ditched Brigida; an even more violent diatribe, not referred to in Pio Paschini's Life, 'Tre illustri prelati del Rinascimento: Ermolao Barbaro, Adriano Castellesi, Giovanni Grimani' *Lateranum*, new ser., XXIII (1957) 43–130, is by the younger Filippo Beroaldo, *Carmina* (Rome 1530), p. 56–56vo, where Adriano is accused of every unpleasant sin one can think of. On the other hand Mr John D'Amico has drawn my attention to Raffaelo Volaterrano's *Commentarii* (Paris 1603), col. 824, where Adriano's abilities are commended. Castellesi was given minor orders at a General Ordination in the Curia, 13 June 1489, A.S.V. Formatori 9, fo. 108; Innocent's order for the annulment was issued on 4 March in the same year.

54. R. Ridolfi, *The Life of Francesco Guicciardini*, p. 8. Rinieri had been bishop since 1502 and held other benefices; E., II. 138, where the date of death has to be corrected.

55. Guicciardini, 'Ricordi', no. xxviii, *Opere inediti*, ed. G. Canestrini (Florence 1857), p. 91.

56. I have discussed this briefly in my contribution to *Itinerarium Italicum*, q.v., pp. 335–41.

57. David Chambers 'The housing problems of Cardinal Francesco Gonzaga', *Journal of the Warburg and Courtauld Institutes*, XXXIX (1976), 21–58. Cf. P. Paschini, 'I benefici ecclesiastici del cardinale

Marco Barbo', *R.S.C.I.*, XIII (1959), 335–54; Giovanni Soranzo, 'Giovanni Battista Zeno, nipote di Paolo II, cardinale di Sa Maria in Portico 1468–1501', *R.S.C.I.*, XVI (1962), 249–74.

58. D. S. Chambers in 'The economic predicament of Renaissance cardinals', discusses mainly the sources of income derived from central funds and distributed through the cardinal's *camerlengo*. There is no doubt that many cardinals were hard up and that even the virtuous looked for benefices. Dr Chambers also makes use of Paolo Cortese's *De cardinalatu*, written at the end of his life and published (at San Gemignano) in 1510. I have also discussed the cardinals more generally in an essay on 'Renaissance Cardinals', *Synthesis*, III (1976), 35–46.

59. For the splendour of some cardinals see Paolo Cortese, *De cardinalatu* (see previous note); and cf. Nesca Robb, 'The fare of princes. A Renaissance manual of domestic economy', *Italian Studies*, VII (1952), pp. 36–61.

60. In general, P. Paschini, *Roma nel Rinascimento* (Bologna 1940); *Codice topografico della città di Roma*, ed. R. Valentini and G. Zucchetti, IV (Rome 1953); F. Castagnoli and others, *Topografia e urbanistica di Roma* (Bologna 1958); and specifically for the Borgo and the Vatican, Magnuson as cited.

61. Besides the works in previous note see Redig de Campos's book cited earlier.

62. Pastor, v. 80.

63. Burke, p. 279.

64. Pastor, v. 69–76.

65. But Alberti's churches at Mantua are recorded.

66. Some interesting remarks and bibliographical references in John Larner, *Culture and Society in Italy 1290–1420* (London 1971).

67. At any rate C. M. Cipolla so argued in *Annales*, II (1947), 317–27. And cf. Brucker, *Renaissance Florence*, pp. 209–10, 293. The chapter on 'The Church and the Faith' in this book is in many ways the most useful introduction to the whole subject of the place of the church.

68. Above p. 20.

69. Above p. 45 and n. 71 to chap. 3.

70. Cf. Thurston, chap. 3 n. 72, who reproduces one or two of the many engravings later produced for pilgrims showing the papal cortège.

71. Cf. Thurston, pp. 73–8.

72. *Commentaries*, ed. Gragg and Gabel, pp. 526–41; on the entry of St Andrew's head and the decoration of Rome which this involved, see Ruth Rubinstein, 'Pius II's Piazza S. Pietro and St Andrews Head', *Essays in the History of Architecture presented to Rudolf Wittkower* (London 1967), pp. 22–33.

73. E. Rodocanachi, *Le Carnival à Rome au XV⁰ et XVI⁰ siècles*, (Amiens 1890) – a brief pamphlet. The subject deserves attention.

74. Cf. Delaruelle, 'La pietà popolare'; C. Ginzburg, 'Folklore, magia,

religione', *Storia d'Italia* 1 (Turin 1972) esp. p. 619. G. Toffanin,
Il cinquecento, 3rd ed. (Milan 1945), pp. 4–8.

75. Jeanne Bignami-Odier, *La bibliothèque vaticane de Sixte IV à Pie
IX* (Città del Vaticano 1973), supersedes earlier accounts; Platina's
register of borrowers (the first to be kept) is reproduced in facsimile
by Maria Bertòla, *I due primi registri di prestito della Bibliotheca
Apostolica Vaticana (Cod.Vat.Lat. 3964, 3966)* (Città del Vaticano
1942).

76. It is highly instructive to turn the leaves of the A.S.V. registers for
the second half of the fifteenth century. Distinctive italic features are
found occasionally in the 1460s or even earlier; but it is only in the
1480s that italic entries become frequent, though older styles persist
and the notaries and clerks could obviously use either style at will;
it is at some later date (about 1500?) that cursive italic becomes *de
rigueur*. It is a great pity that someone with a sharp eye has not
tried to pin down the evolution of a process which was to affect all
European chanceries. It would not be difficult though it would be
laborious.

REFERENCES

This does not include manuscript books and archives; it does include titles of a few works not referred to in footnotes which I have read to my advantage.

Adam, Paul, *La vie paroissiale en France au XIVe siècle* (Paris 1964)

Ady, Cecilia M., *Pope Pius II* (London 1913)

Albano, Hannibali, *Constitutiones synodales Sabinae diocesis* (Urbino 1737)

Alberigo, G., *I vescovi italiani al concilio di Trento* (Florence 1959)
  'Contributi alla storia delle confraternite dei disciplinati e della spiritualità laicale nei sec. XV e XVI', *Movimento*, q.v., pp. 156–253
  'Note in margine a uno studio sulla partecipazione dei vescovi italiani al primo periodo del concilio di Trento', *Italia sacra*, II (1960), 61–72

Ambrasi, Domenico, 'La vita religiosa', in *Storia di Napoli*, III (Napoli Angioina), (Naples 1969), 439–573

Angeleri, C., *Il problema religiosa del Rinascimento* (Florence 1952)

Antonovics, A. V., 'A late XV century division register of the College of Cardinals', *Papers of the British School at Rome*, XXXV (1967), 87–101
  'The library of Cardinal Domenico Capranica', *Cultural Aspects*, q.v. pp. 141–59

Arbesmann, R. O.S.A., 'Andrea Biglia, Augustinian friar and humanist, (d. 1435)', *Analecta Augustiniana*, XXVIII (1965), 154–218

Archiva ecclesiae, II (Città del Vaticano 1959)

Aubenas, R. and Ricard, P., *L'église et la Renaissance*, = Lot and Fawtier, *Histoire de l'église*, XV (Paris 1951)

Bainton, 'Erasmo e l'Italia', *Rivista storica italiana*, LXXIX (1967), 944–951

Banfi, Luigi, ed., *Sacre rappresentazioni del quattrocento* (Turin 1963)

Baptista [Spagnoli] Mantuanus, 'De calamitatibus temporum libri tres', ed. G. Wessels, *Analecta Ordinis Carmelitarum* IV (1917), 5–96

Barbaro, Ermolao, *De coelibatu, de officii legati*, ed. V. Branca (Florence 1969)

Barbieri, G., *Il beato Bernardino da Feltre nella storia sociale del Rinascimento* (Milan 1962)

Battelli, G., 'Archivi ecclesiatici', *Enciclopedia italiana*, I
'Il censimento degli archivi ecclesiastici e la loro tutela durante la guerra', *R.S.C.I.*, I (1947) 113–16, 306–8

Bauer, C., 'Studi per la storia delle finanze papali durante il pontificato di Sisto IV', *Archvio della societa*, I (1927), 319–400

Becker, Marvin B., 'Church and state in Florence on the eve of the Renaissance (1343–1382)', *Speculum*, XXXVII (1962), 509–27

Berdini, beato Alberto, da Sarteano, *Opera omnia*, ed. F. Harold O.F.Obs. and Patrick Duffy (Rome 1688)

Bernardino da Siena, *Opera omnia*, ed. P.P. Colegii S. Bonaventurae 7 vols. (Florence 1950–9)

Bernardino Tomitano da Feltre, beato, *Sermoni*, coll Fr. B. Bulgarino da Brescia, O.F.Obs., ed. P. Carlo Varischi, O.F.M. Cap., 3 vols. (Milan 1964)

Beroaldo, Filippo, *Carmina* (Rome 1530)

Bertoni, Luciano, 'Il "collegio" dei teologi dell' università di Siena', *R.S.C.I.*, XXII (1968), 1–56

Bertòla, M., *I due primi registri di prestito della Biblioteca Apostolica Vaticana (Cod. Vat. Lat. 3964, 3966)* (Città del Vaticano 1942)

Bevacqua, R., *Un grido di allarme e di speranza. Gli archivi ecclesiastici calabresi* (Reggio-Calabria 1969)

Biccelari, F., *Un francescano umanista, il beato Alberto da Sarteano* (Florence 1942); earlier in *Studi francescani*, x (1938)

Bigi, E., 'Ermolao Barbaro', in *D.B.I.*, VI (1968)

Bignami-Odier, Jeanne, *La bibliothèque vaticane de Sixte IV à Pie XI* (in collaboration with Mgr José Ruyschaert, Città del Vaticano 1973)

Billi, Maria, 'Origine e sviluppo delle parrochie di Verona', *Archivio veneto*, ser. 5, XXIX (1941), 1–61

Biondo, Flavio, *Scritti inediti*, ed. B. Nogara (Città del Vaticano 1927)

Biscaro, G., 'Le relazione dei Visconti con la chiesa', *Archivio storico lombardo*, n.s. VI (1937), 117–92

Boccaccio, G., *Genealogia deorum gentilium libri*, ed. V. Romano, 2 vols. (Bari 1951)

Bonmann, O., 'Statuta Bernardiniana di Perugia 1425–6', *Studi francescani* XLII (1965), 278–302

Bossy, John, 'The Counter-Reformation and the people of northern Europe', *Past and Present*, XLVII (1970), 51–70

Bourgin, G., 'La "familia" pontificia sotto Eugenio IV', *Archivio della società di storia patria*, XXVIII (1904), 203–24

Bouwsma, W., *Venice and the Defense of Republican Liberty: Renaissance Values in the Age of the Counter-Reformation* (Berkeley 1968)

Bowker, Margaret, *The Secular Clergy in the Diocese of Lincoln, 1485–1520* (Cambridge 1968)

Boyd, Catherine E., *Tithes and Parishes in Medieval Italy: the Historical Roots of a Modern Problem* (Ithaca N.Y. 1952)

Branca, V., 'Ermolao Barbaro e l'umanesimo veneziano', *Umanesimo europeo e umanesimo veneziano* (Venice 1964)

Brandozzi, Ippolito, O.F.M. Cap., *Il beato Pietro da Mogliano, minore osservante (1435c.–1490). Con due sermoni inediti* (Rome 1968)

Brentano, Robert, 'Bishops' books of Città di Castello', *Traditio*, XVI (1960), 241–54

Two Churches. England and Italy in the Thirteenth Century (Princeton 1968)

Brezzi, Paolo, *Le riforme cattoliche dei secoli XV e XVI* (Rome 1945)

'Lo scisma d'occidente come problema italiana', *Archivio della deputazione romana di storia patria*, LXVII (1944), 391–450

Brucker, Gene, *Renaissance Florence* (New York 1969)

Bughetti, B., 'Documenta quaedam spectantia ad sacram inquisitionem et ad schisma ordinis in provincia praesertim Tusciae circa finem saec. XIV', *Archivum Franciscanum historicum*, IX (1916), 347–383

Burchi, P., *Bibliotheca ecclesiarum Italiae*, I (Rome 1965)

Storia delle parrochie di Cesena, II (Cesena 1962)

Burckardus, Johannes, *Liber notarum*, ed. E. Celani, 2 vols. RR.II.SS. (Città di Castello 1907–)

Burckhardt, Jacob, *Civilization of the Renaissance in Italy*, trans. Middlemore (London 1929)

Burke, Peter, *Renaissance Italy 1420–1540* (London 1972)

Calzolari, C. C., 'L'archivio arcivescovile toscana', *Rassegna storica toscana*, III (1957), 180

Campana, Giovanni Antonio, *Opera Omnia*, (Venice 1495)

Cantimori, Delio, *Prospettive di storia ereticale italiana del ciquecento* (Bari 1960)

Cappelletti, Giuseppe, *Le chiese d'Italia*, 21 vols. (Venice 1844–71)

Capranica, Domenico, with later additions, *Almae collegii Capranicensis Constitutiones* (Rome 1705)

Caro, G. de, 'Francesco Alidosi' in *D.B.I.*, II (1960)

Caron, P. G., *La rinuncia all'ufficio ecclesiastico nella storia del diritto canonico della età apostolica alla riforma cattolica*, (Milan 1946)

Casella, Maria Teresa, 'Una nuova predica del Dominici, *Italia sacra* XV (1970), 369–96

Casini, Tommaso, 'Sulla costituzione ecclesiastica del Bolognes', *Atti e memorie della r. deputazione di storia patria per Romagna*, ser 4, VI (1916), 94–134, 361–402

Castagnoli, F. and others, *Topografia e urbanistica di Roma*, (Bologna 1958)

Castiglioni, Carlo, 'Gli ordinari della metropolitana attraverso i secoli', *Memorie storiche della diocesa di Milano*, I (1954), 11–56

'Un pio consorzio sacerdotale del 1460', *Ambrosius*, XII (1936), 33–7, 313–18

Catoni, Giuliano and Finestri, Sonia, *L'archivio arcivescovile di Siena* (Rome 1970)

Catteneo, Enrico, 'Il battistero in Italia dopo il Mille', *Italia sacra*, xv (1970), 171–95

Caturegli, N., 'La condizione della chiesa di Pisa nella seconda metà del secolo XV', *Bolletino storico pisano*, xix (1950), 17–124

Cecchetti, Bartolomeo, *La repubblica di Venezia e la corte di Roma nei rapporti della religione*, 2 vols. (Venice 1874)

Célier, Léonce, 'Alexandre VI et la réforme de l'église', *Mélanges d'archéologie et d'histoire*, xxvii (1907), 65–124

'L'idée de réforme à la cour pontificale du concile de Bâle au concile du Latran', *Revue des questions historiques*, lxxxvi (1909), 418–435

Cenci, Cesare, O.F.M., 'Antonio da Pereto, ministro generale O.F.M., e i capitoli generali di Roma (1411) e di Mantova (1418)', *Archivum Franciscanum historicum*, lv (1962), 468–500

'Fra Francesco di Lendinara e la storia della provincia di S. Antonio fra la fine del secolo XIV e l'inizio del secolo XV', *ibid.*, 103–92

'Fr. Giovanni Zambotti di Mantova, crocifero, patriarca di Grado (d. 1427)', *R.S.C.I.*, xix (1965), 436–465

'I Gonzaga e i frati minori dal 1365 el 1430', *Archivum Franciscanum historicum*, lviii (1965), 3–47, 201–79

'L'archivio della cancelleria della nunziatura veneziana', *Miscellanea F. Ehrle*, vol. v (Città del Vaticano 1924), pp. 273–330

'Senato veneto – "probae" ai benefizi ecclesiastici', *Spicilegium Bonaventurianum*, iii (1968), 313–454

Cerchiari, E., *Capellani papae et apostolicae sedis auditores causarum... seu sacra romana rota*, 4 vols. (Rome 1919–21)

Cessi, R., 'Paolinismo preluterano', *Rendiconti dell'accademia dei Lincei, classe di scienze morali etc.*, ser. viii, xii (1957), 3–30

Chabod, Federico, *Lo stato e la vita religiosa a Milano nell' epoca di Carlo V*, ed. E. Sestan (Turin 1971)

Chalkéopoulos, Athanase, *Le 'Liber visitationis' d'A.C. (1457–58). Contribution à l'histoire du monachisme grec en Italie méridionale.* ed. M. H. Laurent and André Gouillou (Città del Vaticano 1960)

Chambers, David, *Cardinal Bainbridge in the Court of Rome 1509–14* (Oxford 1965)

'The economic predicament of Renaissance cardinals', *Studies in Medieval and Renaissance History*, iii (1966), 289–313

'The housing problems of Cardinal Francesco Gonzaga', *Journal of the Warburg and Courtauld Institutes*, xxxix (1976), 21–58

'Studium Urbis and *gabella studii*: the University of Rome in the fifteenth century', *Cultural Aspects*, q.v., pp. 68–110

Cheney, C. R., *English Bishops' Registers 1100–1250* (Manchester 1950)

Chimenton, C. *Formazione del chierici in Treviso prima del concilio di Trento*, 2nd ed. (Treviso 1945)

Ciacconius, A., *Vitae et gesta summorum pontificum, necnon S.R.E. cardinalum*, 2 vols. (Rome 1601)

Cipolla, C. M., 'Comment c'est perdue la propriete ecclésiastique dans l'Italie du Nord entre le XIe et le XVIe siècle', *Annales*, II (Paris 1947), 317–27

Cistellini, Antonio, *Figure della riforma pretridentina* (Brescia 1948)

Clergeac, A. *La curie et les bénéfices consistoriaux* (Paris 1911)

Clough, C. H. (ed.), *Cultural Aspects of the Italian Renaissance* (Manchester 1976)

Cochrane, Eric, 'New light on post-Tridentine Italy: a note on recent Counter-Reformation Scholarship', *Catholic Historical Review*, LVI (1970), 291–319

'What is Catholic historiography?', *ibid.*, LXI (1975), 169–90

Contarini, Gasparo, 'De officio episcopi', *Opera omnia* (Venice 1598), pp. 401–31

Conti, Elio, *I catasti agrari della repubblica fiorentino e il catasto particellare Toscano*, I (Rome 1966)

Coradini, F. *La visita pastorale del 1424 nel casentino del vescovo Francesco da Montepulciano* (Anghiari n.d.)

Cortese, Paolo, *De cardinalatu*, (S. Gemignano 1510)

De hominibus doctis dialogus (Florence 1734)

Coulton, G. G., *Five Centuries of Religion*, IV (Cambridge 1950)

Creytens, R., O.P., 'Les cas de conscience soumis à S. Antonin de Florence par Dominique de Catalogne O. P.', *Archivum Fratrum Praedicatorum*, XXVIII (1958), 149–220

'Les vicaires généraux de la congrégation dominicaine de Lombardie (1457–1531)', *ibid.*, XXXII (1962), 211–84

and A. D'Amato, O.P., 'Les actes capitulaires de la congrégation dominicaine de Lombardie', *ibid.*, XXXI (1961), 213–306

Cultural Aspects, see Clough

Cuthbert, Father, *The Capuchins. A Contribution to the History of the Counter-Reformation*, 2 vols. (London 1928)

D'Addario, Arnaldo, review of *L'archivo arcivescovile di Siena* in *Archivio storico italiano*, CXXVIII (1970), 103–10

Aspetti della contrariforma a Firenze (Rome 1972)

Da Alatri, Mariano, O.F.M. Cap., 'La carità cristiana a Roma – il medio evo', *Roma cristiana*, X (Bologna 1968)

Da Bisticci, Vespasiano, *Vite de uomini illustri del secolo XV*, ed. P. d'Ancona and E. Aeschlimann (Milan 1951)

Dalla Santa, Giuseppe, 'L' appellazione della repubblica di Venezia dalle scommuniche di Sisto IV e Giulio II', *Nuovo archivio veneto*, XX (1899), 216–42

'Il vero testo dell'appellazione di Venezia dalla scommunica di Giulio II', *ibid.*, XIX (1900), 348–61

D'Amato, A. M., O.P., 'Sull' introduzione della riforma domenicana nel Napolitano per opera della congregazione Lombarda (1489–

1501)', *Archivum Fratrum Praedicatorum*, xxvi (1956), 249–75 'Vicende dell' osservanza regolare nella congregazione domenicana di Lombardia negli anni 1469–72', *ibid.*, xv (1945), 52–101

D'Amico, S., *Storia del teatro drammatico*, i (Milan 1960)

D'Ancona, Alessandro, *Le origine del teatro italiano*, 2nd ed., 2 vols. (Turin 1891)

Da Nardo, Silvino, O.F.M. Cap., *Sinodi diocesani italiani. Catalogo bibliografico degli atti a stampa 1534–1878*, (Città del Vaticano 1960) *Sinodi diocesani italiani. Catalogo bibliografico degli atti a stampa, con un appendice sui sinodi anteriori all'anno 1534* (Milan 1962)

Da Prati, Pino, *Giovanni Dominici e l'umanesimo* (Napoli 1965)

Debongnie, Pierre, 'Essai critique sur l'histoire des stigmatisations au moyen âge', *Études carmelitaines*, xx (1936), 22–59

Delaruelle, E. 'La pietà popolare alla fine del medio evo', X° Congresso internazionale di scienze storiche, *Relazioni* iii (Florence 1955) pp. 515–37

'Les grands processions de penitents de 1349 et 1399', *Movimento*, q.v., 109–45

Labande, E. R., Ourliac, P. *L'église au temps du grand schisme et de la crise conciliaire'*, 2 vols. = Lot and Fawtier, *Histoire de l'église* XIV (Paris 1962–4)

De Luca, Giovanni Battista, *Il cardinale della S. R. chiesa pratico* (Rome 1680)
Il vescovo pratico (Rome 1675)

Delumeau, Jean, *Vie économique et sociale de Rome dans la seconde moitié du XVᵉ siècle*, 2 vols. (Paris 1957–9)

Del Re, Niccolo, *La Curia romana. Lineamenti storico-giuridici*, 3rd ed. (Rome 1970)

De Maio, Romeo, *Savonarola e la curia romana*, (Rome 1969)

De Negri, Teofilo Ossian, *Storia di Genoa* (Milan 1968)

De Renaldis, G., *Memorie storiche dei tre ultimi secoli del patriarcato d'Aquileia* (Udine 1888)

Dini-Traversari, A., *Ambrogio Traversari e i suoi tempi* (Florence 1912)

Dionisotti, Carlo, *Geografia e storia della letteratura italiana* (Turin 1967)

Domenichi, Domenico de', *Liber de dignitate episcopali*, (Rome 1757)

Dominici, beato Giovanni, *Lucula noctis*, ed. E. Hunt (Notre Dame 1940)

Dondi d'Orologio, Francesco Scipione, *Dissertazione nona sopra l'istoria ecclesiastica padovana* (Padua 1817)

Duex, J. M., *Nikolaus von Kusa*, 2 vols. (Regensburg 1847)

Dühr, Joseph, 'Communions fréquents', *Dictionnaire de spiritualité*, ii (Paris 1953)

Dupré-Theseider, Eugenio, 'Sul "dialogo contro i fraticelli" di S. Giacomo della Marca', *Italia sacra*, xvi (1970), 577–611

Dykmans, M., 'D'Avignon à Rome. Martin V et le cortège apostolique',

Bulletin de l'institut historique belge de Rome, XXXIX (1968), 202–309

Egidi, V. M., 'Il "diplomatico" dell' archivio capitolare di Cosenza' *Calabria nobilissima*, IX (1955), 8–25

Enchiridion archivorum ecclesiasticorum, ed. Dom S. Duca and Simeon A.S. Familiari (Città del Vaticano 1966)

Eubel, Konrad, 'Die provisiones praelatorum während des grossen Schismas', *Römische Quartalschrift*, VII (1893), 405–46

'Die Provisiones praelatorum durch Gregor XII nach Mitte Mai 1408', *ibid.*, X (1896), 99–131

'Welches Verfahren wurde im grossen Schisma beobachtet, wenn ein der einen Obedienz geweihter Bischof zur andern übertrat?', *ibid.*, X (1896), 508–9

Hierarchia catholica, 2nd ed., I–II, (Munster 1913–23)

Evennett, H. O., 'The new orders', *New Cambridge Modern History* (Cambridge 1958), pp. 275–300

ed. John Bossy, *The Spirit of the Counter-Reformation* (Cambridge 1968)

Favier, Jean, *Les finances pontificales à l'époque du grand schisme d'occident* (Paris 1966)

'Temporels ecclésiastiques et taxation fiscale: le poids de la fiscalité pontificale au XIVe siècle', *Le journal des savants*, jan.–mars 1964, 102–27

Fé d'Ostiani Luigi, *Indice cronologico dei vicari vescovili e capitolari di Brescia* (Brescia 1900)

Ferguson, W. K., *The Renaissance in Historical Thought*, (Cambridge, Mass. 1948)

Ferrajoli, Alessandro, 'Il matrimonio di Adriano Castellesi, poi cardinale, e il suo annullamento,' *Archivio della società romana di storia patria*, XLII (1919), 295–306

Ferrara, P., *Luci ed ombre nella cristianità del secolo XIV: il beato Pietro Gambacorta* (Città del Vaticano 1964)

Ferrari, B., *La soppressione della facoltà di teologia nelle università dello stato* (Brescia 1968)

Forcella, Vincenzo, *Iscrizione delle chiese e d'altri edifici di Roma dal secolo XI fino ai giorni nostri*, 14 vols. (Rome 1869–84)

Tornei e giostre, ingressi e trionfali e feste carnavalesche in Roma sotto Paolo III (Rome 1885)

Forchielli, Guiseppe, *La pieve rurale* (Bologna 1938)

'Pieve' in *Enciclopedia italiana*, XXVII (1935)

Foster, Kenelm, O.P., 'Vernacular scriptures in Italy', *Cambridge History of the Bible*, vol. 2, ed. G. W. H. Lampe (Cambridge 1969), pp. 452–65

Fragnita, Gigliola, 'Cultura umanistica e riforma religiosa: il "de officio viri boni ac probi episcopi" di Gasparo Contarini', *Studi veneziani*, XI (1969), 75–189

Fumi, Luigi, 'Chiesa e stato nel dominio di Francesco I Sforza', *Archivio storico lombardo*, LI (1924), 1–74

Gaeta, F., 'P. Barozzi' in *D.B.I.*, VI (1964)

Gaiffier, B. de, 'La mémoire d'André Biglia sur la prédication de S. Bernardin de Sienne', *Annalecta Bollandiana*, LIII (1935), 348–58

Galbreath, D. L., *Papal Heraldry* (Cambridge 1930)

Galuzzi, A. M., O.M., *Origini dell' ordine dei minimi* (Rome 1967)

Gams, P. B., *Series episcoporum* (Ratisbon 1873)

Gasparini, Giuseppina de Sandre, 'La confraternità di S. Giovanni Evangelista della Morte in Padova e una "riforma" ispirata dal vescovo Pietro Barozzi (1502)', *Italia sacra*, XVI (1970), 765–815

Gentile, P., 'Finanze e parlamenti nel Regno di Napoli dal 1450 al 1457' *Archivio storico per le provincie napoletane*, XXXVIII (1913), 185–231

Gilbert, Felix, 'Cristianesimo, umanesimo e la bolla "apostolici regiminis" del 1513', *Rivista storica italiana*, LXXIX (1967), 976–90

Gill, Joseph, S. J., *Eugenius IV, Pope of Christian Unity* (London 1961)

Ginzburg, C., 'Folklore, magia, religione', *Storia d'Italia*, I, ed. G. Einaudi (Turin 1972), pp. 603–76

Giordano, Luigi, *La chiesa di S. Giorgio* [di Chieri] *e la elezione popolare del parroco* (Turin 1896)

Giustiniani, P. and Quirini, P. 'Libellus ad Leonem X P.M.', *Annales Camaldulenses*, IX (Venice 1773), cols. 612–719

Gonnet, Giovanni, *Le confessioni di fede Valdesi prima della riforma*, (Turin 1967)

Gottlob, A., *Aus der Camera apostolica des 15 Jahrhunderts* (Innsbruck 1889)

Grassi, Gioachino, *Memorie istoriche della chiesa vescovile di Monteregale*, 2 vols. (Turin 1789)

Grassis, Paris de, *De caerimoniis cardinalium et episcoporum in deorum diocesibus libri duo* (Rome 1780)

Grayson, Cecil, 'Gentile Becchi', *D.B.I.*, VII (1965)
   'Poesie latine di Gentile Becchi in un codice Bodleiano', *Studi offerti a Roberto Ridolfi* (Florence 1973)

Griffiths, Gordon, 'Leonardo Bruni and the restoration of the University of Rome', *Renaissance Quarterly*, XXVI (1973), 1–10

Guarnieri, R., 'Frères du libre esprit', *Dictionnaire de spiritualité*, ed. M. Viller *et al.* V (1964)
   'Il movimento del libero spirito', *Archivio italiano per la storia della pietà*, IV (1965), 355–650

Guerrini, P., 'Per la storia dell'organizzazione ecclesiastica della diocesi di Brescia nel medio evo', *Brixia sacra*, XIII–XIV (1922–3)

Guicciardini, Francesco, *Opere inedite* ed. G. Canestrini (Florence 1857)

Guillemain, Bernard, *La cour pontificale d'Avignon (1309–1376). Étude d'une societé* (Paris 1962)

Guiraud, Jean, *L'état pontifical après le grand schisme. Étude de géographie politique* (Paris 1896)

Haller, J., *Concilium Basiliense. Studien und Quellen zur Geschichte des Konzils von Basel*, 7 vols. (Basel 1896–1926)

Hatfield, Rab, 'The Compagnia de' Magi', *Journal of the Courtauld and Warburg Institute*, XXXIII (1970), 107–61

Haubst, R., 'Der Reformentwurf Pius der Zweiter', *Römische Quartalschrift*, XLIX (1954) 188–242

Hausmann, F. R., 'Gian Antonio Campana', *D.B.I.*, XVII (1974)

Hay, Denys, 'England and the humanities in the fifteenth century' *Itinerarium Italicum*, q.v., pp. 305–67
'Flavio Biondo and the Middle Ages', *Proceedings of the British Academy*, XLV (1969), 97–125
'Renaissance Cardinals', *Synthesis*, III (1976), 35–46

Heath, Peter, *The English Parish Clergy on the Eve of the Reformation*, (London 1969)

Heers, Jacques, *L'occident au XIV⁰ et XV⁰ siècles. Aspects économiques et sociaux* (Paris 1963)

Hefele-Leclerq = C. J. Hefele, rev. and trans. H. Leclerq, *Histoire des conciles*, VII–VIII (Paris 1916–21)

Heim, Bruno Bernard, *Wappenbrauch und Wappenrecht in der Kirche* (Olten 1947)

Herlihy, David, 'Sancta Maria Impruneta: a rural commune in the late Middle Ages', *Florentine Studies*, ed. N. Rubinstein (London 1968) pp. 242–76
'Veillir a Florence au quattrocento', *Annales*, XXIV (1969), 1338–52

Hoberg, H., *Taxae pro communibus servitiis...1295–1455* (Città del Vaticano 1949)

Hofer, H., *Giovanni da Capistrano* (L'Aquila 1955)

Hofmann, W. von, *Forschungen zur Geschichte der kurialen Behörden von Schisma bis zur Reformation*, 2 vols. (Rome 1914)

Holzapfel, H., O.F.M., *Die Anfänge der Montes Pietatis, 1462–1515* (Munich 1903)

Howell, G. Ferrers, *S. Bernardino of Siena*, (London 1913)

Itinerarium Italicum, ed. H. Oberman and Thomas Brady (Leiden 1975)

Jemolo, A. C., *Chiesa e stato in Italia negli ultimi cento anni* (Turin 1952)

Jones, Philip J., *The Malatesta of Rimini and the Papal States* (Cambridge 1974)

Kaeppeli, Tommaso, O. P., 'Domenicani promossi agli ordini sacri presso la curia romana 1426–1501', *Archivum Fratrum Praedicatorum*, XXXIV (1964), 155–89

Kirshner, Julius, 'Papa Eugenio IV e il monte commune', *Archivio storico italiano*, CXXVI (1969), 339–82
review of Trexler, *Synodal Law* in *Speculum*, XLVIII (1973), 593–7

Knowles, M. D., O.S.B., *The Religious Orders in England*, II–III (Cambridge 1955–9)

Kristeller, P. O., 'Lay religious traditions and Florentine platonism,' *Studies in Renaissance Thought and Letters*, (Rome 1956), pp. 99–102

'Le mythe de l'athéisme de la Renaissance et la tradition française de la libre pensée', *Bibliotheque d'humanisme et de la Renaissance*, xxx (1975), 337–48

'Paganism and Christianity', *Renaissance Thought*, i (New York 1961), pp. 70–91

'The contribution of religious orders to Renaissance thought and learning', *American Benedictine Review*, xxi (1970), 1–55

Kurze, Dietrich, *Pfarrerwahlen im Mittelalter*, (Cologne-Graz 1966)

Larner, John, *Culture and Society in Italy 1290–1420* (London 1971)

Le Bras, G., *Études de sociologie religieuse*, 2 vols. (Paris 1955)

Leccisotti, Tommaso, O.S.B., *I registi dell'abazia di Montecassino*, 8 vols. (Rome since 1964)

'Congregazione benedettina di Sa Giustina e la riforma', *Archivio della società romana di storia patria*, lxvii (1944), 451–69

'Le visite pastorali del cinquecento pretridentino nell'abazia di Monte-cassino', *Italia sacra*, ii (1960), 215–24

Leclerq, J. *Un humaniste érémite. Le bienheureux Paul Giustiniani 1476–1528*, (Rome 1951)

Lefebvre, C., 'Le tribunal de la Rote Romaine et sa procédure au temps de Pio II', *Enea Silvio Piccolomini Papa Pio II. Atti del convegno per il quinto centenario della morte*, ed. D. Maffei (Siena 1968), pp. 199–211

Le Grand, L., 'Archives ecclésiastiques', *Dictionaire d'histoire et de géographie ecclésiastique*, 3 (1924)

Litva, F., S.J., 'L'attività finanziarie dalla Dataria', *Archivum historiae pontificiae*, v (1967), 79–174

Lombardo, M. L., *La camera urbis. Premesse per uno studio sulla organizzazione amministrativa della città di Roma durante il pontificato di Martino V* (Rome 1970)

Lunt, W. E., *Papal Revenues in the Middle Ages*, 2 vols. (New York 1934)

McNair, Philip, *Peter Martyr in Italy: An Anatomy of Apostacy* (Oxford 1967)

Magistretti, Marco, 'Visite pastorali del secolo XV nella diocesi di Milano', *Ambrosius* (1955), 196–214

Magnuson, T., *Studies in Roman Quattrocento Architecture*, (Stockholm 1958)

Maiocchi R, and Casacca, N., *Codex diplomaticus ordinis E. S. Augustini Papiae*, ii (Pavia 1966)

Mallett, Michael, *The Borgias* (London 1969)

The Florentine Galleys in the Fifteenth Century (Oxford 1967)

Mantese, Giovanni, '"Fratres et sorores de poeni tentia" di S. Francesco in Vicenza dal XIII secolo', *Italia sacra*, xvi (1970), 695–714

Marchant, H. J. 'Papal inscriptions in Rome 1417–1527', (London University M. Phil. thesis 1973)

Marcocchi, Massimo, *La riforma cattolica: documenti e testimonianze, figure e istitutione...*, I (Brescia 1967)

Marcora, Carlo, 'Carlo da Forlì arcivescovo di Milano (1457–1461), *Memorie storiche della diocesi di Milano*, II (1955), 255–333

'Frate Gabriele Sforza arcivescovo di Milano (1454–57), *ibid.*, I (1954), 236–331

'Note autobiographiche dell'arcivescovo Giovanni Angelo Arcimboldi', *ibid.*, I (1954), 153–61

'Serie...dei vicari generali della diocesi di Milano (1210–1930)', *ibid.*, VI (1959), 253–82

Marini, Pileo de, see Puncuh

Maroni Lumbroso, A. and Martini A., *Le confraternite romane nelle loro chiese* (Rome 1963)

Martin, F.X., O.E.S.A., 'The Augustinian Order on the Eve of the Reformation', *Miscellanea historiae ecclesiasticae*, II (Louvain 1967), 77–104

'Egidio da Viterbo' (Cambridge Ph.D. thesis 1958)

Martina, G., S.J., review of Ferrari *La soppressione della facoltà di teologia*, *R.S.C.I.*, XXIV (1970), 229–32

Martines, Lauro, *The Social World of the Florentine Humanists* (London 1963)

Massa, Eugenio, 'Giustiniano, Paolo, beato', *Bibliotheca sanctorum*, VII, (1966), 2–10

Mazzuchelli, P., *Osservazione intorno al saggio storico critico sopra il rito Ambrosiano* (Milan 1828)

Meerseman, G., O.P., 'Les dominicains presents au concile de Ferrare-Florence jusqu'au decret d'union pour les Grecs 6 juillet 1439)', *Archivum Fratrum Praedicatorum*, IX (1939), 62–75

'Le origini della confraternita del rosario e della sua iconografia in Italia', *Atti e memorie dell'academia patavina*, LXXVI, part iii (1963–4), 223–56, 301–28

' "In libris gentilium non studeant". L'étude des classiques interdite aux clercs au moyen âge?', *Italia medioevale e umanistica*, I (1958), 1–14

'La riforma delle confraternite laicali in Italia prima del concilio di Trento', *Italia sacra*, II (1960), 17–30

Meneghin, Vittorino, 'Due compagnie sul modello di quelle del "Divino Amore" fondate da francescani a Feltre e Verona, 1499, 1503', *Archivum Franciscanum Historicum*, LXII (1969), 518–64

'Il "mons Euganeus" di Giovanni Barozzi', *Fonti e ricerche di storia ecclesiastica padovana*, II (1969), 11–106

Meoni, Noemi, 'Visite pastorali a Cortona nel trecento', *Archivio storico italiano*, CXXIX (1971), 183–256

Mercati, Angelo, *Raccolta di concordati su materie ecclesiastiche tra la Santa Sede e le autorita civili*, new ed. I (Rome 1954)

Miccoli, Giovanni, 'La storia religiosa', G. Einaudi, *Storia d'Italia*, 2 (Turin 1974), pp. 431–1079

Michaud-Quantin, Pierre, *Sommes de casuistiques et manuels de confessions au moyen age, XII–XVI siècles* (Louvain 1962)

Miglio, Massimo, 'L'umanista Pietro Edo e la polemica sulla donazione di Costantino', *Bollettino dell'Instituto storico italiano per il medio evo*, LXXIX (1968), 167–232

'Vidi thiaram Pauli papae secundi', *ibid.*, LXXXI (1969), 273–96

Minnich, N. H., 'Concepts of reform proposed at the fifth Lateran council', *Archivum historiae pontificiae*, VII (1969), 163–251

'The participants at the fifth Lateran Council', *ibid.*, XII (1974), 158–206

Mirri, Giuseppe, *I vescovi di Cortona*, ed. and revised by G. Mirri (Cortona 1972)

Mittarelli, J. B. and Costadoni A., *see* Giustiniani, P.

Molinari, Franco, 'Visite e sinodi pretridentini a Piacenza', *Italia sacra*, II (1960), 241–79

Mollat, G., 'Contributions a l'histoire du sacré Collège de Clément V a Eugène IV', *Revue d'histoire ecclésiastique*, XLVI (1951), 22–122, 566–94

Les papes d'Avignon, 9th ed. (Paris 1950)

'L'église de France au XIVe et XVe siècles', Fliche, F. and Fawtier, R., *Les institutions françaises au moyen âge*, III (Paris 1962), pp. 339–469

Monaco, M., 'Due eminenti prelati della diocesi Aprutina al servizio della curia romana nel XV secolo: Simone de Lellis da Teramo ed Antonio Fatati da Ancona', *Abruzzo*, XII (1974), 55–72

'Le finanze pontificie al tempo di Clemente VII (1523–34)', *Studi romani*, VI (1958), 278–96

'Il primo debito pubblico pontificio: il Monte della Fede', *ibid.*, VIII (1960), 553–69

La situazione della reverenda camera apostolica nell' anno 1525, (Rome 1960)

Monti, G. M., *Le confraternite medioevale dell'alta e media Italia*, 2 vols. (Venice 1927)

Montini, Giovanni Battista, later Pope Paul VI, 'Gli archivi diocesani e gli archivi parrochiali nell ordinamento della chiesa', *Archiva Ecclesiae*, q.v., pp. 43–55

Moorman, J. R. H., *A History of the Franciscan Order from its Origins to 1517*, (Oxford 1968)

Morçay, R., *Saint Antonin, fondateur du couvent de Saint Marc, archevêque de Florence, 1389–1459* (Paris 1914)

Moroni, Gaetano, *Dizionario di erudizione storico-ecclesiastica*, 103 vols., (Venice 1840–61); *Index*, 6 vols. (Venice 1878–9)

Morpurgo-Castelnuovo, M., 'Il cardinale Domenico Capranica', *Archivio della società romana di storia patria*, LII (1929), 1–146

Movimento, Il, dei disciplinati nel settimo centenario dal suo inizio;

Convegno Internazionale 1960 (Spoleto 1962) = Dep. di storia patria per l'Umbria, app. al *Bolletino*, no. 9

Muratori, L. A. (the 'new' Muratori), *Rerum italicarum scriptores*, various texts q.v., (Città di Castello 1900–)

Niero, A., 'Ancora sull'origine del rosario a Venezia e sulla iconografia', *R.S.C.I.*, xxviii (1974), 465–78

'La mariegola della più antica scuola del rosario di Venezia', *ibid.*, xv (1961), 324–36

'Statute della confraternita di Santa Maria della Misericordia di Chirgnano (Venezia)', *ibid.*, xx (1966), 289–409

Nimmo, Duncan, 'The Franciscan Regular Observants 1368–1447 and the Divisions in the Order 1294–1528' (Edinburgh University Ph.D. thesis 1974)

Oliger, Paul Remy, O.F.M., *Les evèques réguliers* (Paris 1958)

O'Malley, John W., S. J., *Giles of Viterbo* (Leiden 1968)

'Man's dignity, God's love and the destiny of Rome, a text of Giles of Viterbo', *Viator*, iii (1972), 389–416

'Preaching for the pope', *The Pursuit of Holiness in late Medieval and Renaissance Religion*, ed. C. Trinkaus and H. Oberman (Leiden 1974), pp. 408–43

Origo, Iris, *The World of San Bernardino* (London 1963)

Orlandi, S., *S. Antonino*, 2 vols. (Florence 1960)

Palermino, Richard, 'Platina's "History of the Popes"', (Edinburgh University M.Litt. thesis 1973)

Palmarocchi, Roberto, 'Lorenzo de' Medici e la nomina cardinalizia di Giovanni', *Archivio storico italiano*, cx (1952), 38–54

Panella, A. 'Per una guida storica degli archivi ecclesiastici' *Pubblicazioni degli archivi di stato*, xix (1955), 267–78

Partner, Peter, 'Camera papae: the problems of papal finance in the later Middle Ages', *Journal of Ecclesiastical History*, iv (1953), 55–68

The Papal States under Martin V (London 1958)

'The "budget" of the Roman church in the Renaissance period', *Italian Renaissance Studies*, ed. E. F. Jacob (London 1960), pp. 256–78

Paschini, P., 'Fattori di decadenza nell'Aquileia del quattrocento', *Aquileia nostra*, vii and viii (1936–7)

'I benefici ecclesiastici del cardinale Marco Barbo', *R.S.C.I.*, xiii (1959), 335–54

Il carteggio fra il cardinale Marco Barbo e Giovanni Lorenzi (1481–90), (Città del Vaticano 1948)

'Ludovico, cardinale camerlengo', *Lateranum*, new ser., v (1) (Rome 1939)

'I monasteri feminili in Italia nel '500', *Italia sacra* ii (1960) 31–60

La beneficenza in Italia e le "Compagnie del divino amore" nei primi decenni del cinquecento, (Rome 1925)

Roma nel Rinascimento, (Bologna 1940)

'Tre illustri prelati del Rinascimento: Ermolao Barbaro–Adriano Castellesi, – Giovanni Grimani', *Lateranum*, new ser. xxiii (1957), 11–196

'Una familia di curiali: i Maffei di Volterra', *R.S.C.I.*, vii (1953), 344–76

'Una familia di curiali nella Roma del quattrocento: i Cortesi?, *ibid.*, x (1957), 1–48

Pastor, L. von, *History of the Popes*, ed. and trans. F. I. Antrobus and others, vols. i–x (London 1891–1910)

Storia dei papi, trans. and ed. A. Mercati and P. Cenci (Rome 1942–)

Ungedruckte Akten zur Geschichte der Päpste, i (Freiburg 1904)

Pellicia, G., *La preparazione e ammissione dei chierici ai santi ordini nella Roma del secolo XVI* (Rome 1946)

Pesce, L. *Ludovico Barbo, vescovo di Treviso*, 2 vols. (Padua 1969)

Petrocchi, Massimo, *Una 'devotio moderna' nel quattrocento italiano? ed altri studi* (Florence 1961)

Piana, C., 'Il diaconato di Fra Girolamo Savonarola', *Archivum Fratrum Praedicatorum*, xxxiv (1964), 343–8

'Promozioni di religiosi agli ordini sacri a Bolagna (1341–1508)', *Spicilegium Bonaventurianum*, iii (1968), 1–312

Pius II, *Commentaries*, ed. and trans. F. A. Gragg and L. C. Gabel, 'Smith College Studies in History', xxii xxv, xxx, xxxv, xliii (Northampton, Mass. 1937–57). And see above chap 1, n. 33.

Aeneas Sylvius Piccolominus, *De gestis concilii Basiliensis Commentariorum libri ii*, ed. and trans. Denys Hay and W. K. Smith (Oxford 1967)

Piva, E., 'Venezia e lo scisma durante il pontificato di Gregorio XII' *Nuovo archivio veneto*, xiii (1897), 135–58

Platina, B., *Vita Christi et omnium pontificum*, RR.II.SS., ed. B. Gaida, (Città di Castello 1912–32)

Pobladura, Melchior A., O.F.M. Cap., *Historia generalis ordinis fratrum minorum capuccinorum*, i (1525–1619) (Rome 1947)

Polenton, Sicco, *Scriptorum illustrium Latinae linguae libri xviii*, ed. B. L. Ullman, Papers of the American School in Rome, vi (Rome 1928)

Polonio, Valeria, 'Crisi e riforme nella chiesa genovese ai tempi dell' arcivescovo Giocomo Imperiale (1439–52)', *Miscellanea di studi storici*, i (Genoa 1969), 265–363

Pontieri, E., 'La Calabria del secolo XV e la rivolta di Antonio Centeglia' *Archivio storico per le province napoletane*, xlix (1926), 5–154

Per la storia del regno di Ferrante I d'Aragona, re di Napoli (Naples 1969)

Poole, R. L., *Lectures on the History of the Papal Chancery down to the time of Innocent III* (Cambridge 1915)

Posenato, P., 'Chierici ordinati a Padova dal 1396 al 1419', *Fonti e ricerche di storia ecclesiastica padovana*, ii (1969), 11–106

Practica cancellariae apostolicae, (Rome 1503)

Priuli, Girolamo, *I Diarii*, ed. A. Segre and R. Cessi, 4 vols. of which vol. 3 not published, RR.II.SS., (Città di Castello–Bologna 1912–41)

Problemi di vita religiosa in Italia nel cinquecento = Bologna convegno 1958 and *Italia sacra*, II (Padua 1960)

Prodi, Paolo, 'The structure and organization of the church in Renaissance Venice: suggestions for research', in *Renaissance Venice*, ed. John Hale (London 1973)

Prosdocimi, L., *Il diritto ecclesiastico nello stato di Milano dall' inizio della signoria viscontea al periodo tridentino* (Milan 1941)

Pullan, Brian, *Rich and Poor in Renaissance Venice* (Oxford 1971)

Puncuh, Dino, 'L'archivio capitolare di San Lorenzo ed il suo nuovo ordinamento', *Bolletino ligustico*, VIII (1956), 13–20

Il carteggio di Pileo de Marini arcivescovo di Genova 1400–1429 *Atti della società ligure di storia patria*, new ser. XI (= LXXXV, Genoa 1971)

Quirini, P. see Giustiniani, P

Raponi, O.S.A., 'Il cardinale agostiniano Alessandro Olivia di Sassoferrato (1407–63)', *Analecta Augustiniana*, XXV (1962), 89–143, XXVI (1963), 194–293

Rashdall, Hastings, *The Universities of Europe in the Middle Ages*, ed. Powicke and Emden, 3 vols. (Oxford 1936)

Rationes decimarum Italiae. See above p. 110

Redig de Campos, Dioclecio, *I palazzi vaticani* (Rome 1967)

Reeves, Marjorie, *The influence of Prophecy in the later Middle Ages: a Study of Joachism* (Oxford 1969)

Richard, P., 'La monarchie pontificale jusqu'au concile de Trente', *Revue d'histoire ecclésiastique*, XX (1924), 413–56

Ridolfi, R., *Life of Girolamo Savonarola*, trans. C. Grayson (London 1959)

Life of Francisco Guicciardini, trans. C. Grayson (London 1967)

Robb, Nesca A., 'The fare of princes: a Renaissance manual of domestic economy', *Italian Studies*, VII (1952), 36–61

Rodocanachi, E., *Le carnival à Rome au XV⁰ et XVI⁰ siècles* (Amiens 1890)

Roover, R. de, *Money, Banking and Credit in Medieval Bruges* (Cambridge, Mass. 1948)

Ross, J. B., 'G. Contarini and his friends', *Studies in the Renaissance*, XVII (1970), 192–232

Rossi, G., 'Un vescovo scismatico della chiesa ventimigliese', *Archivio storico italiano*, XII (1893), 139–48

Roth, Philip, *The Jews in Renaissance Italy* (New York 1959)

Rubinstein, Nicolai, *The Government of Florence under the Medici, 1434–1494*, (Oxford 1966)

Rubinstein, Ruth, 'Pius II's Piazza S. Pietro and St Andrew's Head', *Essays in the History of Architecture presented to Rudolph Wittkower* (London 1967)

Russo, Francesco, *Storia dell' arcidiocesi di Cosenza* (Naples n.d., c. 1956)

Saggi, Ludovico, O. Carm., *La congregazione mantovana dei carmelitani fino alla morte di Battista Spagnoli (1516)* (Rome 1954)

Sambin, Paolo, 'Chierici ordinati a Padova alla fine del trecento', *R.S.C.I.*, II (1948), 381–402

'Altri chiericati ordinati a Padova nella seconda metà del secolo XIV', *ibid.*, VI (1952), (386–407)

'L'abate Giovanni Michiel (d. 1430) e la riforma di S. Giorgio Maggiore di Venezia', *Italia sacra*, XVI (1970), 483–545

L'ordinamento parrochiale di Padova nel medio evo (Padua 1941)

'Nuove iniziative di pubblicazione di storia della chiesa in Italia', *Archiva Ecclesiae*, q.v., pp. 179–88

Studi di storia ecclesiastica medioevale, *Deputazione di storia patria per le Venezie: miscellanea di studi e memorie*, IX (I) (Venice 1954)

Salutati, Coluccio, *De seculo et religione*, ed. B. L. Ullman (Florence 1957)

Sarpi, P., *Opere*, ed. G. and M. Cozzi (Milan 1969)

Scritti giurisdizionalistici, ed. G. Gambarisi (Bari 1955)

Sbriziolo, Lia, 'Le confraternite veneziane di devozione – saggio bibliografico e premesse storiografiche', *R.S.C.I.*, XXI (1967) 167–97, 502–42

'Per la storia delle confraternite veneziane dalle deliberazioni misti (1310–1471) del consiglio dei Dieci: Ie scuole dei battuti', *Italia sacra*, XVI (1970), 715–63

'Note su Giovanni Dominici I', *R.S.C.I.*, XXIV (1970), 4–30

'Venezia sacra', *ibid.*, XX (1966), 451–71

Scarisbrick, K. J., 'Clerical Taxation in England 1485–1547', *Journal of Ecclesiastical History*, XI (1960), 41–54

Schmitz, L., 'Die libri formatorum der Camera Apostolica', *Römische Quartalschrift*, VIII (1894), 451–72

Schmitz, Philibert, O.S.B., *Histoire de l'ordre de Saint-Benoît*, III (Maredsous 1948)

Shearman, John, 'The Vatican Stanze: functions and decoration', *Proc. Brit Acad.*, LVII (1971), 369–424

Soranzo, Giovanni, 'Giovanni Battista Zeno, nipote di Paolo II, cardinale di Sa Maria in Portico 1468–1501, *R.S.C.I.*, XVI (1962), 249–74

Matteo Bosso di Verona, 1427–1502. I suoi scritti e il suo epistolario (Padua 1965)

Sorbelli, Albano, *Il commune rurale dell'Appenino emilano nei secoli XIV–XV* (Bologna 1940)

La parrochia dell'Appenino emiliano nel medio evo (Bologna 1910)

Sozzini, M., *Consilia*, 5 vols. (Venice 1574)

Stella, Aldo, 'La proprietà ecclesiastica nella repubblica di Venezia dal secolo XV al XVII', *Nuova rivista storica*, XLII (1958), 50–77

Stephens, John N., 'Heresy in Medieval and Renaissance Florence', *Past and Present*, LIV (1972) 25–60

Tacchi-Venturi, Pietro, S. J., *Storia della compagnia di Gesu in Italia*, I, parte prima, 2nd ed. (Rome 1951)

Taccone Galucci, D., *I regesti dei romani pontefici per le chiese della Calabria*, (Rome 1902)

Tamburini, Filippo, 'Il primo registro di suppliche dell'archivio della sacra penitenziaria apostolica (1410–11)', *R.S.C.I.*, XXIII (1969), 384–427

Tangl, M., *Die päpstlichen Kanzleiordnungen von 1200–1500* (Innsbruck 1894)

Tassi, Ildefonso, O.S.B., *Lodovico Barbo (1381–1443)* (Rome 1952)

'Un collaboratore dell'opera riformatrice di Eugenio IV: Giovanni de Primis', *Benedictina*, II (1948), 3–26

Tenenti, Alberto, *Il senso della morte e l'amore della vita nel Rinascimento* (Turin 1957)

Thomassin, Louis, *Ancienne et nouvelle discipline de l'église touchant les bénéfices et les bénéficiers...*, 4 vols. (Paris 1678–81)

Thompson, A. Hamilton, *The English Clergy and their Organisation in the later Middle Ages* (Oxford 1947)

'Diocesan organisation in the Middle Ages: archdeacons and rural deans', *Proceedings of the British Academy*, XXIX (1943), 153–94

Thurston, Herbert, S. J., *The Holy Year of Jubilee* (London 1900)

Tierney, Brian, *Foundations of the Conciliar Theory* (Cambridge 1968)

Toffanin, G., *Il cinquecento: storia letteria d'Italia*, 3rd ed. (Milan 1945)

Töth, P. de, *Il beato cardinale Niccolò Albergati e i suoi tempi*, 2 vols. (Aquapendente 1934)

Tomei, P., *L'architectura di Roma nel quattrocento* (Rome 1942)

Toussaert, J., *Le sentiment religieux en Flandre à la fin du moyen âge* (Paris 1963)

Tramontin, S., Niero, A. Musolino, G., Candiani, C., *Culto dei santi a Venezia*, (Venice 1965)

Tramontin, S., 'Un programma di riforma della chiesa per il concilio Lateranense V: il "Libellus ad Leonem X" dei Veneziani P. Giustiani e P. Quirini', *Venezia e i concilii*, (Venice 1972), 67–93

Trexler, Richard C., 'Death and testament in the episcopal constitutions of Florence', *Renaissance Studies in Honour of Hans Baron*, ed. A. Molho and J. A. Tedeschi (Dekalb, Illinois 1971)

Economic, Political and Religious effects of the Papal Interdict on Florence 1376–1378 (Frankfurt am Main, 1964)

'Sacred images in Florentine religion', *Studies in the Renaissance*, XIX (1972), 7–41

Synodal Law in Florence and Fiesole (Città del Vaticano 1971)

Trinkaus, Charles, *In Our Image and Likeness*, 2 vols. (London 1970)

Ullman, B. L., *The Humanism of Coluccio Salutati* (Padua 1963)

Ughelli, F., *Italia sacra*, 2nd ed. by N. Coleti, 10 vols., (Venice 1717–22, Reprinted Bologna, 1972–4)

Valentini, R. and Zucchetti, G., ed., *Codice topografico della città di Roma*, IV (Rome 1953)

Varese, Claudio (ed.), *Prosatori volgari del quattrocento* (Milan 1955)

Venard, Marc, 'Recherches sur le recrutement sacerdotal dans la province d'Avignon', *Annales*, XXIII (1968), 987–1016

Vian, Nello, 'Il beato Bernardino da Feltre in edizioni e studi recenti' *R.S.C.I.*, XXIV (1970), 193–203

Villari, P., *La storia di Girolamo Savonarola e de' i suoi tempi*, 2 vols. (Florence 1859–61)

Visite pastorali a Milano. Inventario, ed. Ambrogio Palestra (Florence 1971)

Voigt, Georg, *Enea Silvio de' Piccolomini als Papst Pius II*, 3 vols. (Berlin 1856–63)

Volaterrano, Jacopo [Gherardi], *Il diario romano*, ed. E. Carusi, RR.II.SS. (Città di Castello 1904–11)

Volaterrano, Raffaello [Maffei], *Commentarii rerum urbanorum libri* XXXVIII (Paris 1603)

Walker, J. B., '*Chronicles' of Saint Antoninus* (Washington 1933)

Walsh, Katherine, 'The observant congregation of the Augustinian Canons in Italy, *c.* 1385–*c.* 1465 (Oxford University Ph.D. thesis 1972)

'Papsttum, Kurie und Kirchenstaat im späteren Mittelalter: neue Beiträge zu ihrer Geschichte', *Römische historische Mitteilungen*, XVI (1974), 205–30

Weinstein, Donald, *Savonarola and Florence: Prophecy and Patriotism in the Renaissance*, (Princeton 1970)

Weiss, Roberto, *Humanism in England during the Fifteenth Century*, rev. ed. (Oxford 1957)

Un umanista veneziano, Papa Paolo II (Venice 1957)

Widloecher, N., *La congregazione dei canonici regolari Lateranensi: periodo di formazione (1402–1483)* (Gubbio 1929)

Wilmart, A., *Codices Reginenses Latini*, II (Città del Vaticano 1945)

Woodward, W. H., *Vittorino da Feltre and other Humanist Educators* (Cambridge 1897)

Zabughin, V., *Storia del Rinascimento cristiano*, (Milan 1924)

Vergilio nel Rinascimento italiano, 2 vols. (Bologna 1921)

Zafarana, Zelina, 'Per la storia religiosa di Firenze nel quattrocento: una raccolta privata di prediche', *Studi medievali*, ser. 3, IX (1968), 1017–113

Zonta, G., *Francesco Zabarella, 1360–1417* (Padua 1915)

INDEX

Modern authors referred to in text and notes are not normally indexed, and notes are only indexed selectively.

Abbreviators, College of, 85–6
Abruzzi, 65
administrationem, in, grants of bishoprics, 18–19
Adrian VI, pope, 38
Agnus Dei, 69
Alba, Carretto bishops of, 19
Albergati, Niccolò, 12–13, 54, 56, 81
Alberti, Leon Battista, 107
Alexander V, pope, 29, 30, 31
Alexander VI, pope, 35, 36, 37, 42–3, 78, 87–8, 92
Alfonso V, king of Naples, 15, 35, 83
alum at Tolfa, 38–9
Amadeo, duke of Savoy, *see* Felix V
Ammanati, Giacomo, cardinal, 35, 102
Ancona, 47
Angelico, Fra, b., 15
Angelus, 69
anticlericalism, 65
Antonino, S., 12, 15, 50, 53, 56, 57, 64, 92, 94–5
Aosta, see of, 27
Apulia, 65; Basilian monks in, 59
Aquileia, patriarchate of, 14, 29
Aragon, Aloysio d', cardinal, 37
Aragon, Giovanni di, cardinal, 37
Aragon, kingdom of, 82, *and see* Naples
archbishoprics in Italy, 12
archives, church, in Italy, 4–7, 50, 128 n.17, 129 nn.22, 23
archives, papal, 109, 133 nn. 31, 35
archdeacon, cathedral dignity, 21
archpriest, in cathedral chapter, 21–2

Aretino, Pietro, 63
Arezzo, bishop of, *see* Pazzi, C. de'
Ariano, see, exchange, 17
atheism, 65, 92
Augustinian Hermits, 60, 74
Ave Maria, 69
Avignon, papacy at in fourteenth century, 18, 26, 28, 34, 46; after 1417, 54

baptism, 21, 23–5, 135 n.64
Barbaro, Ermolao (d.1471), bishop of Treviso and Verona, 13, 94, 103
Barbaro, Ermolao (d.1493), patriarch of Aquileia, 95
Barbo, Ludovico (d.1443), bishop of Treviso, 71, 75–7, 88, 97, 99
Barbo, Marco, cardinal, 14, 35, 99, 105
Barbo, Pietro, cardinal, *see* Paul II
Barnabite Order, 80
Barozzi, Pietro, bishop of Padua, 95
Bartolomeo di Lendinara, 94
Basel, Council of, 30–3, 39, 71, 83–5
Basilian monks in S. Italy, Congregation of, 59
Basso, Girolamo, cardinal, 35
Becchi, Gentile, bishop of Arezzo, 156 n.48
béguines, 98
Belley, see, exchanged, 17
Benedict XIII, 13, 28, 30
Benedictine Order, 75–6
Benevento, archbishopric, 12
Berdini da Sarteano, Alberto, b., 95
Bergamo, 14, 21
Bernardino da Feltre, S., 68, 79, 93, 96

Bernardino da Siena, S., 60, 68, 70, 73, 80, 96
Bessarion, Cardinal, 59
Bianchi movement, 66, 70
Bible, and literature, 92–4, 97; in Italian, 149 n.22
Biglia, Andrea, 95
Biondo, Flavio, 1, 45, 102
bishops, nature of consecration, 44–5; background of, 19–20, 31–2, 99–101; and reform, 81–2; see archives, church, and exchanges
Bitonto, see, exchanged, 17
Bleeding Hosts, 90
Boccaccio, Giovanni, 93–4
Boccanegra, bishop of Ventimiglia, 30, 31
Bologna, 47
Bologna, confraternities in, 67, 81
Bologna, diocese, 12–13, 17
Bologna, ordinations, visitations, synods, 50, 54, 56
Bonaventure, S., 92
Boniface VIII, pope, 41
Boniface IX, pope, 28, 29, 31, 60, 88
Borgia family, 26; Cesare, cardinal, duke of Romagna, 35, 36, 87; Juan, duke of Gandia, 87; Pedro Luis, duke of Gandia, 35; and see Alexander VI, Calixtus III
Borgo, Rome, 47, 105
Borja, Alonso, see Calixtus III
Borlandi, Orlando, archbishop of Florence, 15
Borromeo, Carlo, cardinal, 57
Bosso, Matteo, 95
Bramante, 47, 90
Brescia, see of, 21–2, 50
Bruges, Pragmatic Sanction of, 83
Bruni, Leonardo, 42
building, church, in Renaissance, 106
Burckard, Johann, master of ceremonies, 42, 107
Burckhardt, Jacob, and Renaissance, 91–2

Calabria, 59, 65
Calandrini, Filippo, cardinal, 35
Calixtus III, pope, 15, 26–7, 35, 41–2, 83, 89, 109

Camaldoli, Order of, 58–9, 85
Campana, Gian-Antonio, bishop of Cotrone, 103–4
Campidoglio, Rome, 105
Cancelleria, Rome, 105
Canigrani, Filippo de', 53
Capestrano, Giovanni, S., 70
capitulations, election, 28
Capocci, Niccolò, cardinal, 81
Capranica, Domenico, cardinal, 31, 53, 62, 81–2, 100
Capuchin Franciscans, Order of, 60, 78
Cardinals, College of, 27–8, 34–7, 43, 86–7; see conclaves, concistory
Carmelite Order, 60, 74
carnival, 107
Castellesi, Adriano, cardinal, 104–5, 156 n.53
Castiglione, Branda, cardinal, 81, 107
Castiglone Olona, 107
Caterina Fieschi Adorno, Sa, 80
cathedrals and baptisms, 23–4
Cava, monastery, 21
Cavalli, Jacopo de', bishop of Vercelli, 29
Celestine V, pope, 41
celibacy and matrimony, 102–5
Cesari, Alessio, bishop of Chiusi, 30–1
Cesarini, Giulio, cardinal, 100
Cesena, diocese, 24
Chalkéopoulos, Athanasius, 59
Chambéry, 27
chapters, cathedral, 20–2
charity, 67, 79–81
Charles V, emperor, 16, 38
Charles VII, king of France, 33
Chiaravalle, abbey, 14–15
chiericati, 22–3
Chiusi, see of, 30–1
church in Italy, wealth of, 100
Ciacconius (Chacon), Alfonsus, 1
Cibò, Giovanni-Battista, cardinal, see Innocent VIII
Cibò, Lorenzo, cardinal, 36
Cibò, Maurizio, 36
Città di Castello, see, exchanged, 17
Città Castellana, see of, united with Orte, 13
claustration, 58, 62–3

Clement VII, pope, (d.1394), 16, 27–8, 29, 30
Clement VII, pope (d.1534), 37, 47, 101
clergy, regular, 58–64, 74–6
clergy, secular, 20–5, 49–57, 52–3; *see* ordinations
Colet, John, 94
Coleti, Niccolò, 2–3
Cologne University, 53
Colonna family, 35
Colonna, Prospero, cardinal, 34
commendam, in, grants, 18–19, 58, 74–5
Common Life, Brethren of the, 97–8
common services, 10–11, 18, 33
communion, 64, 79–80, 92
conciliarism, 8, 32–3, 85
conclaves, 37–8, 138 nn.44, 45
concistory, secret, 45–6
Condulmer, Francesco, cardinal, 34
confession, 25, 79–80, 149 n.21
confraternities, 66–7, 70, 78–80
Congregations and reform, 74–5, 76–7
Constance, Council of, 11, 13, 29, 32, 42, 83–5
Contarini, Gasparo, cardinal, 95
Corpus Christi, Feast of, 90, 147 n.92
Correr, Antonio, cardinal, 75
Correr, Gregorio, elected bishop of Verona, 13
Corsignano, *see* Pienza
Corsini, Amerigo, bishop of Florence, 15
Cortese family, 103
Cortese, Paolo, 103
Cortona, visitations, 50
councils, *see* Basel, Constance, Fifth Lateran, Pisa, Trent; *and* conciliarism
Cremona, see of, 14
Cross, sign of, 64
Crusade, 35, 39, 86
curia, papal, 34, 41–8; *see* Offices and curia
Cusa, Nicholas of, 86

da Bisticci, Vespasiano, 101

da Forlì, Carlo, archbishop of Milan, 13
Damian, St Peter, 93
da Ponte, Jacopo, 29
Dati, Leonardo, 60
dean, in Italian chapter, 21–2
de Brogny, Jean, cardinal, 42
Dedel, Adrian, cardinal, *see* Adrian VI
Degna, Zaccaria, bishop of Ventimiglia, 30
della Rovere family, 35–6
della Rovere, Cristoforo, cardinal, 35
della Rovere, Domenico, cardinal, 35
della Rovere, Francesco, *see* Sixtus IV
della Rovere, Giuliano, *see* Julius II
de Luca, cardinal G. B., 10
d'Estouteville, Guillaume, cardinal, 42
devotio moderna in Italy, 97–8
dimissory, letters, 54
discipline, *see* flagellation
dispensations, 39
Domenichi, Domenico de', 45, 86
Dominican Order, 20, 68; reforms in, 60–1, 74, 76–7, 88–9
Dominici, Giovanni, 60, 76, 88, 93–4
Donadei, Giacomo, bishop of L'Aquila, 30–1
Dragonara, diocese, 11
drama, sacred, 70

education, *see* clergy, seminaries
election, capitular, 12–13
Erasmus, 85, 95, 97, 109
Este family, 82; Ippolito d', cardinal, 37
Eucharist, 25; *see* communion, mass
Eugenius IV, pope, 15, 22, 26–7, 31, 34, 39, 43, 47, 55, 63, 67, 70–1, 83, 85, 89, 99, 109
exchanges of bishoprics, 16–18, 133 n.31

Fano, 64
Felix V, antipope, later cardinal, 30, 37, 83
Ferrara, chapter at, 21; heresy at, 71
Fieschi, Ibleto, bishop of Vercelli, 29
Fieschi, Jacopo, bishop of Ventimiglia, archbishop of Genoa, 30

Fieschi, Lodovico, cardinal, 29
Fiesole, visitation, 50, 56
flagellation, 66–7
Florence, 36, 47, 56, 60, 63, 66, 68, 76–7, 85; see and province of, 9, 12, 15–16, 50
Forcilioni, see Antonino, S.
Forlì, see, exchanged, 17
Formatori, see ordinations
France, 46
Francesco da Paola, S., 60, 78
Francis, St, 72–3, 93
Franciscan Order, reform in, 20, 60–1, 73–4
Fraticelli, ix, 66, 74
Frederick III, emperor, 89
Free Spirit, Brethren of the, ix; see Porete, Marguerite
friars, 59–61, 73–4, 85; see Dominican Order, Franciscan Order
Friuli, during Great Schism, 29

Gallipoli, see, exchanged, 17
Gandia, dukes of, see Borgia, Juan and Pedro Luis
Geneva, bishops of, 37
Gennaro, S., miracle of liquefaction, 69, 90
Genoa, church in, 30, 66, 76, 79–80
Gerson, Jean, 98
Gesuate Order, 70–1, 78, 81
Gherardi, Jacopo (Volaterrano), 102–3
Gherardini, Leone, 77
Ghirardo, Maffeo, elected patriarch of Venice, 14
Giacomo della Marca, S., 70
Giles of Viterbo, cardinal, 95–7
Gisalberti, Matteo de', bishop of Vercelli, 29
Giudici, Bartolomeo de', bishop of Ventimiglia, 30–1
Giustiniani, Lorenzo, patriarch of Venice, 98
Giustiniani, Paolo, and Pietro Quirini, 'Libellus' of, 63–4, 75, 84–5, 95–7
godparents, 25
Gonzaga family, 60, 82; Francesco, cardinal, 37, 105; Sigismondo, cardinal, 37

Greek monks, see Basilian
Gregory XII, pope, 13, 27, 29, 32, 42, 83–5, 99
Guarino da Verona, 95
Guicciardini, Francesco, 104
Guicciardini, Rinieri, bishop of Cortona, 104
Giovanni da Capestrano, S., 73

Henry IV, emperor, 84
Henry VIII, king of England, 38, 40, 104
heresy in Italy, ix, 65–6, 70–1
Holy Blood, 90
Holy Name, cult of, 68
Holy Year, see Jubilee
humanities and reform, 97; and episcopal promotion, 100; see Renaissance patronage

Impati, Bertrando, O.F.M., bishop of Ventimiglia, 30
indulgences, 39
Innocent VII, pope, 28, 29, 36, 40, 43, 104
Inquisition, papal, 65
Ippolito, Niccolò, bishop of Ariano, etc., 17
italic handwriting, 109, 158 n.76
Italy, limits of, ix–x, 8, 27, 131 n.2; 'nation', 8, 127 n.7

Jesuit Order, 64, 80
Jews, 68
Joachim of Flora, 92
John XXIII (d.1419), 13, 29, 31, 41–2
John XXIII (d.1963), 8
Jubilee, 107
Julius II, pope, 38, 40–1, 42, 43, 47–8, 84, 96, 101

Kempis, Thomas à, 93, 98

Ladislas, king of Naples, 33
laity, 64–71
Lamb and Flag, see Agnus Dei
L'Aquila, see of, 30
Lateran Canons, Congregation of, 77–8, 85, 89–90
Lateran, see St John Lateran
Lateran Council, Fifth, 84–5

Latin and Italian in curia, 42
Lavello, see, exchanged, 17
law and episcopal promotion, 100
lay and clerical careers, *see* marriage and celibacy
Lecceto, Augustinian Hermits at, 74
Leo X, 16, 37, 43, 60, 63, 73, 84–5, 101–2
Lesina, diocese, 11
Levant, Italian mendicants in sees in, 20
Liguria, 29
Lombard Congregation, *see* Dominican Order, reform in
Lucera, bishop of (Antonio Niccolò), 30
Luther, 78, 109

Maffei family, 102
Maffei, Gherardo di Giovanni, 102
Maffei, Mario, bishop of Aquino, 103
Maffei, Raffaelo (Volaterrano), 102
Maffei, Timoteo, 94, 96
magister palatii, and sermons before pope, 96
Malatesta family, 29, 32
Malatesta, Sigismondo, 31
Marinacco, Pietro, bishop of Ventimiglia, 30
marriage and celibacy, 44–5
Marsi, see of, 19
Marsili, Luigi, 98–9
Martin V, pope, 30, 31, 32, 33–4, 39, 41–2, 43, 45, 47, 69, 76–7, 109
mass, 24–5, 64, 69, 92
Medici family, 60; Filippo de', bishop of Pisa, 57; Piero di Cosimo, 15; and see Clement VII *and* Leo X
Messina, 62–3
Michelangelo Buonarotti, 101, 105–6
Michiel, Giovanni, bishop of Verona, 14, 35
Milan, dukes of, *see* Visconti, Sforza
Milan, see and archdiocese, 12, 22, 46, 50, 53, 67
Minims, Order of, 60, 78
Modena, see, exchanged, 17
Mondovì, see, exchanged, 17
monks, 58–9
Montecassino, abbey, 15, 21, 76

Monte Corvino, see, exchanged, 17
Montefiascone, chapter at, 21
Monti di Pietà, 68
More, Sir Thomas, 97
Motula, see, exchanged, 17
Muratori, L. A., 7
Musatto, Albertino, 93
mysticism, 97–8

Naples, 46, 69
Naples, kingdom of, 11–12, 15, 30
Nardini, Stefano, cardinal, 13, 53, 82, 100
Nardò, monastic cathedral, 21
'nations', at councils, 83
Nepi, see, united with Sutri, 13; exchanged, 17
nepotism, papal, 34–7
Neroni, Giovanni, archbishop of Florence, 15–16
Nicholas V, pope, 34–5, 41, 47, 89, 101, 105, 109
notarial records of bishops *acta*, 50
nuns and nunneries, state of, 61–3

Observant reforms of religious, 60–1, 73–4
offices at curia, sale of, 18–19, 38–9, 43–5
Oratorians, 80
Oratories of Divine Love, 79–80
ordinations of clergy, 50–6, 140 nn. 2–4, 142 n.26
Orsini family, 35; Rinaldo degli, archbishop of Florence, 16
Orte, see of, united with Città Castellana, 13
Orvieto, 46; see exchanged, 17

Padilla, Francisco de, 2
Padua, diocese of, 23, 50, 53–4, 71
paganism of Renaissance, 92, 106
Palazzo Venezia, Rome, 105
Palladini, Jacopo, bishop of Florence, 15
Panciera, Antonio, patriarch of Aquileia, 29
Panormitanus (N. de Tudeschi), 83
Papal States, 33, 38, 40, 47, 84
Paris University, 53
parish in Italy, development of, 23–5

parish priests, election of, 24, 108, 135 n.59
Parma, *domus baptizatorum*, 135
Parma, see, exchanged, 17
parrochia, see parish
Paul II, pope, 14, 15, 27, 34, 35, 43, 85-6, 89-90, 99, 107, 109
Paul V, pope, 41
Pavia, see of, 53-4
pawnshops, *see* Monti di Pietà
Pax, the, 69
Pazzi, Cosimo de', bishop of Arezzo, archbishop of Florence, 16
Penne and Atri, see, exchanged, 17
Perugia, see of, 46, 47, 81
Petrarch, Francesco, 94
Philip Neri, St, 80
Piacenza, see of, 50, 57
Pico della Mirandola, Giovanni, 66
Piccolomini, Aeneas Sylvius, *see* Pius II
Piccolomini, Antonio, bishop of Siena, 19
Piccolominini, Francesco, bishop of Siena, 19
Piedmont during the Great Schism, 29
Pienza, 9, 13, 19, 106-7, 101, 109
pieve, see parish
Pisa, see of, 16, 50, 53, 57-8, 64, 66; exchanged, 84; *conciliabulum* of, 33, 84; Council of, 29, 31
Pistoia, see of, 56
Pius II, pope, 13, 15, 26, 32, 35, 39, 47, 55, 86-9, 101, 104, 107, 109
Pius III, pope, 38
Platina (B. Sacchi), 1, 85-6
plenitude of power, papal, 88-90
poetry and classics, 92-4
Poggio Bracciolini, G.-F., 42, 45, 103
Pomponazzi, Pietro, 97
popes, place in the Italian Church, viii-ix; in Italian politics, 16, 36, 38-40; public display, 40-1, 45-6, 107-9; reform of church, 82-90, 151 n.51, 152 n.56; Renaissance patronage, 109; *see* conclaves, curia, Papal States
Porete, Marguerite, 70-1
Porta del Popolo, Rome, 105
possesso, see popes: public display

poverty, 67, 79; apostolic, *see* friars
preaching, 67-8, 70
precentor, cathedral dignity, 21
priests-regular, Orders of, 78, 80
priests, shortage of, 25
'primicerius', cathedral dignity, 21-2
princes and church reform, 82
Priuli, G., 62
processions, *see* Popes, display
property of church in Italy, 65
propitiatory acts, 69
proprietory churches, 18
prostitution, 62-3, 152 n.4
protonotaries, status of, 86
provision to bishoprics in Italy, 12
provost, cathedral dignity, 21-2
pyx, *see* Tabernacle

Querceto, Camaldolese nunnery, 63
Quirini, Pietro, *see* Giustiniani, Paolo

Raphael, 90, 106
Ravenna, archdiocese, 12
Raymond of Capua, O.P., 60, 88
reform and the Reformation, 48; *see* bishops, popes, princes
regress, right of, 18-19, 75
religious Orders, *see* clergy, regular
Renaissance patronage by Italian clergy, 101-9
resignationes in favorem, 18-19, 75
Riario, Girolamo, 36
Riario, Pietro, cardinal, 16, 35
Riario, Raffaelo, cardinal, 105
Rimini, Malatesta Tempio, 106-7
Rivato, Tomasso, bishop of Ventimiglia, 30
Rochetaillée, Jean de la, cardinal, 42
Rome, 46-8; in reforming thought, 96-7; in Renaissance, 105, 107, 109; *see* Borgo, Campidoglio, Palazzo Venezia, Porta del Popolo, St John Lateran, Sa Maria della Pace, Sa Maria Maggiore, S. Paolo fuori le Mura, Santo Spirito, Sistine Chapel, Vatican
Rosary, 69
Rossano, see, exchanged, 17

Sabina, see of, 50
saints, 24, 68-9, 80-1

St Andrew's Head, 107
S. Bartolomeo, Church of, at Benevento, 12
S. Broxio, church of, Padua, 24
S. Giorgio in Alga, monastery in Venice, 75, 85
Sa Giustina, Congregation of, 70, 75-7, 85
St John Lateran, Rome, 45-6, 78, 89
S. Lorenzo, nunnery at Padua, 54
San Marco, Dominican convent, Florence, 60
Sa Margherita, church of, Padua, 106
Sa Maria della Pace, Rome, 90
Sa Maria di Fregionaia, monastery, 77
Sa Maria Impruneta, town and Florentine cult of Virgin, 69
Sa Maria Maggiore, Rome, 46
Sa Maria de Tripozemeta, Basilian monastery, 59
Saint-Marthes, S. and L., 2
S. Paolo fuori le Mura, Rome, 76
San Paolo a Ripa d'Arno, monastery, 58
St Peter's Basilica, Rome, 41, 46, 48, 105
Santo Spirito, hospital in Rome, 67
Salutati, Coluccio, 94, 103
Salviati, Francesco, archbishop of Pisa, 16
Sandei, Felino, 17
Sansoni, Raffaelo, cardinal, 35
Sapienza, University of Rome, 53, 85
Sarpi, Paolo, 83
Sarsina, see, exchanged, 17
Savonarola, Girolamo, 6, 54, 66, 68, 77
Savoy, 29
Scarampo, Lodovico, cardinal, 15, 34
scholarship, church, in Italy, 3-8
scholasticus in cathedrals, 53
Secret Archives of the Vatican, see archives, papal
seminaries, in Rome and elsewhere, 81-2; and see clergy, education
sermons, 96-7; and see preaching
Sforza family, 60, 77, 82; Ascanio, cardinal, 15, 37, 105; Francesco, duke of Milan, 83-4; Gabriele, archbishop of Milan, 13
Sicily, 59

Siena, see of, 9, 19, 47, 50, 68
Sigismund, emperor, 29
Sixtus IV, pope, 15-16, 35, 39, 43, 58, 86-8, 90, 101-2, 107, 109
Sixtus V, 37
sodomy, 62
Sutri, see of, united with Nepi, 13; exchanged, 17
Synods, episcopal, 50, 141 n.7

Tabernacle, 69
Taranto, see, exchanged, 17
Tarentaise, province of, 27
Tek, Ludwig duke of, patriarch of Aquileia, 29
Telese, see, exchanged, 17
Teramo, see, exchanged, 17
Teramo, bishop of (Marino de Tocco), 30
Termoli, see, exchanged, 17
tertiaries of mendicant orders, 98
Theatine Order, 80
theology in Italian education, 53; in episcopal promotion, 100
Thomas Becket, St, 148 n.3
titles to benefices, 51, 54
Tortona, see of, 81
Traversari, Ambrogio, bishop, 50, 58-9, 63, 75, 95, 99
Trent, Council of, 6, 19, 20, 24, 65, 83, 92, 109
Trevico, see of, 19
Tudeschi, Niccolò de, see Panormitanus
Tuscany, 64

Udine, 29
Ughelli, Ferdinando, 2-4, 19
Ughi, Matteo, bishop of Cortona, 30
unions of bishoprics, 9, 13
universities and clergy, 52-3
Urban VI, pope, 27-8, 29, 30, 34, 46

vacabilia, see offices, sale of
Vatican Archives, 26
Vatican Council, First, 97
Vatican Library, 109
Vatican Palaces, 40-1, 47-8, 90, 105
Venetians and reform, 76-7, 85-6, 95, 99
Venice, patriarchate, 12

Venice, 13–15, 27, 29, 34–5, 62, 66, 68–9, 70–1
Ventimiglia, see of, 29–31
Vercelli, see, exchanged, 17
Verona, see of, 13–14, 22, 24, 53, 57
Vicenza, see of, 14, 79
Virgin Mary, cult of, 69, 108
Visconti family, 13, 82; Francesco Maria, duke of Milan, 14; Giangaleazzo, duke of Milan, 33; Giovanni Maria, duke of Milan, 82; Ottone, archbishop of Milan, 22
visitations, episcopal and regular, 12, 50–1, 58–61, 140 n.5, 141 n.6

visitations *ad limina*, 46
Vitelleschi, Giovanni, cardinal, 15
Viterbo, 40, 46–7
Volaterrano, *see* Gherardi, Jacopo *and* Maffei, Raffaelo

Wadding, Luke, 2
Waldensian church, ix, 66
Wharton, Henry, 2
Wolsey, Thomas, cardinal, 38

Zabarella, Bartolomeo, cardinal, 15
Zeno, Giovanni-Battista, cardinal, 14, 35, 105